A vivid, grueling, step-by-step ret
true story of faith, hope, and love fi
World Trade Center. Will inspire ̶ ̶ ̶, ̶ ̶ ̶̶ ̶ ̶̶ ̶ those without hope
and those who seek to help others in jeopardy.

Oliver Stone
Film director, producer, and screenwriter
Director, *Platoon* and *Born on the Fourth of July*

My father used to say we are defined in life not by how we handle the
things that go well, but the things that do not. Having sadly covered so
many tragedies, I know they can destroy us or define us. In this
beautiful book, Will and Michael point us to our better angels, and our
better selves, because "everyone has a World Trade Center." But not
everyone gets through it or has a guide like this one to deal with it. Even
20 years out from the horror of 9/11, they remind us life isn't always
fair but our strength to deal with it is always there. We just have to see
it and get over the pride that prevents so many of us from learning from
it. They even provide the road map.

Neil Cavuto
Anchor, Fox News and Fox Business

Dr. Moats lays bare the human heart and soul of Will and Allison Jimeno
in this marvelous exposé of pain and suffering as a result of the 9/11
disaster. We can only imagine their shared experience in tragedy and
upheaval, but we also experience their faith and trust in God which is
part of the fabric of their lives. The range of human emotions doubt,
fear, anger, forgiveness and spirituality are all expressed in a moving
and compelling manner as a result of this dreadful event in our history.

Rev Msgr. Kevin Flanagan
Pastor Emeritus, St Lawrence R.C Church, Chester N.J.
Will and Allison Jimeno's Pastor and friend

Sunrise Through the Darkness is a transformational journey into one of
America's most dreaded milestones—9/11. But it is much more than a
recording of that notorious history; it is a profoundly intimate,
intensely heart-rending story of one man's experience of 9/11 as a Port
Authority police officer and first responder. The subject of that story,
William Jimeno, presents readers with the most gripping "blow-by-

blow" account of the thoughts, feelings, and sensations of what it was like to attempt to save lives and pay the ultimate price of near death on that fateful day that they are ever likely to witness. And what emerges is a highly inspiring meditation on healing, a "reordering" as distinct from "disordering," as co-author Moats keenly observes, that will expand the horizons of anyone who has known great pain in life, and who has desperately fought to redefine that pain. Which includes just about all of us, does it not?

Kirk Schneider, PhD
Psychologist and author of *Awakening to Awe* and
The Depolarizing of America: A Guidebook for Social Healing

After combat deployments to Iraq and Afghanistan as a Green Beret, this book and the author's struggles really resonated with me. As a Physician Assistant, I will recommend this book to my many patients in the military that are struggling with the same battles and the trauma of war.

Brett TerBeek, MPAS, PA-C
US Army

Sunrise Through the Darkness is one of the first books of its kind to interweave the journey of trauma and recovery through the unique perspective of a survivor, a loved one, and a clinician. Paramount in this story is the triumph of humanity overcoming even the most egregious of wounds. Will echoes the same sentiment we as clinicians try to illustrate to clients; trauma is not a competitive badge on display. Will's accounts of the events of 9/11 combined with Dr. Moats' experientially guided questions evoke many spontaneous emotions in the reader. Although following Will's struggle to reorient himself after suffering physical, emotional, and spiritual wounds is courageous, the boldest account of courage is Will and Allison's vulnerability in sharing their story and journey with the world. That is the true testament to faith, hope, and love; being vulnerable enough with your own wounds to help others toward recovery with theirs.

J. Blair Cano, PsyD, MSCP
US Navy veteran

During my son's four-year leukemia battle, my wife was fond of a quote: "A burden shared is divided, and joy shared is multiplied." Will's story is extraordinary. Short of meeting the man in person, it's almost unbelievable. His season of suffering and path to restoration are at once both uplifting and heart rending, but the vulnerability he shares is the necessary ingredient to finding healing and wholeness. One of the darkest spiritual temptations to believe is that you are alone. You are not alone. Reading Will's story will help you find the hope that lies beyond yourself, and to help you move toward the path leading to renewal.

Chaplain, Major Caleb Clark
United States Air Force

Michael Moats and Will Jimeno immerse us in an extraordinary story of survival while illuminating a path of healing reinforced with humility, faith, and love. This book actively encourages gentle introspection. As my own losses and traumas surfaced, I have allowed myself to process them anew, with more compassion, acceptance, and forgiveness--not only for the situations, but ultimately for myself. *Sunrise Through the Darkness* serves as a beacon of hope for anyone who has experienced life's challenges of pain, loss, and trauma, particularly for those of us who have chosen to answer the call of helping others.

David Wilson, Battalion Chief
Drexel Heights Fire District

Sunrise Through the Darkness

A Survivor's Account of Learning to Live Again Beyond 9/11

by William Jimeno
with Michael Moats, PsyD

Colorado Springs, CO
www.universityprofessorspress.com

Sunrise Through the Darkness: A Survivor's Account of Learning to Live Again Beyond 9/11
by William Jimeno with Michael Moats, PsyD

First Published in 2021, University Professors Press. United States.

ISBN (Hardcover): 978-1-955737-00-5
ISBN (Paperback): 978-1-939686-99-2
ISBN (eBook):   978-1-955737-01-2

University Professors Press
Colorado Springs, CO
www.universityprofessorspress.com

Cover Photo: "Colorado Plains Sunrise" by Michael Moats; "New York Skyline" by Shutterstock
Front Cover Image designed by Allison Jimeno
Cover Design by Laura Ross

Authors' Notes

Will

The events contained in this book are true. Reconstructed from memory, past notes, research, an interview with Scott Strauss, and the help of my wife, Allison, this is my account of the tragic events of September 11, 2001, and my subsequent recovery. The dialogue is not verbatim, but it is intended to capture as much as possible the accuracy and spirit of what was said at the time. Others may remember things differently; I can only speak from my experience. Many names are mentioned in this book to show respect, honor, and appreciation. However, the absence of names in no way reflects the contrary. There are so many people, named and unnamed; each is a thread in the tapestry of this story and my life.

Michael

Reading this book may be therapeutic, evoke emotional distress, or both. Although it may have a therapeutic effect, it is not intended as a substitute for therapy. If it evokes emotional distress, please reach out to a local behavioral health provider or emergency room (if needed) to assist in processing this experience rather than struggling alone. Our hope is that we can share, grieve, and grow together in our individual and collective traumas.

Note: Explicit language, intense situations, and descriptions of death and dying are included. Please use discretion with age appropriateness.

Dedication

To my wife Allison for being my soulmate and a pillar of strength and unconditional love. To my beautiful Bianca and Olivia, you are both the very best gift I could have ever been blessed with, and you both make me so proud to be your father. You are my legacy.

To my 37 fellow Port Authority Police of New York and New Jersey brothers and sister. I swore to *never forget*, and as long as I breathe and walk this earth, I will speak of your bravery and sacrifice on that fateful day of September 11, 2001. God bless each of you and your families:

- Police Officer Christopher Amoroso
- Police Officer Maurice Barry
- Police Officer Liam Callahan
- Lieutenant Robert Cirri
- Police Officer Clinton Davis
- Police Officer Donald Foreman
- Police Officer Gregg Froehner
- Police Officer Thomas Gorman
- Police Officer Uhuru Gonja Houston
- Police Officer George Howard
- Police Officer Stephen Huczko, Jr.
- Inspector Anthony Infante
- Police Officer Paul Jurgens
- Sergeant Robert Kaulfers
- Police Officer Paul Laszczynski
- Police Officer David P. LeMagne
- Police Officer John Lennon
- Police Officer John Levi
- Police Officer James Lynch
- Captain Kathy Mazza
- Police Officer Donald McIntyre
- Police Officer Walter McNeil
- Director of Public Safety Fred V. Morrone
- Police Officer Joseph Navas
- Police Officer James Nelson
- Police Officer Alfonse Niedermeyer
- Police Officer James Parham
- Police Officer Dominick Pezzulo

- Police Officer Bruce Reynolds
- Police Officer Antonio Rodrigues
- Police Officer Richard Rodriguez
- Chief James Romito
- Police Officer John Skala
- Police Officer Walwyn Stuart
- Police Officer Kenneth Tietjen
- Police Officer Nathaniel Webb
- Police Officer Michael Wholey

To my Port Authority Police Department (PAPD) brothers who gave on that day and beyond, only to die from exposure to the toxins from the rescue effort. Your commitment and sacrifice to bring home our brothers and sisters will *never be forgotten.*

- Police Officer John Cortazzo
- Police Officer Paul Pallas
- Police Officer Steven Tursellino
- Police Officer Charles Barzydlo
- Police Officer James Kennelly
- Police Officer Mark Meier
- Police Officer Michael Teel
- Police Officer William Leahy
- Detective Thomas Inman
- Sergeant Lawrence Guarnieri
- Sergeant Vincent Oliva
- Lieutenant Robert Jon Brant
- Lieutenant William Doubraski

~ William Jimeno

To my fellow first responders, who are willing to bleed physically and emotionally for the sake of answering the call to serve. I know what you give so that others can remain safe in their shielded view of pain and danger. I dedicate this book to you as my way to reach back to you. Your courage and sacrifice come at a cost; please do not carry that cost alone.

Table of Contents

Acknowledgments

Michael
I would like to acknowledge my wife, Annie, for her tireless support of me, my writing, and my passion in caring for others. To University Professors Press (https://universityprofessorspress.com), thank you for breaking with your traditional path of publishing predominantly academic publications and partnering with us in a shared desire to reach out to those that may not otherwise reach out for themselves. All our intertwined lives depend on one another. Thank you to Rodger Broomé, a fellow clinician, retired police officer, and fireman, for being a reader of this work and offering additional perspective. To Allison Jimeno, thank you for lending an extra set of eyes and editorial assistance. You definitely did more work than what you signed on to do. You are very much appreciated!

Will
I would like to take this opportunity to acknowledge and thank some incredibly important people in my life. I mention them throughout the book, but I cannot mention them enough to express the amount of gratitude I have for them.

To my beautiful wife and soulmate, Allison, without your love, support, and patience, I could have never found my sunrise. Allison, I owe you so much, and I try every single day to give back to you as you have given to me with your love and support. Te Amo!

To Bianca and Olivia, thank you for being my reasons for fighting so hard to battle my darkness. You have both grown into beautiful young women who make your mother and me so proud, and you truly are my legacy. I love you both beyond what words can express. War Eagle!

To my parents, William and Emma (aka Papito and Gizmo), thank you so much for bringing me to the United States of America and instilling in me the desire to be a good person and a proud American, while also never letting me forget our Colombian heritage, which has made me a better person. I have been able to give back to our precious United States of America through my service and my multicultural background, and for that I am forever grateful to both of you. I love you with all my heart.

To Karen, my baby sister; her wonderful husband, Doug; and my nephew, Gavin, thank you so much for always being so supportive of me and our family without question. You are a huge part of my life, and I am grateful to have you all in my life. Karen, I love you, and I'm blessed to have you as my sister.

I want to wholeheartedly thank the men and women who are without a doubt the reason I am able to be here today, walking and talking. Starting off with my Sergeant, John McLoughlin—John, without you I would not be here today. Your expertise and leadership are the major reasons I'm alive and writing this book and continuing to try to help other people through my experiences. I cannot fully express to you my gratitude and my love. You will always be my hero, and the world is a better place with men like you in it.

Antonio—A-Rod, I think of you every single day. I'm forever grateful for you, for being a true brother in blue, and not a day goes by without thinking of you and your sacrifice. I am here today because of you. I love you, brother, and may you rest in peace. To your beautiful wife, Cristina, who has been a beacon of hope for me—your support and advice over the years has been something I've taken to heart and have used to fuel my recovery. Thank you, Cristina, you truly are an example of a warrior. With all that you have lost, you still give so much to this world through your examples of strength and love, raising your two beautiful children. I love you.

Chris Amoroso—you were the guy I or any other cop would go through a door with, no questions asked. Your heroic actions that day helped people make it home to their families, and even being injured never stopped you from doing your duty and what you loved—and that was being a cop. We are blessed to have that photo from the *Daily News* photographer that captured your bravery and self-sacrifice. You are an example to live up to, and I miss you, brother. You represented the PAPD with *Pride – Service – Distinction*. Love you, Chopper!

Dominick Pezzulo—Dom, not a day goes by without thinking of you and what you did for our team. Your sacrifice is something I have no words for except, I love you, brother! I start off my day by looking at your picture, as well as those of Antonio and Chris, and it reminds me to live life in a good and fulfilling way so I can honor you and the guys. You truly are what John 15:13 means: "Greater Love hath no one than this, that a man lay down his life for his friends." You are missed, and that pain will never go away from my heart. I will never forget you, and you have my admiration, respect and, most of all, my love.

Jason Thomas, David Karnes, and the civilian who went back to

Brooklyn without looking for any recognition, after being there that evening and helping to locate John and me—thank you so much. You truly are heroes and great Americans; I love you guys.

Scott, Paddy and Chuck—You are three of the bravest men I know. Words cannot express the gratitude that I have for you. You are proof that there are good men who are willing to step up when evil strikes. You are my heroes, and you exemplify the true meaning of humility. I am blessed to have you in my life and proud to call you my brothers and fellow Americans! I love you all! Thank you from the bottom of my heart!

To the medical staff at Bellevue hospital, including Drs. James Cushman, Philip Wolinsky, Nirmal Tejwani, David Roccaforte, Lee Tessler, Maria Raven, Julie McLaughlin and all the countless nurses and physical therapists—thank you so much from the bottom of my heart for your love, your caring, and your expertise. It is a major part of my recovery. I love you all!

To all my physical therapists from Kessler Rehabilitation Institute: Dawn Texas, Scott Zuckerman, Michelle Beltran, Dawn Quipers, Joe Reda, Brian and Maria Malachy—thank you so much! You helped greatly in my recovery, and you are true heroes. Continue to do your good work in helping others to regain their lives back. I love you guys!

To all my fellow police officers of the Port Authority Police of New York and New Jersey—thank you from the bottom of my heart for being there in my darkest moments and beyond. I am proud to have been a Port Authority police officer, and each and every single one of you are heroes, not only those who were there on September 11th, but all of you who continue to serve and protect the people of New York and New Jersey and this country, as they come through all our facilities in New York and New Jersey. Remember, you are true heroes. Sometimes you don't hear that enough, but I'm here to tell you that you are, and I appreciate you and love and respect you. I wish you a safe career.

To the countless rescue workers, from the Port Authority Police Department, New York City Police Department, New York City Fire Department, and every other agency that came out that evening to help rescue my sergeant and I—thank you! I have had the honor to meet some of you in passing over the years, but I will never truly know each one of you. I thank you wholeheartedly for putting your life on the line to make sure that two cops, two Americans, two human beings made it home to their families. I thank you, and I appreciate your actions that day, as well as what you did for us and, more important, for America and humanity.

I want to thank our friends and neighbors in Clifton, NJ who, when I returned home, truly supported us, inspired us, and uplifted us! Thank you so much!

Thank you to all our friends and neighbors in Chester, NJ. Chester welcomed us with opened arms. It's a beautiful town, and I'm blessed to live here, where one of my fellow Port Authority police officers, Gregg Froehner, lived. He made the ultimate sacrifice on 9/11. He was such a great part of the community. I'll try to do my best to uphold his memory in our town. Chester is as American as you can get. I love that we fly our flags down Main Street on the 4th of July, have Memorial Day parades, and have a beautiful monument in honor of Gregg Froehner at Chubb Park. Men like Gregg, and all those we lost on September 11th, remind us that freedom is not free, but there are men and women willing to give the ultimate sacrifice to keep us free. For that, I am thankful.

I want to thank my outdoor community, M. R. James and his beautiful wife, Janet, as well as Will and Jimmy Primos and the entire Primos family. I want to thank my family at Mossy Oak: Toxey Haas, "Cuz" Strickland, Bill Sugg, and the entire staff that I have been blessed to call my friends and extended family. Last, but not least, thank you to Billy Dowen and Jess Moats for your love, support, and friendship. You all have been my outlet, my peace, and have played an instrumental role in my recovery. I thank you for that and love you all very much!

I want to thank the people who helped me face my PTSD: Peter Killeen of the Port Authority PBA, and Deborah Mandel, who truly helped me find my path to happiness. Debbie, you will never be forgotten, and I love you.

Last, I would like to thank UPP for their stepping outside their wheelhouse in doing this book. I truly appreciate UPP for making it possible to share my story and help people to find happiness.

From Will and Michael

Although we have acknowledgments specific to each of us, collectively we have not forgotten the many individuals from Ground Zero, the Pentagon, and Flight 93 that died that day as they had set out to live their daily lives. It is important for us to recognize the many lives lost years later as a direct result of assisting in the search and rescue mission, the cleanup. We also recognize the paid members and volunteers that continued to be supportive in their roles in the months following that tragic day. To our fellow police, firefighter, and EMS brothers and sisters—we may fight like siblings, but we mourn as family. Additionally, we would like to acknowledge all the boat captains and crews that mobilized in a matter of minutes to evacuate approximately 500,000 individuals in the following nine hours.

Setting the Context: Before and After

It is our hope that *Sunrise Through the Darkness* is experienced as more than simply a book; we hope it is a book of hope and transformation. As you prepare to experience September 11th from before, beneath, and beyond the collapse, we want to invite you to engage in an activity intended to deepen your experience of this book and potentially yourself. Take a few minutes to complete the following activity[1] before you begin reading the rest of the book. This will be presented again in the activity section at the end, to be completed after you have finished reading.

Before reading this book, complete the following sentences below:

On September 11th, 2001,

I thought:

I felt:

I was:

It held:

---

[1] Adapted from an activity in Hoffman, L., & Moats, M. (2015). *Capturing Shadows: Poetic Encounters Along the Path of Grief and Loss (Poetry, Healing, and Growth Series)*. University Professors Press.

Preface

Sunrise Through the Darkness is a book that was 20 years in the making; we just didn't know it at the time. Will was at work, doing what he had been called to do, and Michael was 1,800 miles away, getting ready for work and watching the morning's news unfold. We didn't even know each other at the time. Nevertheless, everyone's hearts were present in New York City on September 11, 2001. It took a tragedy, but the noise of life fell away as people connected in silence to feel deeply the human suffering happening before our eyes. It's one of those times that everyone can tell you where they were and what they were doing when it happened. The attacks had their own impact on our remembering, but almost everyone will remember how differences no longer mattered for that brief time. Without losing our uniqueness, we also were one.

It was human beings going to work that went into the buildings on the morning of 9/11; it was human beings that went into the buildings after the planes hit, to go to work; and it was human beings who worked to help bring loved ones back to their families, both dead and alive. It's so important to remember that people of all races, genders, ages, economics, and nationalities were affected that day. They were killed, injured, traumatized, showed courage, were compassionate, cried together, helped one another, clung to one another, and showed the power of shared humanity in the face of evil, destruction, and intense cruelty.

As a police officer, Will sometimes saw the evil that people are capable of, even though nothing could have prepared him for what he was about to see and experience. As a clinical psychologist, Michael sees the life-changing consequences in people's lives due to heinous acts of disregard. Both have been called to professions of serving others that do not allow for rose-colored glasses. However, both Will and Michael also are privileged to see the beauty in people and in their perseverance for living. It's not about choosing one or the other but understanding the relationship between darkness and light.

Tragedy comes in many forms, including imposed and self-inflicted. If we can take one message from the feelings present on the morning of September 11th, let us take the message that we are in this together, regardless of need or role. If I am a civilian who was helped out, I will reach back and help someone else. If I am a first responder who helps others, I will allow others to help me. There is no room for shame in tragedy or trauma, but somehow shame needlessly exists and often gets in our way of seeking the help we need.

At 9:59 am, Will was running toward a hallway leading to a freight elevator, while Michael watched in disbelief from his living room as the South Tower began collapsing upon itself. Will didn't ask for this to happen or the resulting consequences, but he made a series of decisions about how he was going to respond. He took what he had learned from many others and utilized it to help him create a path back to living. He offers his pain, his struggle, and his daily fight to create something from the rubble of 9/11 in honor of his team.

Michael shares the same belief in giving to others from what has been invested in him. He shares with his clients that his ability to sit in their darkness comes from the gifts of others who have sat with him in his times of pain and despair. Both Will and Michael want to offer this message of hope to anyone dealing with their own tragedy, pain, struggle, or darkness. We honor those who have given to us by reaching back out to others. Love of humanity doesn't have a specific face and isn't limited by time. Our lives are finite, but our gifts of interconnectedness give meaning and support in a multidimensional path. If you can reach out to care for others, then you can also reach to be cared for by others.

The reason we speak specifically to first responders is because they are often the last to ask for help. Additionally, this is why we included a chapter speaking specifically from the voice of a spouse—Will's wife, Allison. Because we may not have had the tragedy directly impact us physically or because we are still alive, sometimes we tell ourselves we have no reason to feel the way we do. This couldn't be further from the truth, and begins to drive us deeper into despair. Just because we, as first responders, utilize a certain amount of denying the self to serve others, it does not equate to denying the self as some sort of badge of honor. In fact, we do more damage to those we serve (e.g., family, clients, patients, friends, departments) by denying our needs—by denying our pain.

Rather than integrate the three primary voices of Will, Allison, and Michael, we chose to enhance the distinction of each to value the experience and perspective that each brings. Will and Allison's stories could easily be synthesized, but we did not want Allison's experience to be absorbed by the intensity of Will's dramatic details, which is something that easily happens with couples when one partner is involved in a traumatic event. Both have their own experience of the trauma and resulting consequences, but usually one voice is much more present in their shared story, leaving the other to deal with their own pain with a greater sense of denial or feeling of being undeserving of attention. Will and Allison both had an incredible amount of support, which is not always the case for people, but their struggles are still easily connected with and offer companionship for those who currently are looking for a way to make their own path toward the sunrise.

Read carefully and take time to digest each chapter. Listen for subtleties of faith, hope, and love throughout. If something causes you to pause, ask yourself what it was, why it was, and how you can apply this in your life. However you choose to engage this message, just like life it's up to you. Perhaps ask yourself why you made this choice or that choice. At the end of the book, there are reflective exercises, poems, and resources for your availability. You've had the courage to put yourself in harm's way for the sake of serving others, have witnessed the ugliness of what people are capable of doing to one another, or have survived emotional and/or physical pain that you didn't think was possible. Yet here you stand. Your ability to remain standing under the weight of what you carry is already a testament, no matter how messy it's been or felt. You are still here. One of the commonalities of being human is suffering. We do not get out of this life without scars. You are not alone.

If we are human, we suffer. If we suffer, we need care, and we need connection. The farther we separate ourselves from one another through uniform, skin color, gender, age, nationality, ethnicity, economics, or career, the more damage we are prone to do to ourselves and others. September 11th reminded us of humanity in the face of evil and pain. That reminder came at an extremely high cost. Let us not forget!

Foreword

My name is Mauricio Henao. I am 34 years old, and I was born in the United States. My parents are originally from Colombia, and I'm the youngest of three children. In 2008, I enlisted in the Marines and was part of the infantry's Fleet Anti-terrorism Security Team (FAST), where I did most of my travels, including to the Middle East. In 2013, after five years of active duty, I was honorably discharged and began college to pursue a bachelor's degree in business. Immediately after, I continued my studies, completing an MBA at Fairleigh Dickinson University, which is where I first met William Jimeno.

After the military, transitioning back to the civilian world was challenging. It was a struggle to get my mind and spirit in the right place because I hadn't accepted the fact that I was scared and not feeling well. Even after being diagnosed with PTSD (Post Traumatic Stress Disorder), I really didn't take it seriously. I refused to accept the diagnosis because it felt like I was being labeled as mentally challenged. I told myself, "Oh well, I'm sure I'll be okay if I just don't think about it and move forward." Unfortunately, it just doesn't work like that. Some of my symptoms of PTSD were nightmares, occasional moments of angry outbursts for no apparent reason, and waking up profusely sweating. Depression was also now a part of my life, and it made me not want to go anywhere. I still refused to get help.

By mid-fall semester 2013, I remember a veteran telling me to go seek help at the VA (Veterans Affairs), but I ignored his suggestion. A short time after, students were invited to the auditorium to meet one of the survivors from 9/11, Mr. William Jimeno. There was something about his story that connected with my spirit. He asked the audience if we had any questions. I raised my hand and asked him, "How do you deal with PTSD?"

Will responded, "Unfortunately, there is no cure. We just have to learn how to live with it. However, remember these words: Faith... Hope... and Love."

In 2014, I was going through my darkest moments; I was afraid and still not wanting to seek help. I was not sleeping at all, due to being afraid of getting nightmares. Some of my military friends were suffering in the same manner and, unfortunately, took their own lives. I began to withdraw from my life even further. I didn't want to attend class. I didn't want to see family. I would just sit in my room. I had very little money for food, and I spent most nights crying and asking myself, "What is going on? Why am I feeling this way?" I constantly shook with fear and isolated myself from everything.

One night I felt that I had no other choice but to go to the emergency room at the VA because I wasn't feeling well. I was very weak from not eating or sleeping. The VA told me that I needed to stay for a few days so the doctors could complete a mental evaluation. The way the nurse spoke to me, I knew something wasn't right. They put me on a floor with other veterans who were struggling with PTSD. I have never forgotten my roommate at the hospital. He was an army veteran who shared with me that he tried to take his own life. He had placed his own pistol under his chin and pulled the trigger, but because of how he angled the weapon, the bullet exited through his mouth. He was fortunate to survive, but he lost most of his front teeth.

There were so many stories of veterans who are going through a lot because of PTSD. Another night, the doctors had to use force on a veteran to ensure he had an evaluation. I can still remember hearing those screams at night. I had no idea what to do at the time. I felt there was no peace inside of me and that no matter how much the doctors could do about my condition, it was not going to be enough. So, one night I had a memory flash, and it was Will Jimeno's story and remembering how he had positioned himself in the form of a cross, thinking it was his final moments. However, he was eventually saved by two Marines. Faith, Hope, and Love were the words that came to my mind. Faith, Hope, and Love were the words that stuck with me while in the hospital.

After a week in the hospital for treatment, I was finally able to go home. They gave me a lot of medicine and follow-up care with the doctors, but Faith, Hope, and Love were the primary things I needed to move forward. I was renewed. I was happy to come back with a relaxed mentality and ready to move forward. Other veterans started asking me how I was able to maintain a sense of happiness and not let this evil (PTSD) take over my soul. With a smile I told them "Faith... Hope... and Love."

In 2015, I was privileged to hear that William Jimeno was returning to the auditorium to give his speech—the one I heard during my darkest moments. I walked in with a smile, stood in the back, and listened to his story. When he asked if anyone had questions, I didn't hesitate to raise my hand and introduce myself. I shared that his story, his words, and his wisdom were what saved me during those nights in the hospital. Since then, I share my story with other veterans and civilians to let them know what helped me get out of the dark and follow the light.

Part of the story that Will shared with us was to remember that a couple of Marines saved him on 9/11. The irony of his story is that he saved a Marine with these same words: "Faith… Hope… and Love."

Mauricio Henao

USMC

New Jersey

Introduction

Have you ever wanted to die or just disappear from the pain of life? If the answer is yes to either of these questions, you are not alone, even though it may feel like it. Port Authority Police Officer William "Will" Jimeno had not experienced such pain until September 11, 2001. On that day he felt his life leaving his body as he lay beneath the debris of the collapsed World Trade Center's 220 stories. Feeling helpless and feeling hopeless, he began expressing gratitude for his existence and for the people he loved; he had accepted that his life would end on that day. The edge of death ebbed and flowed throughout the day, and hope had seemingly run out, or so he thought.

The story of Will Jimeno and Sgt. John McLoughlin's survival and rescue on 9/11 was told in Oliver Stone's movie, *World Trade Center*. However, this was only the beginning of the fight for their lives and journey in healing. It had taken years for some of Will's injuries to mend; others, like the ones that were unseen, are still a work in progress. This book is part of that healing process. Although medically retired from the Port Authority of New York and New Jersey, his life's meaning of serving and protecting has been and still remains ingrained in his being. September 11th challenged Will to change how he lived out his meaning, and walking an unknown reconstructive path was significant in finding his way back to living life, rather than simply surviving it. Speaking to new police graduates, first responders, NFL teams, and school children, Will has taken this historic and personal tragedy and created a message of hope that is relatable to anyone struggling with a situation that causes feelings of helplessness or hopelessness. It is a direct message from Will to the reader that *you are not alone*. You are more than your struggle, and you are more than your pain. You are needed in this world.

Trauma comes in many forms. First of all, let's simply define trauma as an injury. In the physical world, it could be a bruise, a broken bone, a crushing injury, a gaping cut, or a host of other examples that cause damage to the physical body. They may be ranked in severity by how much risk of dying each causes but, beyond safety, the subjective experience is what matters to each person, with each injury. The same is true with the invisible wounds, or traumas, to a person's psyche.

Whether we are talking about being embarrassed in front of our peers, being neglected as a child, experiencing rape, having been involved in war, or having seen someone die, the same is true in understanding and valuing the subjective experience of the traumatized person. Trauma is not competitive, and it becomes *a part* of one's life narrative. However, it does not have to become one's *entire* life narrative.

First responders are known for going in where others are fleeing. They have repetitive exposure to intense, gruesome, life-threatening, sorrowful, and life-changing experiences. Who are these first responders? Definitions may vary depending on who's writing them, but our definition of first responders are those that willingly step into situations in which they may get bloody, battered, see the fullness of evil, and sacrifice their rose-colored glasses so that others may feel safer, protected, and sleep more soundly at night. We are speaking of our military, police, firefighters, paramedics, doctors, and nurses. This list is not exhaustive and is open to interpretation, but this is the lens from which we are working.

The weight of what they carry so others will not have to can come at a high cost. The inability or not knowing how to process, grieve, and find a healthy place for the reality of their days and nights can cause substance abuse issues, higher rates of divorce and domestic violence, health issues, and higher rates of suicide.[1] In 2017, 103 firefighters died by suicide versus 93 in line-of-duty incidents. There were 140 police officers that died by suicide compared to 129 in the line of duty.[2] Keep in mind that these are the people that are involved in gunfire, structural fires, high-speed chases, rescue situations, and the threat of physical violence. Yet, more police and firefighters died by suicide than as the result of their high-risk careers. In 2018, there was an average of 17.6 Veteran suicides per day.[3] A systematic literature review assessing doctor suicides over a 10-year period, albeit with a broader definition,

---

[1] Ilgen, M., & Felicia Kleinberg. (2011, January 20). *The Link Between Substance Abuse, Violence, and Suicide. Psychiatric Times, 28* (1). https://www.psychiatrictimes.com/view/link-between-substance-abuse-violence-and-suicide; *VA.gov: Veterans Affairs.* Substance Abuse in Veterans. (2011, December 22). https://www.ptsd.va.gov/understand/related/substance_abuse_vet.asp.

[2] Hayes, C. (2018, April 12). *'Silence can be deadly': 46 officers were fatally shot last year. More than triple that—140—committed suicide. USA Today.* https://www.usatoday.com/story/news/2018/04/11/officers-firefighters-suicides-study/503735002/.

[3] Office of Public and Intergovernmental Affairs. (2020, November 12). *VA.gov | Veterans Affairs.* Va.Gov. https://www.va.gov/opa/pressrel/pressrelease.cfm?id=5565

showed an average of one completed suicide every day.[4] Although a straight comparison of numbers in the general population may seem like there is a higher suicide rate in the civilian sector, when the number of completed suicides per 100,000 of each domain is evaluated, the data quickly show the significance of our concern for those that are caring for us while often feeling very alone in their struggles.

The loss of life from suicide is too great, and we are reaching out to each and every reader of this book to share that there is hope, even when it doesn't feel like it. A single match can defy darkness, and the story of Will Jimeno can be a match that starts lighting the way. This is not a simple motivational speech. It is a lived testimonial to the strength of the human spirit, no matter how battered and broken it may feel. Will shares how his rescue was only the beginning of his battle. He had physical wounds that were visible and required assistance in helping him heal. However, he also had invisible wounds to his soul. Reaching out for help was not something that came easily. Allowing the help proved to be even harder. Thankfully, he did both and is able to use his pain productively to help others. He brings an experiential perspective of survival on 9/11 and his continued healing process from the immense loss of that day. In *Sunrise Through the Darkness*, Will partnered with his friend, Michael Moats, in an effort to break down the stigma, the fear, and the preconceived ideas about mental health and PTSD, which can become barriers to seeking help.

Will and Michael have been friends for over 17 years, and they share a passion for serving their communities: Will, a retired Port Authority police officer; and Michael, a clinical psychologist serving military members and their families. They have both witnessed the best and the worst in what people are capable of doing for, as well as to, one another, causing both to feel the weight of the responsibilities of their respective callings. Even being surrounded with colleagues, partners, family, and friends, being a first responder can feel isolating and lonely. Whether one is restricted by privacy matters or if the details of the story are just not appropriate to share, many first responders are carrying a burden of collective trauma that can become an emotional marsh of pain, guilt, and shame.

Some may wonder what kind of shame a first responder could feel, considering that the nature of their jobs is to serve, to save, and to protect. Shame can come in many forms, but some of the most prevalent

---

[4] Anderson, P. (2019, May 29). Physicians Experience Highest Suicide Rate of Any Profession. *Medscape.* https://www.medscape.com/viewarticle/896257#vp_1

are things that had to be done (e.g., taking a life), things that could not or were not done (i.e., saving a colleague/partner), the compiled list of secondary trauma experiences (e.g., carnage, injuries of humanity), and having to ask for help (i.e., when the rescuer needs rescuing). The most common reason we have seen in suicidal ideation in first responders is hopelessness due to shame, lack of support (externally or self-imposed), and fear of potential consequences with one's career (e.g., licenses, security clearances, loss of employment). Therefore, they often suffer in silence to the point they believe their only remaining choice is suicide.

Although the darkness of hopelessness may make it hard to see beyond the perceived horizon, know this; there are always opportunities as long as life is present. Suicide takes away any of the unknown and unrealized choices waiting on the other side of this moment. The darkness will say that this is your future and is all that will ever be. The weight of hopelessness distorts one's view and creates weariness of the soul. The lie Michael continues to hear in his office is that individuals contemplating suicide thought others would be better off without them or their burdens (i.e., their darkness), in which they erroneously internalized their burdens as an identity: "I am the burden." When working with the family members of someone that has completed suicide, the truth of how much they were loved and how much they are missed is what is left, as well as the pain of their absence and the haunting question of *why*? Their loved ones still had unused hope for the person that is now and forever gone.

Will lived through a horrific experience and still lives with some of the consequences today. The costs will forever be a part of his life's narrative, but he is the author of the remaining pages. He shares that he considered ending his life. This consideration was more a desire to escape the mental anguish than a desire to die, but he also shares his journey to each day's sunrise through the darkness. Will openly admits his successful fight to go beyond surviving and actually *live* could not have been done alone; it was only through reaching out that he's been able to take back some of what he lost that day and to give back to others. He could not see or imagine the gifts that followed that horrific day. How much he would have missed had he given up. Regardless of the situation, we have both been able to see the gifts within the pain, which is a concept that can only be truly understood through experience.

Michael frequently shares with his clients that the only reason he is able to sit with them in their darkness is because of the many people that invested in his life and taught him what it means to live, which is not some form of pathological happiness but lived lessons of smiling with your whole body, grieving with your whole heart, remembering that messy is better than not trying, trusting what is known over what is felt, never letting go of one's "why," and—probably the most important (Michael's compass)—never to lose sight of humanity in others and especially in the mirror.

Regardless of one's faith, there is a lesson that can be gleaned from the Christian scripture, Mark 12:31 NIV, "Love your neighbor as you love yourself."[5] If a first responder could use this to show care for others like they do when they answer the call, then perhaps they can show the same care and compassion for themselves and the toll their jobs take. Maybe reaching out could become bidirectional. Will and Michael are reaching out; will you reach back?

It has been 20 years since that tragic day on September 11th. There is an entire generation that was either not born yet or too young to remember that day unfolding. We are also speaking to this new generation. Never forget the pain that hate can cause. Never forget the uplifting power of love, compassion, and self-sacrifice. Never forget that an immigrant cop ran alongside his fellow native-born cops and firefighters into a building full of US citizens, immigrants, and foreigners—all human. Never forget that there is hope as long as there is air in our lungs, even when it doesn't feel like it.

This book may be focused on first responders, but it is not exclusive to first responders. Trauma is trauma, and we can all learn from one another. Additionally, the intent is to provide information through connection and sharing rather than being an exhaustive, theoretical resource on trauma. Use this book however it may be of benefit. It is laid out in a format that allows the reader to use it as a living companion, a book in which we share our stories and offer an opportunity to walk with us as you look within yourself. We included the experience from Will's wife, Allison, to shed light on vicarious trauma and to give voice to those who often suffer alongside their loved ones in quiet anonymity. We also want to provide some insight about the human side of therapy, including offering some questions and activities as an opportunity for self-exploration. Some may find the questions and activities useful, others may have no interest in them at all. Either way is fine. The point is that we each have a unique path to

---

[5] *New International Version Bible.* (2011). The NIV Bible. https://www.thenivbible.com (Original work published 1978)

take in this life, and the journey of living, reading this book, working through pain, or finding what is meaningful for each of us is an existential responsibility to be decided each day and, at times, like in this story, each minute. Choose today, choose this hour, choose this minute, if need be, to walk through whatever darkness you are experiencing and keep going toward your sunrise.

Chapter One

I Wanted to Die

"Sometimes even to live is an act of courage." — Lucius Annaeus Seneca[1]

My life was leaving my body, and it was all right. I was physically, mentally, and spiritually exhausted. I wanted to give up. I wanted to die. Thirteen hours could not do justice to the intensity of the compounding trauma that would seize me: the innumerable losses of life; the horrifying images and sounds; the persistent, fragile balancing act between life and death; the relentless pain; and the death of my friends. It was all just too much, and it was time to let go. At least that's what I thought at the time. How easy it would have been to just let go and escape the pain, especially without having any way to know what the next moment, day, or even the next twenty years would offer. It has been worth all the pain. I am so glad that I didn't give up!

We spend much of our lives under the illusion of having control. What a joke! Sure, we have power to affect, responsibility for choice, and sometimes just dumb luck, but control? If that's what I believed previously, September 11th permanently changed that thinking error. In less than a day I went from excited anticipation to wanting to die. There was no way to plan for this, and there sure as hell was no script to follow. The smallest decisions—knowing and unknowing—took me on a ride that was unimaginable. I had almost called in the night before to take a personal day to hunt, only to change my mind before bed. It's almost comical... almost. Even after twenty years, it may be hard to believe, but I can wholeheartedly say this, "I wouldn't change having been there. In spite of the pain, I was doing what I was called to do. I served with the best!"

To be a part of something greater, to be a Port Authority Police Officer and to serve the people of New York and New Jersey had been a dream that took six years to achieve. It was in my blood and nothing

---

[1] Krokou, D. (2018). Power Quotes: For Life, Business, and Leadership. Business Expert Press.

was going to stop me. Even as a child, I loved watching Popeye the Sailor Man. He helped others and fought bullies, which was pretty cool. John Wayne and Clint Eastwood soon followed. Their strength and bravery in times of crisis and moments that were seemingly doomed to failure were motivating and represented the kind of man I wanted to grow up to be. That never-give-up mentality fit with the lessons my parents modeled when coming to this country from Barranquilla, Columbia, as well as instilling in us faith in God and love for our family, our community, and our country. Maybe that's where my fascination with the uniform came from as I grew, especially police and military uniforms. This country has given so much to me and my family, and I was taught that blessings come with responsibility. The uniform I wore represented that responsibility of giving back, of serving others.

Now, to be a police officer and to be part of the Port Authority of New York and New Jersey, I had arrived. Not only was it my dream job, but it afforded me the income to better provide for my beautiful wife, Allison, daughter, Bianca, and our unborn daughter, who was yet to be named. Every day was a new day full of opportunity, and every night I rested in the love of my family and the blessings in my life. This night, September 10th, 2001, was no different.

Reflections

The reader may choose to use the end-of-chapter reflections to process what they are reading, what they have experienced, or for greater empathy for a loved one. This is not intended to replace professional therapy; rather, it is made available as an opportunity to stir thought, create greater awareness of emotions, increase awareness of experiences, and assist in personal growth. You may choose to simply reflect, to journal the answers, or to skip some or all of them entirely. Additionally, you may choose to stay in the flow of reading before coming back to these questions. Choose how you will experience this book.

1) Notice what you felt in your body.
2) Notice your thoughts and what images became present for you.
3) What did you feel emotionally?
4) Was there something you wanted to do while reading this chapter?
5) Do you need to pause, breathe, reflect, or grieve in this moment before continuing?

(Continue practicing these as you read forward. Begin to increase your awareness in the moments. They can either simply be noticed or written down.)

Chapter Two

Just Another Day, Until It Wasn't

"Life can change so fast, so unexpectedly. Love when you can, while you can, as much as you can." — Mandy Hale[1]

The alarm clock blared and violated the early morning silence. It was 4:50 am. The night was never long enough, but rolling out of bed was met with a daily sense of enthusiasm. The morning routine was pretty much the same: a shower, a shave, and kissing my ladies goodbye for the day. Allison was now almost seven months pregnant, and I kissed her and her belly. There was no conversation, just a moment of love before she drifted back asleep and I headed to Bianca's room. Bianca was four years old, and she held my heart in her tiny little hands. Life really was good, and every morning I just had such a feeling of gratitude. My family was good and about to get bigger. I was a cop, and we were in our first home, which we had just purchased six weeks prior. I was living my dream. Like most mornings, I literally kind of skipped down the steps of our home's wooden porch.

An early 20-minute ride from Clifton, New Jersey to the Port Authority Midtown Bus Terminal, the largest in the country and busiest in the world, provided a daily opportunity to appreciate the sunrise and the awakening of the city. What a beautiful morning! With only nine months on the job, I excitedly walked from the parking lot, crossed the alley, passed 9th Avenue, and entered the bus terminal, passing the police desk before heading down to the locker room for the daily changing into my uniform and some friendly trash talk with my fellow brothers in blue. The locker room was another place that felt like home, even if it didn't smell like home.

The locker room was similar to ones in a high school. Inside to the right were some weights that the guys could use for a quick workout

---

[1] Hale, M. (2019). *You Are Enough: Heartbreak, Healing, and Becoming Whole* (Reprint ed.). FaithWords.

before or after shift. There were rows of beige lockers, and mine was all the way at the end of the aisle right next to the bathroom. Inside the door of my locker was a picture of Bianca as a toddler sitting in a Tupperware box. She put a smile on my face every time the locker door was opened. This smelly, functional space is where I made the transition from civilian to police officer, perhaps more symbolically than literally, because I felt being a police officer was more of who I was as a person than simply a profession. I was surrounded by men who had my back and by a picture of the little girl that I loved dearly.

I laid my cell phone next to my wedding ring on the top shelf. Officers were not supposed to carry their cell phones with them, even though I sometimes did. This morning I had decided to leave it behind, figuring I would pick it up during my 10:15 break. Why? Who knows, but that was one of many mundane decisions that would have never been given a second thought on any other day; it was a decision that still makes me shake my head 20 years later. Next to the phone was my wedding ring. Wedding rings were often taken off for safe keeping because officers would sometimes during arrests get into altercations in which their hands would get banged up and swell, causing them to have to get their rings cut off. Suited up and stowed away, I went upstairs for roll call.

It was just a normal day. Everyone lined up in the typical four rows, memo books in hand. First line of the tour: *0700 Roll Call*. Assignments were handed out for the day, updated information was shared on missing children and wanted criminals, and any new, pertinent information was given to assist the officers in making the day as productive and safe as possible. Unfortunately, no one knew the evil that was already in play, hidden in the silence of a normal, beautiful New York day. There were no warnings.

I was given Post 3-5, the corner of 42nd and 8th Avenue. The streets were already humming with traffic, horns, and the chatter of people. Many mornings started with a detour to grab a cup of coffee with my classmate and fellow patrolman, Dominick "Dom" Pezzulo, but this time it was skipped in favor of heading straight to our posts. Dom was known for being a great guy and one that always had another officer's back. He was stationed at Post 5, on 8th Avenue between 41st and 40th, and I was one block up 8th between 42nd and 41st. We were tasked with helping people with information, aiding anyone with a health or medical issue, and, of course, making sure people were safe from any crime.

The bus terminal was a busy place, especially in the early morning and late afternoon hours, better known as *the rush*. People from New Jersey, New York, and nearby commuter states, not to mention the tourists, came into the bus terminal. A daily, steady flow of people by the thousands came out of the doors for about an hour before slowing down.

Like on any other day, I answered tourist direction questions, roused the usual homeless people that slept there overnight—whom I came to know and build relationships with—and watched for the everyday opportunists attempting to ease tourists of their valuables. I stood under a long canopy, leaning against the taxi post and looking to my right toward the corner of 42nd Street and 8th Avenue. We had worked our patrols for about 90 minutes when I noticed Sgt. Bill Ross and Officers McNerney and Sanchez looking into the sky. Sgt. Ross was pointing at something, following its movement with his fingers. While I was watching them intently, a large shadow passed rapidly over the intersection of 42nd and 8th Avenue, lasting only a second. With no sound beyond the street noise, the shadow came and went, which seemed weird but not enough to stop them from going back to the day's business. It seemingly was a blip in an otherwise routine morning.

Only a few minutes passed before the radios crackled with a call for everybody to 8-40, which means all officers are to return to the police desk. An 8-40 is a rare thing to happen, so with a hurried step I crossed over 41st toward Dominick. We walked into and through the main lobby of the bus terminal.

"Willy, something bad must have really happened for us all to get called back," Dom said.

"Yeah."

Willy was the name that only my parents or people from my childhood used. People knew me as Will since I had joined the Navy—that is, except for Dominick. I had a lot of respect for him. He was older than most of the newer cops, having just made the cutoff for the Academy at 35. He had previously been a teacher at Lehman High School in the Bronx, but he became a police officer to provide a better income with better benefits for his family. Dom was just an all-around solid guy. He was my brother; he was my friend.

Side by side, we quickly made our way through the crowd. Although there was a respect for our pace and purpose, it was still a normal day. No one was yelling or running. The only chaos was that we knew something had happened that needed attention. Coming around the police desk that sits high up on the right, I glanced over at the gathered sergeants and lieutenants and saw Sgt. John McLoughlin. Perhaps it was because I knew an 8-40 was serious that I internally heard the voice of Petty Officer 2nd Class, Darrin Smeback, say, "When a bad situation arises always follow somebody entering that knows what they're doing so your chances of getting out are greater. Stick tight to those that can teach you how to be better and to be a leader." Sgt. McLoughlin "Sarge" was one of those leaders that had proven himself to be the kind of guy that I would follow.

John was a 19-year veteran with the PAPD who had been an Emergency Service Unit (ESU) operator and a SWAT guy. He was a professional. Before 9/11, Sarge assisted with some calls, helped process drug busts, and willingly shared his experience with the newer officers. However, he wasn't one for babysitting. He told his officers, "You guys are in charge of the law; you carry a weapon. Make sure you do your jobs well." He didn't mind if we wandered off a bit to talk with one another as long as our posts were clean and we were immediately available to any citizen or fellow cop in need. He was matter of fact, and he was consistent.

As I walked past the desk, something was different. I could see the concern on Sgt. McLoughlin's face, which was unsettling, and I thought, "Man something really serious must have happened." We continued down the hallway and to the left into the break room, which we called the reserve room, where there were couches, tables, gun lockers, and a big television. Entering the room was the first awareness I had about what caused this recall. The big screen showed that Tower 1 of the World Trade Center had taken a hit and had a gaping hole with billowing, black smoke rolling out of it. Sgt. Ross, who had earlier been pointing up to the plane passing overhead, stared at the television and said, "Those are terrorists." Had there been any confusion whether or not this was a small commuter airplane, the sheer size of the hole cleared up any doubt that this was indeed a commercial plane. His words reminded me of a lesson we were taught in the Academy involving the 1993 attack on the World Trade Center. The senior officers warned that they believed the terrorists would make another attempt in the future. The unfortunate but poignant words stuck in my mind and even deeper in my heart; "it's a target-rich environment." The realization that this really was a terrorist attack sunk in fast and hard. In a quick moment, I grabbed the pay phone to call Allison. It was a fortunate connection because the phone lines were already being overloaded and many calls were not going through. She was working as an executive assistant to the president of a manufacturing company in Carlstadt, New Jersey, just a short distance from our home.

"Hey, Al, something bad happened."

"Yeah. Do you know if Bill DeCota (a mutual friend) is okay? Have you heard anything?" she immediately asked, having heard about a plane hitting the Trade Center on the radio while commuting between their daughter's daycare and arriving at work.

"I don't know."

"Do you know if he's at work?" she asked, still focused on their friend.

"I don't know. A plane hit the Trade Center," I responded.

"Yeah, we're watching it on TV. Do you think he'd be there yet?" Allison asked again.

"I don't know," I responded again.

"Do you know what floor his office is on?" she inquired with anxious persistence.

Just then Inspector Fields and Lt. Kassimatis came into the room. "Listen up! When we call your name, get on the bus we commandeered on 9th Avenue. We're going to go down to assist the evacuation at the World Trade Center.

"I gotta go. I gotta go."

"Okay," she replied, and we both hung up.

Not only had it been the shortest conversation she had with me, but she told me later that she noticed that I didn't say I love you. I always said I love you. Allison felt the absence of what she had grown used to expecting from me, but she also felt a small sense of relief, thinking that I was at the bus terminal and not at the World Trade Center.

Without saying a word, Dominick, myself, and Mike "Mikey" Robles, a senior cop who had a lot of time on the job, didn't wait for our names to be called. Dom and I followed Mikey down the escalators and out to 9th Avenue where a city bus was waiting. All the passengers and their luggage had been removed, and they were standing on the sidewalk in disbelief and confusion. Since the three of us were the first guys out, we sat in the front and the others piled in right behind us, filling most of the bus. Sgt. McLoughlin came out and got into a Port Authority Police Suburban; Inspector Fields got in on the passenger side, and Sgt. Feeley got into the back seat. The caravan traveled down 9th Avenue, with Sgt. McLoughlin leading the way. In the middle of this intense transition, a moment of levity cut through as the bus driver was obviously reliving his high school dream of driving with no rules. He not only was running red lights and ignoring other various driving laws, he was given a police escort with lights and sirens. He was definitely into it and with the full support of the police.

"Let's go! Let's do this!" he shouted.

Some were discussing what little they knew and trying to wrap their minds around it, and others were unsuccessfully trying to get calls through to their loved ones. I asked, "Yo, Dom, can I use your phone?"

He didn't respond and kept fiddling with his phone.

"Dom, come on man, I need to call Allison."

Dominick, having already tried to call his wife, barked, "Bro, it's not working!" Dom was a gentleman. He never seemed to get angry about anything. He had never snapped at me, but we were all on edge. "I've been trying to get through to my wife. Nothing's getting through," he followed up in his normal tone.

The bus was cutting through the village and was still about two lengthy blocks away from the Trade Center when we saw our first glimpse of what was to come. It was only the beginning. Down a side street lay this man. He looked deceased. A New York City Fire Department (FDNY) ambulance was on scene and working on the gentleman, but he looked dead from our viewing point. We all fell silent as we passed by, and the bus continued up another block to Barclay Street. Oddly enough, the block was void of civilians between the injured man and where the bus stopped to let everyone off. Our normal was now anything but normal.

Nevertheless, we arrived on scene, and it was time to go to work.

Reflections

1) Do you need to pause, breathe, reflect, or grieve in this moment before continuing?
2) Make a list of moments/actions that registered as rationally or emotionally significant.
3) Review your list of moments/actions and separate them into supportive, motivational, painful, regretful, meaningful.
4) Which moments/actions fit into multiple lists?
5) Do you need to pause, breathe, reflect, or grieve in this moment before continuing?

Chapter Three

Into the Darkness

Believe you can and you're halfway there. — Theodore Roosevelt[1]

Police and Fire were setting up staging areas. Each department was gathering its people and beginning to make plans. Lieutenant Murphy joined Sergeant Ross and Lieutenant Kassimatis and were directing everyone to stand by for orders. We were still trying to comprehend the scene before us. I looked up and was struck by the overwhelming amount of paper floating in the air, like a parade with confetti, but instead of confetti it was a sky full of file cabinet contents wafting amongst the smoke and dust. The destruction to the North Tower, more commonly called Tower One, was massive and unreal. I looked to my 11 o'clock position and saw fire on the corner of Tower 2. The damage appeared to have been caused by deflected projectiles from the plane hitting Tower 1, not knowing that both towers had been hit by separate aircraft. Tower 2 had been hit sometime during our getting on the bus and transitioning to the scene. Taken in by the tremendous amount of debris falling, I wasn't prepared for what I was about to experience and would never be able to unsee. A senior officer, Ronnie Delmar, who had been in the '93 bombing said, "Look! They're jumping!"

I could clearly see people jumping out of this smoke-filled hole. Some were jumping by themselves, and some were holding hands. My god, it was such a helpless feeling watching so many people jumping, trying to escape their pain. From the veil of the black smoke each suddenly appeared and soon vanished. With each person I could not help but think of the rippling of a pond as a pebble is thrown in. Each person falling to their death was someone's mother, brother, father, sister, and the rippling of loss just kept going. They kept jumping, and I watched them until they disappeared behind Building 6. It was

---

[1] Roosevelt, T. (2000). *A quote by Theodore Roosevelt.* Goodreads. https://www.goodreads.com/quotes/9997-believe-you-can-and-you-re-halfway-there

heartbreaking! I was not alone in the surreality. Words of bewilderment and compassion could be heard, and the tears forming in Officer Delmar's eyes are with me today. The last person I saw jump is still vivid in my mind. The man had blond hair, was wearing a pinkish shirt with khakis, and he jumped straight out with his arms spread open and his feet together, like a cross. My eyes were locked on him until he disappeared behind the building.

While my stomach sunk, something in my chest fired up. This is why I became a cop, to help people. No matter how small I felt in this situation, here I was, and I was ready. Standing in front of something unimaginable, I thought of two people I knew that may be in the buildings: Bill DeCota, the Director of Aviation for the Port Authority, and the mother of my friend Jeremy Jacobs. It is funny how the mind works. I was standing in front of buildings that hold thousands of people, and initially, all I could think of is that I had to get in there to find Bill and Mrs. Jacobs.

"I need volunteers!" Sgt. McLoughlin's bark snapped me back into the task at hand. His request was followed with the need for people trained in using Scott Air-Paks. The Air-Paks are the same air tanks the firefighters wear. It's not common to see a police officer wearing an Air-Pak, but Port Authority officers are cross-trained for law enforcement in two states, as well as in firefighting because they are the first responders at airports and other facilities and have to be prepared to handle all situations.

Sgt. McLoughlin looked around and yelled, "I don't want to hear any bullshit. I just need guys that know how to use it."

Since Dom, myself, and another of our classmates, Antonio Rodrigues (A-Rod), had just graduated in January and had recent training, we volunteered. It felt unique that we had been part of the 100th graduating class just months prior at the Marriott World Trade Center. Now we were standing here again, but this time there was no celebrating. There were no smiles. This time the situation was real, very real, and our training would be put to the test.

"Okay, that's a team," declared Sgt. McLoughlin, and we started running toward the building. Debris was everywhere: papers, large chunks of concrete, pieces of metal, and shattered glass. It was everywhere! As we ran toward the building, I looked over my shoulder and could see some firefighters and the rest of our guys standing by. I knew this was temporary and they would be as involved as our team, but for that moment it felt like we were going into a massive battle alone. The fear was becoming very present as we moved forward. We could see remnants of what we believed was from the skin of a plane, as well as human remains strewn about. The absence of people on this street felt eerie. Nevertheless, the team continued forward past a set of stairs (the set of stairs later named "Survivor Stairs") to an entrance that gave us access to the mall level of the World Trade Center.

The World Trade Center consisted of seven buildings. However, the two most notable were the Twin Towers, two huge buildings of 110 stories each. They were once the tallest buildings in the world, for almost a year in the 1970s, and they were connected by an underground mall level, also known as the concourse, full of shops and eateries. This was the area that our team of four were about to enter and that would give us access to the lobbies of both towers. Sgt. McLoughlin called out, "Jimeno, grab our PR24s (batons), our memo books, and our hats, and run them to the suburban. I parked it right on the corner, and then run back and meet us inside this lobby at the E-Room," which was one of many emergency rooms within the World Trade Center that held all the necessary gear for first-responding situations, such as helmets, axes, first-aid kits, defibrillators, and Scott Air-Packs.

I gathered everyone's equipment and ran toward Church Street. There were things falling from the sky that could have killed me. If there were any doubts, the damaged suburban that had been hit by concrete since being parked was a stark reminder. The roof and hood of the vehicle had been crushed, but the passenger side window was open, so I ran to the vehicle and put the items in the front seat. I could see a picture of Bianca inside my overturned hat. It was common for cops to put pictures of family in their hats to keep family close to them. There was too much going on to linger and the falling debris ushered me to stay close to the buildings. It was quite an unimaginable sight to see thousands of people being herded down Church Street, some running and some walking, but all trying to get somewhere other than here. I, on the other hand, turned back toward the Towers and took cover by entering Building Five, making my way back toward the team. As I entered the building, a lady came up to me, "Officer! Officer! Don't forget the day care center." The day care center in the complex had been in full swing when the plane struck.

"We'll make sure they're taken care of," I reassured her and then continued toward the E-room rendezvous.

"Sarge, Sarge, there are kids in here."

"It's all right. They've already been evacuated," he, in turn, reassured me. "Gear up."

Antonio had already put on a bunker coat and his Scott Air-Pak. Dominick had on his Air-Pak. There were no more bunker coats, so I put on an Air-Pak as Sgt. McLoughlin put on his yellow coat and a blue helmet. Per training, we checked each other's Paks. As real as it had been up to this point, strapping on the equipment and going through the checks caused our hearts to race. We were in the mouth and about to go into the belly. The team members looked at one another other and gave the reminder that we would not separate from each other no matter what happened. I was putting on perp gloves, which were gloves that were used to protect officers during pat-downs, medical issues, or numerous other daily functions that could have exposed them to things better left untouched, when Antonio said, "Jimeno, don't put your gloves on. If you get near a fire, they'll melt on your hands."

"Good point. Thanks!" I said while quickly removing the gloves.

Antonio was another one of those guys that just made the age cutoff coming into the PAPD, although he already had four years of service on the NYPD. It was not the first time he offered experienced advice to me, as it was his nature to look out for his buddies and fellow officers in whatever way was needed. Besides being a great cop and friend, he was an amazing artist and had a beautiful Portuguese accent. We were glad to have him on our team because he had just come back from a trip to Portugal and transferred from afternoons to days; this was his first day shift since making the change.

"We're going downstairs to the police desk to get more equipment," informed Sgt. McLoughlin.

Standing at the desk was a detective who had brought in a piece of the plane's fuselage. It didn't matter that we already knew a plane had caused this damage to the building. It was still beyond our comprehension that we were staring at a huge piece of a plane on the floor. Sgt. McLoughlin told us, "Find a mail cart and gather more equipment."

Even though we didn't know what the plan was yet or where we were exactly going, we started loading lights, axes, and oxygen tanks. Part of the reason we didn't need to know all the details was because of our belief in Sgt. McLoughlin. He helped set up security at the World Trade Center after the '93 bombings. He knew the buildings like the back of his hand.

We collected the gear, and the team was now on the move. Sgt. McLoughlin led the way, I pushed the cart, and Dominick and Antonio paralleled the cart. Pushing the cart back to the elevator, I couldn't help but think, "Aren't we supposed to stay off of the elevators during a fire?"

Even though we had gone down that same elevator, for some reason gaining elevation created an uneasy awareness within me that I hadn't noticed on the way down. I kind of chuckled to myself that I was glad it was a short trip up. The team exited to the right and made their way around the escalators that took people down to the PATH train.

There was a steady flow of people coming from Tower One, and they were helping one another. Even though there were a few people running and yelling, most were making their way in a single file across the marble floor through broken glass and a couple inches of water from the broken pipes. There was an FBI agent guiding people as the team walked by. Two civilians, a Black man and a White man, were carrying a blonde female that had a deep cut on her leg. I remembered feeling the presence of an overwhelming sense of love for one another in the human interplay that was displayed in the midst of chaos. I was impressed with their bravery and felt my motivation rise to a new level of courage because I knew people were depending on us to get them out safely.

The team approached a crossroads where we could go right toward Tower 1 or left toward Tower 2. It was here that we encountered another team of Port Authority police officers pushing their own cart of equipment. The officer pushing the cart was another classmate of ours, Walwyn "Stewie" Stuart. He also had transferred over from the NYPD, and during the academy his wife, Thelma, had given birth to their first little girl, Amanda. Stewie always had a smile on his face, always.

"Man, this is crazy, right?" Stewie asked.

"Yeah, it's somethin'," I replied. We chatted a bit while waiting for our sergeants to finish discussing the game plan. I think it helped calm our nerves to just be guys and talk about nothing of too much importance.

Sgt. McLoughlin said, "Let's go."

The teams turned in their respective directions and began to separate. Stewie and I turned toward each other to give a fist bump.

"Stay safe."

"You, too, brother." I couldn't have known that this would be the last time we would see each other.

Another familiar face, Christopher Amoroso, came walking up to the team. Chris was a big guy, and he was the kind of guy, the kind of cop, that people would never hesitate to put their lives in his hands. He loved the job; he loved to serve. As cops, we would say, "He's the kind of guy I'd go through a door with." He was also my on-the-job training (OJT) officer following the academy.

"Hey, Sarge, can I join you," Chris asked, in more of a declarative way but with enough respect to make it sound like a question.

"Are you all right," we asked, looking at the deep cut beneath his eye. Apparently, he had already saved four people and had been hit by a piece of falling debris during the rescues.

"I'm all right, guys. We've still got a lot of people to get outta here."

"Okay, Chris, fall in," Sgt. McLoughlin gave the nod and our team continued in the direction of Tower 2. We stopped just before the revolving doors leading into the lobby by the elevator banks. Next to us was a Ben & Jerry's ice cream shop. The shop may not be important to the story, but ice cream is always relevant in life.

"You guys come with me; Jimeno stay here with the cart. We're going downstairs to another E-room and get some more equipment."

They went down to Jimmy Lynch's office, the primary police officer in charge of safety at the World Trade Center, a position previously held by Sgt. McLoughlin. Jimmy took his job seriously, and he was there to serve no matter the cost. He had been in the building that day completing medical paperwork from a recent knee surgery when the attacks occurred. He wasn't supposed to be there that day in an official capacity, but when he realized the buildings had been hit, he immediately responded to his post. That's just who he was.

The guys gathered additional Air-Paks, lights, axes, and anything else they thought they might need. The team at least felt like they were better prepared to assist in getting people out. There was a big job to do, and additional trips back down for equipment would have wasted precious time.

While I was waiting, I remember looking into the lobby of Tower 2, and I could just see people. It was more chaotic here. I saw people on the ground who had passed. I saw people running in the opposite direction toward an exit that opened up to Liberty Street, and I heard our cops shooting the large glass windows out on the other side so that more people could get out quickly. I felt scared. I was being bombarded with images and sounds that evoked strong emotion, but I had to keep it together to do my job. There were two distinctive sounds: concrete hitting the ground and human bodies hitting the ground. Both were extremely loud popping sounds, but I remember hearing the distinct sound of human bodies landing on the pavement. Other people were getting killed by the bodies falling on them as they exited the buildings. The sounds were relentless, and I remember saying to myself, "Man, I'm fucking scared!" Because now I'm standing by myself looking at what's going on, and there was really nobody near me, but I could see the command center of Tower 2 to my left where there were some firefighters and cops standing. All of a sudden, I had a bald-headed Port Authority police officer wearing a Scott Air-Pak and sweating heavily approach. His name was Bruce Reynolds, and although we had never met before, I knew of and recognized him. Bruce was assigned to the George Washington Bridge (GWB). It was one of our senior commands at the time, which meant you had to have 15+ years on the job to even be offered the assignment. Those were all the salty dogs. It was a great gig, and one that was well earned. I had seen pictures in *The Bergen Record*, my local newspaper, of this Port Authority cop saving jumpers from the George Washington Bridge, and that cop was Bruce.

"Reynolds, GWB (George Washington Bridge)," Bruce called out as he approached.

"Jimeno, BT (Bus Terminal)."

He leaned up against a stand and said, "What a mess, huh?"

"Yeah. This is bad," I responded.

Bruce calmly looked at me and said, "You know what, kid, it's gonna be a long day today, but we're going to bring a lot of people home."

Even though I had already served in the Navy, as a young cop I needed that reassurance from a seasoned officer. I felt the significance of being supported by and feeding off my fellow officers, especially when tough times hit.

"Here comes the team," I stated, drawing attention to Sgt. McLoughlin and the guys returning from the lower level E-room.

"Be safe," Bruce said as he turned and walked back toward the command center. Much like Stewie, I did not know it would be the last time I would see him, or that Bruce had come directly over from the GWB and wasn't even supposed to be in the building due to a health condition from a previous incident while on duty. That's just who he was, the kind of officer that put his life on the line and took the time to talk with a young officer in the middle of chaos.

The team loaded everything in the cart, and I started pushing it again. Heavily geared and heavily sweating, I continued to push, aided by the adrenaline rush that my brain ordered up to accommodate the situation. Antonio took notice and told me, "Will, let me push the cart? You have been pushing since the police desk. If you get tired, you won't be any use once we get to where we are going."

I was not only appreciative, but Antonio's loyalty was something I had grown used to and could count on. Still not knowing Tower 2 had been hit, we continued transitioning from Tower 2 to Tower 1. We had made it another 20 yards straight down the concourse where the team stopped to talk to other emergency personnel, consisting of firefighters and an Emergency Medical Technician (EMT).

Sgt. McLoughlin called out to them, "Be careful. We just came from Tower 2. The elevator shafts down at the B1 level are showing some buckling."

The firefighters nodded and walked on, and Sgt. McLoughlin started communicating over the radio as the team stood awaiting the next command. Antonio was behind the cart, or at the six o'clock position; to the left stood Christopher Amoroso; I was directly in front of the cart; Dominick Pezzulo was in the 1 o'clock position; and Sgt. McLoughlin was at 11 o'clock. Off to our right was a hallway leading to an elevator. A call-out over the radio from Inspector Fields asked for the team's position. Sgt. McLoughlin responded, "We're in the concourse, and we're heading to 1," when a deafening boom immediately drew all our attention.

I looked up and could see and feel the whole building violently shaking like we were in some sort of special effects scene in a movie. A fiery blast the size of my house filled the lobby of Tower 2. I could feel that I was just standing there, completely confused by what felt like a bad dream. The building was coming apart, and I was terrified.

"Run! Run to the elevator!" Sgt. McLoughlin shouted as he pointed toward a hallway to our right that led to a freight elevator. Dom started running, and I followed close behind him. I glanced back and could see Sgt. McLoughlin on the move, too. There was one goal: get to that elevator. The lights started flickering, and the air started to fill with a brown debris cloud. I couldn't help but think, "Will, what have you gotten yourself into?" Everything was happening lightning fast, but there was also a slow-motion clarity. I could see Dom entering the hallway and turning slightly to his left, and for a split second I thought I could see light. From within I heard, "Run toward the light and remember our promise that we would not leave each other." Following Dom's lead, I started turning to the left when I felt something pick me up and slam me to the ground. Whatever it was tossed me into a reclining position like I was lying back on my couch, except not so much. The position was right, but I was trapped under something heavy. My training taught me to first call out for assistance through my radio. Reaching for my lapel mic with my left hand, I yelled out the call, "8-13! 8-13! Officers down! We're getting hit with concrete! We're at the Trade Cent-"

Something fell and hit my hand, ripping the mic away. More debris started falling, and I grabbed my helmet, trying to protect myself as best as I could. The helmet was already strapped on, but I was taking intense hits. One of the shots knocked my helmet loose, tearing the chinstrap from my neck. What the hell was big enough to rip a leather chinstrap? More and more concrete kept pummeling me, and then, nothing. Total silence. Total darkness.

Reflections

1) Are there parts of this chapter that you find personally meaningful?

2) Are there times in your life that you have willingly walked into the darkness for a cause greater than oneself? Do you know why?

3) Do you need to pause, breathe, reflect, or grieve in this moment before continuing?

Chapter Four

Willy, Don't Forget

Greater love hath no man than this, that a man lay
down his life for his friends. — John 15:13 KJV[1]

The dust and smoke began to give way to the light. There was a hole about 20 feet above me, and I could begin to see that I was in a cavern of sorts. On top of me was a large piece of concrete, pinning me down from my upper left torso, across my midsection, and covering my legs; the left leg I was pinned flat, and my right leg was partially bent, with the added enjoyment of being wrapped in metal. As I took inventory of my body, the pain on my left side started to make itself known. I had partial mobility, with my left arm able to bend at the elbow and move my hand. I also had full use of my right arm and torso.

In front of me, beyond my feet, was solid concrete. It was pretty much the same to the right, but there was two to three feet of space, which felt like a mansion compared to the rest. To the left, I could see Dom, face-down in a push-up position. Out of sight about 15 feet beyond the concrete at my feet was Sgt. McLoughlin. He had been pinned in a fetal position. His presence became known when he yelled from under the debris, "Sound off! What's everybody's condition?"

"Pezzulo!"

"Jimeno!"

Anticipation was met with silence. Hope was left lingering in that empty space awaiting the voices of Rodrigues and Amoroso. It was a painful silence.

Dom spoke up and said, "Hey, I'm okay, but I'm stuck."

"I can't move; I've got concrete on me. I'm being crushed over here," I replied. The pain bit me again. I started calling out, "Chris! A-Rod!...Amoroso! Rodrigues!" I yelled it again and again, but the only answer I heard was from Dom.

"Willy, they're in a better place."

---

[1] *King James Version Bible.* (2011). The KJV Bible. https://www.biblehub.com.

The harshness of that reality was tough. We knew we had lost two great men who were also brothers, fathers, sons, cops, and great Americans. They were just gone. Why were we still here and they just were gone? They just vanished. That was just too much to have to absorb so quickly. Thankfully for us, Sgt. McLoughlin was a seasoned professional that kept his focus in spite of the situation. He called out again for a status update on our conditions.

Dom said, "I'm stuck, but I think I might be able to get out of here."

"I can't move," I restated. "I've got a lot of concrete on me, and it's painful." It felt like there were 10 Chevy Suburbans piled one on top of the other, and I was the jack stand. As the pain started to hold my attention hostage, the intensely loud beeping of my Scott Air-Pak started going off. They are engineered to do so when it registers a lack of movement for a period of time to assist a downed first responder in alerting others and helping them be located. This piercing sound was going off right in my ear, and I could do nothing to shut it off or remove the Air-Pak. To add to the annoyance, Dom's started going off. I thought of some new English words and maybe some Spanish ones too to describe my frustration. However, my frustration soon gave way to fear. I'm staring at Dominick, and more and more Air-Pak beepers are starting to engage and sound off. They were coming from above us, and it sounded like hundreds of them. I thought, "Why are there hundreds of people not moving? Were all the first responders dead?"

Thankfully, while the alarms were blaring, Dom was shimmying, contorting, and persistently working at removing his Air-Pak so that he could maneuver his way from beneath the debris that had been holding him down. Moving at all was no easy task in this compact space full of heavy objects and sharp, protruding limitations. However, Dom managed to free himself, crawl across my face, and was now crouched to my right side in a small opening. Looking up, he could see the hole I had seen.

Dom looked around and said, "Sarge, I think I can climb up and go get help."

"No. You've got to get Jimeno out, and then the two of you can get me out."

"But Sarge, I can go get help!" reasserted Dom.

"No! You'll never be able to find us again."

It felt like a kick in the gut to Dom. Even though Sgt. McLoughlin had reason behind his decision, it was hard for Dom to wrap his head around it.

"Willy, I've got a family at home."

"So do I. I've got a daughter and one on the way."

We continued to talk about it, and it was clear Dom struggled with what he thought was the right choice for him to do. As a man, it made sense to get out and try to find help with the hope of returning home, but as an officer he was called to stay with his team and try to save them. True to Dom, he followed orders and tried to help fellow officers that couldn't help themselves. It made sense tactically, but the rational doesn't always comfort the emotional.

"Willy, I'm gonna stay and get you out," Dom assured me. "Hey, Sarge, I'm gonna get Jimeno out."

"Good. Hurry up! Try to get him out."

Dom dug in and started trying to work this immense piece of building off of me. It was an impossible task, but Dom tried anyway. To add to this Herculean task, a piece of rebar was wrapped around my foot. The other end of the metal had another piece of concrete connected to it that Dom started trying to break free. He was a strong guy, and he pulled back on the chunk of material until his hands slipped off. Inevitably, the block sprang back onto me.

"Shit!" I said grimacing. It hurt, but there was no other choice. Again and again, he pulled. Again and again, it sprang back.

"Dom, you're beating the shit out of me," I said in a half painful grunt and half laugh.

Dom fell back into a sitting position laughing because the absurdity was just too funny to ignore.

"Yeah, I'm kicking your ass!" He had tried for about fifteen minutes to get me even slightly freer than I had been, and all he managed to do was to beat me up some more. But it was in our laughter together that showed we had accomplished more in our effort than if he had even removed the block. We were partners. We were friends. We were in this together.

"If you're gonna kick my ass, then hurry up and get it done," I joked.

Dom exhaled as the mood shifted, "Willy, I can't get you out."

An intense wave of fear washed over my body. All I could think of was, "Holy shit! He can't get me out! We are in a bad situation, and he can't get me out." This thought in my head had barely finished when another enormous, explosive sound shattered the moment. Again, my internal voice spoke, "This is it. We're gonna die!"

Dom had just enough room to crouch in the area on my right, so he positioned himself to brace for the impact he knew was coming. I crossed my arms over my chest making the Sign Language symbol for *I love you* with both hands. This was something I did with Allison and

Bianca, and I hoped that if they found me, they could tell Allison so that she would know I was thinking of her in my last moments. It was the first time I had been able to think about my family with any depth since we arrived on scene. It had been about the mission, survival, and my teammates up till now. When all of that seemed lost, I rested in my love for my family.

Debris started coming through the openings, and the ground was rumbling all around. Larger chunks and dust began filling the cavity we occupied making it hard to see. I looked to my right and could barely make out Dom. Dom was getting peppered with the same debris when something large hit him, sitting him down like a rag doll. The already small opening was rapidly filling in more and adding more weight onto us. I screamed out and could hear Dom yelling, too, but he sounded different, as if there was something muffling him. From beyond my feet, I heard Sgt. McLoughlin screaming in pain, the kind of screeching that would have made a bystander nauseated. Sgt. McLoughlin was already pinned in a fetal position under immense weight, but now he was taking direct hits on top of the debris, crushing him even more.

Similar to the first collapse, the intensity of the chaos went from overwhelming to silence. This time though the silence included sounds of pain from us. Catching my breath, I looked over to Dom who was just a couple of feet from me. He was caked in dust and looked like a statue. The crimson red against the pale dust on his face made it clear that he was bleeding from his mouth. His muffled voice and spitting blood was evidence that Dom had suffered massive internal injuries when that last piece of building hit him. Dom was trying to speak, but I could only hear murmuring.

"Dom! Dom! Are you okay?" I yelled.

Softly, Dom replied, "No, Willy, I'm dying."

"Hold on, Dom! Hold on!"

Dom continued to spit the blood from his mouth, and he said, "Willy, don't ever forget I died trying to save you guys."

"Dominick, I will never let anyone forget this."

Dom raised his voice slightly and called out to Sgt. McLoughlin, "Sarge, can I get a -38?" In the middle of dying he was cracking a joke, asking if he could get a "break" (i.e., Port Authority Police Code 8-38).

Sgt. McLoughlin, still enveloped in pain, could tell by Dom's voice it was serious, and he held his groans and responded to Dom, "Yeah, you can have a -38."

Dominick, with the little remaining strength he had in his body, pulled out his sidearm. He said, "I love you, Willy."

"Dom, I love you."

Dom raised his arm toward the hole to the outside world and fired a shot off in a last-ditch effort to alert anyone that his team was still down there. His body slumped, and his gun dropped to his side. He was gone. I could see my friend give his last breath trying to save us, and now I could also see him just a couple of feet away, dead.

"Sarge, Dom's dead! Dom's dead!" I painfully cried out.

Sgt. McLoughlin, still moaning in pain, still leading his team, said, "Keep focused! Keep focused! Can you get out?" He kept asking different questions or giving different commands to keep me from falling into despair and losing focus on *our* survival.

"I understand. He's gone, but you need to stay focused!" Sgt. McLoughlin asserted.

His words felt harsh, but it got me to start thinking in the direction of doing what was possible. I tried to reach for my weapon but couldn't get it out. My body was starting to swell due to the compression of the building crushing my body. The exhaustion was getting the best of me, and it took a toll every time I moved. But I saw a small chunk of concrete I could reach. Maybe I could chip away at this massive block on me? I sure didn't have many options, so why not try? It didn't take long to see this wasn't going to get me anywhere, so I started taking inventory again. Radio gone. Who knows where the hell that thing went. Weapon, inaccessible. Flashlight, buried. Handcuffs, well, I can get to the primary pair in the front, but the backup cuffs in the back are buried. So, I took out my cuffs from the front and started trying to chip away at the block. With every swing I felt like I was running a marathon. My thirst was intense. I'm not sure how long it had been since I drank anything, but I knew I had a mouth full of concrete dust and smoke. Bringing my focus back to the cuffs, I'd take a few swings and then a break; a few swings and then a break. I finally had to set the cuffs down and rest, but when I reached for them again, I couldn't find them. I thought, "Where the hell did they go? I just sat them right on top of my chest.

Frustrated, I called out, "Sarge, what do we do now? What's next?"

"Jimeno, we've never trained for anything like this."

Not satisfied with the answer, I continued with the questioning, "Well, Sarge, what's going to happen to us?"

"They're not going to come in and look for us. If it's what I think it is up there, they're going to have to secure the scene and make sure there are no other bombs or anything," Sgt. McLoughlin explained, still under the assumption this was a result of car bombs. "We're just going to have to keep trying to stay alive."

"What can we expect now?"

"Listen, basically what will likely happen is that we will suffer from compartment syndrome. Our bodies will probably poison themselves, and if they don't get to us by morning, we're probably going to die," he said in his straightforward, professional manner.

I didn't like what I heard, but it still brought me some comfort at least knowing what to expect. I focused, looking for ways to help myself. I decided to shout periodically in case someone could hear us from above.

"PAPD! Officers down! There's men down here!" Over and over I yelled, only to receive silent responses. "PAPD! Officers down!"...

Out of nowhere a ball of flames fell from above, almost hitting me. I hadn't seen any sign of fire until it was coming at me. I thought, "Are you kidding me?" Fire is the one thing I didn't like having to mess with. We were cross-trained in police and firefighting duties, but I was scared of fire and didn't want anything to do with it, especially when I was trapped and it was falling next to me. As weird as it seemed, the flames were not only hitting near me, but they were also rolling in my direction. A familiar smell hit me; it was jet fuel. That smell had been imprinted on me from my Navy days. I knew that if the flames caught my uniform on fire I couldn't do anything to stop it, and I would burn alive. I was yelling and moving as much as possible to avoid the flames. I could feel the burning on my arm and knew it was going to take hold of the uniform.

In shear desperation I yelled out to Sgt. McLoughlin, even though there was nothing he could physically do. "Sarge, Sarge, there's fireballs falling in here! I'm gonna burn alive!"

The only thing Sgt. McLoughlin could do was to again try to keep me fighting by saying, "Stay focused! Stay focused! Try to put the flames out."

I continued to do whatever evasive maneuvers I could, but there just wasn't much ability to move. With no pattern to them falling they hit, rolled my way, and then just disappeared shortly before hitting my sleeve. I didn't understand why this happened, but I was sure grateful for whatever stopped them.

Pow!... Pow! Pow!... Pow!

"What the hell!" I yelled. Not only was the fire threatening to burn me alive, but it heated up Dom's weapon enough to start firing it off. It was only a couple of feet away, next to his body. With only about 18 inches of space above me and on most sides, I could literally see sparks right above my face with every shot.

Again, with no other way to describe it, I desperately called out, "Sarge, Dominick's gun is going off!" After all I had gone through in those hours, rational thought gave way to fear. I placed my hand over the side of my head hoping that if a bullet hit me that it might take some of the impact. I knew better, but I had to try something. Pow!...Pow!...silence. The weapon finally emptied itself.

"Holy shit! I've just been shot at, and I'm still alive!" I thought. It also became a stark reminder that I had not worn my vest that morning, thinking I would grab it at my 10 o'clock break. Allison would be so pissed if she knew. Thankfully, it was months later that she found out. She had been so supportive in agreeing to buy this ultra-lightweight vest when money had been tight. Right then, I would gladly have faced her anger because I would have been with her, at home.

I was somehow still holding it together. I didn't know how, but I was. At this point I had been crushed, lost two teammates in the first collapse, watched another one die next to me in the second, had been burnt, and had been shot at in close quarters, all within a few hours. It was ridiculous, and the totality of it just could not be absorbed.

"PAPD! Officers down! There's men down here!" There was still daylight left, and I was going to try my best to use it all up. Sgt. McLoughlin and I kept each other alert by talking to each other. We tried our best to distract from the situation and the pain to focus on survival. Time was our friend; time was our enemy. Sarge couldn't move, but I could a little, so I kept at it.

I began to work at my weapon again. With sloth-like movements I still couldn't get it out of the holster, but this time I was able to eject the magazine. This was important because the Smith & Wesson 5946s were built so that the gun would not fire without the magazine in place. Also, I could now use the magazine to try to chip away at the concrete slab holding me down. Fatigue made that a short effort, and I had to set it down. Unfortunately, the magazine must have traveled through the same magical portal as the cuffs because I could no longer find it either. With nowhere to go, I thought I would make another attempt at removing my weapon. My hands were now looking like the puffy Michelin Man, so working the holster was even more difficult. Somehow, someway, the weapon released. I slowly pulled up and tried to point it out toward the hole above to shoot like Dom had. I kept trying to pull the trigger and was frustrated with it not firing. "Seriously?" It finally dawned on me that I had earlier ejected the magazine. Well, if it wasn't going to shoot, I might as well use it to start chipping at the concrete again.

With each attempt at something new, I found renewed strength to try. However, this quickly faded with movement. I had to set the gun down. When I reached back for it, I couldn't find it.

"Fuck!" Because of the swelling in my hands I could not tell the difference between rocks or a weapon. Everything felt the same, and there was little feeling left in my fingers. "Where the hell is everything going?" Needless to say, I felt defeated. The light of day appeared to wane, and the two of us began to talk again.

Sgt. McLoughlin said, "My name is John."

"I'm Will."

First-name introductions are common and seemingly insignificant in most relationships, but cops have a culture of using last names. I did not know him as John. He only knew me as Jimeno. Additionally, here was my superior initiating this informality. Where others may take it for granted, it was huge for me, and Sarge was leading us to a different level of relationship that would help us survive.

We started talking about our families; John shared that he had four children. I told him about my four-year-old daughter, Bianca, with another child on the way. Both of us prayed together, and we tried to keep each other's spirits up. Much like my attempts to chip away at the concrete, John kept trying to call on a radio that only offered static in return. Regardless of the impotent outcomes, trying and hoping kept us focused on surviving and our hopeful rescue.

At times throughout the day, John went silent. I knew John was in pain, so silence meant he was potentially drifting toward sleep, which was not good. I called out to him, sometimes with some colorful words, to keep him awake.

"Get up, Sarge, get up!"

"I'm here, Will."

John did the same for me. Both of us were barely hanging on, and as teammates we were doing the only thing in our power: watch each other's backs.

"Will, we have to keep each other awake. If we sleep, we die."

The struggle to stay awake and to stay alive continued. Somewhere in the distance we heard another boom similar to the ones we experienced earlier, but this was further away. Shots were being fired, and it sounded like a raging gun battle. With all the events of the day and now this, I thought, "Oh shit! We're at war; I hear shooting." It turned out that the ammunition supply from Building 6 was on fire.

All that had happened and was continuing to happen was too surreal to comprehend. At times it felt like a dream, albeit a bad one, but then I would be jolted into reality, usually due to pain. The bad movie continued, and night began to settle in. We tried to keep the conversation up between us, but exhaustion was taking its toll. I had come to a point where I wanted to give up—I wanted to die. This was the most pivotal point for me. Dominick, Antonio, and Chris were dead. I was in so much pain, and I had been through hell. As darkness descended, so did my hope. I just wanted to close my eyes and give up. I wanted to surrender to death.

Being Catholic, I began to pray my final prayer. "God, thank you for 33 great years here on earth. Thank you for my mom and dad who brought me to this beautiful country. Thank you for my sister, Karen. Thank you for my wife, Allison. Thank you for my little girl of four years. God, I'm gonna ask you for two things. First, since I won't be there, please let my mother-in-law and my mother be present when Allison gives birth, and somehow, someway make it possible for me to see our baby being born. Please allow me to somehow touch her and look over her since I will not be able to hold her and be with her." I didn't know how it was possible, but I was believing in it. I also felt that everyone unjustly killed by those cowards that day would go to heaven: first responders and the civilians that were just trying to provide for their families. I thought that it was likely I would die, and if I did, I was proud to die as a police officer, a family man, and as an American, doing the right thing.

Pulling a business card from my pocket, I wrote a final note that said, "I love you, Allison." I had to press hard and carve the words into the back of the card because this new pen I had, which supposedly wrote upside down, didn't work. It was important to me that Allison felt loved, even in my death. I wanted her to know I loved her and hoped that she would, one day, meet a good man that would offer her the kind of love she and my daughters deserved. I finished the message and put the card back in my pocket, hopefully, to be found later. Now that I had handled my earthly duties, I turned my thoughts toward heaven. It may sound silly to some, but the second thing I asked to receive was for God to give me a glass of water because I was so thirsty from all the smoke, gravel, and dust. With my prayers spoken and my love for Allison and Bianca written, I closed my eyes.

Reflections

1) Are feelings of empathy, judgment, the need to save, or the need to avoid coming up for you? Do you know why?
2) Are there any of your relationships where you have left things unsaid that need to be said?
3) Do you need to pause, breathe, reflect, or grieve in this moment before continuing?

Chapter Five

Jesus and the Marines

*Birds sing not because they have answers but because
they have songs. — African proverb*[1]

I don't know if I had a vision, if I fell asleep, or if I had one leg over the threshold of death, but I saw a person walking toward me with a glowing, white robe. This figure had no discernible face but had brown hair down to his shoulders. In the distance over his left shoulder was a beautiful, tranquil pond with trees around it. Over his right shoulder was an endless sea of tall grass. As this figure walked toward me, I no longer felt pain and a peace came over me. I knew who this was. It was Jesus, and He was carrying a bottle of water cradled in His left arm. All of a sudden, I came to and felt a fire in my belly. Something came over me. The pain was present, but I thought if I gave up now I would be giving up on a lot. First and foremost, I knew I was closest to the hole to the outside. If I gave up and died, no one would be able to hear John, and he would die, too. Secondly, I would be giving up on getting home to my family; I had to make it back to Allison, Bianca, and my unborn baby girl. I thought, "How could I possibly give up on all of that and let the terrorists win? No way! I will not give up on my family; I will not give up on my country! I've got to keep fighting for America and the good that we represent." I knew I had to keep going, but the last thing that hit me was that if I gave up now, I would be giving up on myself.

My passion came through as I yelled to John, "Sarge, we're gonna get out of this fucking hellhole, or we'll die trying!" I had made my decision to live or die with peace, knowing I had given it everything that I had. This decision helped me regain focus and drive, but I was still in a battle that involved pain, suffering, heat, and thirst.

Prior to this vision I was trying to get out. Now I was trying to stay alive. I decided it was time to mentally go to my Rolodex of positive

---

[1] Walsh Anglund, J. (2021). *A Cup of Sun: A Book of Poems by Joan Walsh Anglund.* Harcourt. (Original work published in 1967).

things in life—things that inspired me. One thing that offered itself up was deer hunting. Since I had originally planned on taking a personal day today to go hunting, I told myself to imagine getting set up in my deer stand before sunrise and prepare to do an all-day sit, which is tough. It at least gave me a distraction from the situation and a place to put some of the pain, which was constant and intense. It never left. Everything in me said I should move the position of my body to get some relief, but I did not have that option. So, I had no choice but to feel the consistency of the pain that was offset by the stabbing jolts of intensity. If there was any choice at all in that moment, it was to use the imagery of hunting to place some of it in a more positive reframe. Call it a mind hack or whatever, but it helped.

Allison, Bianca, my unborn child, my parents, and my sister—I went through each of them and thought about memories lived and yet to come. And then there was John. We kept striking up conversations, some longer than others, some shorter, but we kept holding shared hope in our words. Conversation, memories, hopes, and prayers were the only things we could share to comfort and support each other. I started thinking about an earthquake earlier that year in Turkey. I remembered seeing on the news a little girl about three years old surviving and being pulled from the rubble three or four days after the quake. I thought, "If that little girl could survive, and John and I were supposed to be these tough cops, then we have to survive." I knew the comparison was silly, but it also helped for a little while.

Next on my Rolodex was a clip from the movie *G.I. Jane* with Demi Moore. There was a part where they were doing Navy SEAL training, and they were doing flutter kicks on the beach. The main character who plays the Master Chief was shouting out, "Pain, pain is your friend! Pain is your ally! Pain will keep you angry! It will keep you fighting! The best part of pain is that it lets you know you are alive!" I used this to hang on when the pain shot through me. With each wave I said, "You are not dead. You are alive."

The day kept offering moments of hope intermingled with moments of fear or confusion. As I settled into the hope of still being alive, still having the opportunity to fight, I heard more gunshots and felt the ground begin to rumble again.

"Oh my God. There's that sound again," I called out to Sarge. I didn't know it at the time, but other buildings above were still shifting and collapsing. What I knew was that one thing I could count on was the fact that I was still breathing. Everything else was subject to change. Matter of fact, not knowing what change was coming was the other thing I could count on. However, I decided to focus on being alive.

A couple of more hours had passed when I felt a droplet of moisture hit my face. I wasn't sure if it was water or oil, but I knew it was wet. It was coming from a small-diameter pipe above me. I fought through the pain to reach up and grab the pipe, shaking it to get whatever moisture it offered, just to moisten my lips. When I released it, the pipe sprang back and hit something metal, making a metallic ping.

John said, "What was that?!"

"I don't know. It's just a pipe that's above me."

"Keep doing that."

I kept trying, but it took me about fifteen minutes between each pull just to get enough energy to attempt it again. I didn't know how many times I could do it, but I kept doing it for what felt like forever. It was exhausting. During a resting period, I asked John to put a message out over the radio that Officer Jimeno would like his wife to name their baby Olivia, and tell Allison that I love her. This was important to me to try because prior to this whole tragedy, we had been in a deadlock over the name. I wanted either Sierra or Alyssa, and Allison wanted Olivia. John honored my wishes by relaying the message over the static of the radio. I could then hear the radio crackle again as John sent a message out to his wife telling her he loved her and the kids. John and I resumed struggling through the pain and doing everything in our power to survive. It was a long, painful evening.

Around 8 pm that night, I thought my imagination was playing tricks on me because I heard someone calling out in the distance.

"United States Marine Corps! If anyone can hear us, yell or tap!"

It wasn't my imagination, and I gave it all I had and yelled, "PAPD! Officers down!"

The voices kept getting closer, "Keep yelling! We can hear you!"

"PAPD! Officers down! PAPD! Officers down!"

The shouts grew closer and louder. I knew they had to be right on top of us. A light shined through a little hole to my left side, one I didn't even know was there. The light was hitting my left hand, but they couldn't tell the difference between my hand and the concrete because of being caked in dust. It was the perfect camouflage at the most imperfect time. The rubble and I had become one.

I shouted, "Port Authority Police! We have men down! I'm Officer Jimeno! My sergeant is down here! We've been trapped for a long time...please help us!"

"We're Marines! We're going to help you!"

I thought, "Holy shit, the Marine Corps is here? We must be at war!"

I took advantage of the military connection and yelled out, "Hey, I'm former Navy! We used to carry Marines on my ship. Please don't leave us!"

"We're not gonna leave you, buddy!" the Marine declared.

"Can you see me?" I asked.

"Not yet. Make some movement."

I frantically moved my hand back and forth. I was buried on my left side, but had movement in my elbow and hand, and I was using all of it. "I'm moving my hand. Can't you see it?"

"No, we can't see you!"

"Holy shit! I'm fucking right here!" I exclaimed.

The fear and frustration was unreal. Here they are right on top of me, so close, but not close enough to see me. Eternity passed in a couple of minutes of trying, and I had to try something else. Putting my caked index finger and thumb into my dry, debris-filled mouth I somehow moved my fingers enough to get a collective droplet of spit.

"This has to work..." I thought. Rubbing the spittle into the palm of my hand I partially cleaned a small area, revealing a muted flesh toned circle. Having already used more hope than I knew I was capable of, I put my hand out again, waving the little fleshy area like a beacon.

"We got you! We can see you!"

"Oh, thank God!" I couldn't believe it. I could not believe we were finally found. The joy was overwhelming and a welcome relief.

I yelled, "Sarge, the Marines are here! They found us!"

"That's really good, Will," John said in an exhausted tone.

I laid my head back down and could hear the men talking above. I heard the two Marines, Jason Thomas and David Karnes, and a civilian (who chose to remain anonymous). They directed the civilian to go back down the pile to notify available responders of the men trapped while they stayed and attempted to dig down to us. The civilian ran into some firefighters and reported that two Marine Reservists were on the pile trying to dig down to two cops that were found buried alive. It was just what the firemen needed to hear. They connected with the New York City Police Department Emergency Service Unit (NYPD-ESU) Truck One, which is their SWAT team. Cops started scrambling up the pile in the direction he had given and met up with the Marines. Knowing he had done all that he could, this unnamed civilian decided it was time to return home to Brooklyn.

Thomas and Karnes kept digging and talking to me, and they directed the ESU toward our location. Two voices became many voices. It was a welcome sound.

"We made it," I thought, as my relief began to be washed away with fear. It was the first time I had been able to let go, even a little, and fear quickly found me. I started thinking, "Now they found us, and I'm, like, okay. So now what happens? Am I going to hold on long enough for these guys to be able to get in here?" The reality of how much this hole resembled a tomb was now exceptionally hard to ignore.

Reflections

1) Are there parts of this chapter that you find personally meaningful for your life?
2) What role does spirituality (regardless of belief affiliation) play in your life, especially during/after a crisis?
3) Is it possible that feelings of helplessness in your life are just that—feelings? Is there more you can do? Do you let feelings become your facts?
4) What is your *why* in life today? If all was stripped away except for a single reason why you fight for life, what would it be (no matter how big or small)?
5) Do you need to pause, breathe, reflect, or grieve in this moment before continuing?

Chapter Six

So Many Patches, Just One Goal

My humanity is caught up, is inextricably bound up, in
yours. — Archbishop Desmond Tutu[1]

I could see a light coming down this little hole to my right, but it was being partially obscured by dust being kicked up. That hole was incredibly tight, but here crawls this guy. He was crawling through concrete, sharp metal, electrical wiring, and rebar. It was so hard to see, but eventually there were three men making their way through this unstable mess of potential death. The first one to me was Scott Strauss, a member of the NYPD-ESU Truck 1, who led the operation. Making his way behind Scott was Chuck Sereika, a civilian who had been a paramedic and was there to offer whatever help he could. They both had bald heads, and that was the primary view I had for the next few hours.

Scott and Chuck were literally on their bellies because there wasn't much room, and they couldn't stand up. Only one person could fit in the hole that led to me, and they literally were on their sides with their hands above their heads, pulling themselves closer and closer. Each inch of advancement was a result of scratching and clawing at the rubble before passing it back. Behind them was a light in the dark void, which was Paddy McGee, another member of the NYPD-ESU Truck 1. He stayed a little behind them, near the elevator shaft that our team had originally run toward. During the collapse it had broken in such a way that made a hole exposing the shaft, and they were using it to dump debris down as they removed it from around me. Rock by rock, chunk by chunk, they passed it back, making their way to me and using it to clear any space possible around me. It was amazing to think that this shaft had broken in such a way that provided both a hole they were using to clear debris, and it had fallen in such a way to create the cavern that partially shielded us from the immense devastation, ultimately

---

[1] Tutu, D. (1999). *No Future Without Forgiveness.* First Image Books.

saving our lives. A few feet in any direction was the difference between life and death. And now the guys were making progress, literally, in inches. The smoke and dust was thick, and Scott and Chuck changed positions every few minutes. It was hot as hell!

"Hey, Medic, what's your first name?" Scott asked, seeking something more relational, considering the intensity of their shared situation.

"Chuck."

"Hey, Chuck, I'm Scott."

Debris was falling down onto my face from the guys above trying to clear an additional path down. I was so thankful for what everyone was doing, but I was also weary of having a mouth full of concrete dust. "Hey, Marine, stop digging there. It's falling in on Will." Scott yelled.

The digging stopped.

"Hey, Marine, you got something else I can call you other than Marine?" Scott similarly asked.

"Staff Sergeant Karnes," he responded matter of factly.

I'm not sure if Scott chuckled or grunted while moving debris, but he just kept digging. When in crisis, events often seem to take longer than they are, but this was not the case that night. These men, in spite of their limiting environment, were consistently moving closer. I felt Scott reach out and touch me for the first time. I was so tired, so exhausted, that I wanted to just give myself over to Scott. I could feel myself passing over the baton of responsibility for my life. My heart rate shot up, and I began to hyperventilate. Gasping for air, I thought, "Oh shit! I'm losing it!" It felt like my heart was going to explode. I was scared, and I was confused.

"Hey, you gotta get yourself under control!" Scott yelled. "You're going to give yourself a heart attack. Focus! Slow your breathing."

I couldn't understand why my body just seemingly went out of control. After all, the calvary was here. We were being rescued. I could literally touch the guys that were going to help me, and I felt relieved until I didn't. It felt like another chunk of concrete hit my chest, but there was no concrete; there was no understandable reason for the pressure in my chest. "What the hell is my body doing?"

"Hey man, you've got to keep focused. You have got to keep focused," Scott sternly advised as he administered oxygen.

I heard Scott loud and clear, and it helped me to start to slow my body. Just because the guys were there, I still had a responsibility for my own rescue. I was not alone, but I still had a job to do.

I worked on slowing my body down. I thought of positive things and breathed in the oxygen. My respirations and heart rate began to slow. We used the oxygen periodically to manage moments of anxiety, but most of the time I didn't need it. What I did need was water.

"I am so thirsty. Do you have any water?"

"It's coming." Scott reassured.

While the three rescuers had been making their way down the hole and beginning to clear some rubble, word had spread, and it had spread fast. First responders from different departments, states, and organizations were showing up to assist from above. They were making a human chain of hundreds of men and women, like us, who had a heart for serving. There were two of their brothers that needed them, and they, again, walked into danger to do all they could to save us. Water started being passed up the line until they got some bottles down below into *the hole*.

I began gulping like a madman, to the point of coughing it up. That was the best damn water I had ever tasted.

"Ease up, Jimeno" Scott reminded me.

It had been ten hours since I had had any fluids, except for the oily drips from the pipe. I had been surrounded by smoke and dust and had a ton of it poured all over my face and head. This water was a welcome sensation that brought some relief and renewed energy.

It's incredible what the body can withstand. I couldn't even remember the difference between having concrete on me and not having concrete on me. It was a weird thought, but I realized we had become part of the building. With all the destruction, debris, smoke, and dust, we were simply breathing with the building. In the initial collapse and in the second collapse, I coughed every once in a while, but the smoke didn't seem to bother me, which was incredible because these guys were choking on the smoke. They were having a hard time breathing. For whatever reason, my body hadn't reacted to the toxic, airborne irritants. Even though the rescuers were having a hard time without the oxygen, it didn't stop them. They just fought through it and kept focused.

Chuck, Scott, and Paddy finally cleared enough debris to start working on me. Scott moved across the slab that was resting on me.

"Aaaaahhhh!" I screamed in pain like I had never heard myself scream before. Beneath the crushing wall my body had been swelling. Compartment Syndrome was not starting; it had taken hold, and the added pressure of Scott on me was excruciating. Scott tried to maneuver himself and my leg again with the same result, nothing productive but screams. I thought to myself, "Oh my God, how are we going to do this? Every time he touches me it's painful." I knew there was no way to do this without going through more hell. I looked up and could see the hole above me. I couldn't tell how they had made their way in, but I knew freedom was 20 feet from me. I realized that if I kept screaming, it was just going to slow everything down, and I was ready to get out. I worried about how much time John had left. John had been silent since he heard they had been found.

"Can you get my partner out first?" I asked.

Scott paused for a moment, "No, we have to get you out first."

I told myself I had to shut up and eat the pain. I knew the faster they worked the faster they could get to John. Chuck slithered up and inserted an IV, using duct tape to hold it in place. Those two bald heads just kept twisting, turning, and wiggling around.

At one point, Scott secured my weapon and handed it back to Paddy.

"Gun coming up."

A few seconds later someone from above called down, "I got it. It's a Glock."

"No! It's a Smith and Wesson!" I yelled back.

In typical New York fashion they're yelling back down, "Who the fuck cares!"

They all started laughing. Scott chuckled and asked, "You're fucking almost dying, and you're worried about what type of weapon it is?"

"Well, I was just being accurate about the facts."

We passed the time by talking about our families and just some general small talk. There was a lot of opportunity for any of us to die, but there was also still time to be human with one another. Being human with one another, what a treasure. That's what they brought down into the middle of a crushing, burning, and jagged debris field, their humanity.

"Look, I'm going to take you guys out for a nice steak dinner when you get me out of here," I told them.

"Sounds good."

It was a perpetual ebb and flow between the pleasure of sharing stories and razzing one another and the frustrations of the situation. They were coughing, dry heaving, and persistent in their mission. The guys continued to work on me, and they were literally digging me out by hand, like a couple of groundhogs. They kept calling for different tools to be brought up the line and down into the hole to assist in the rescue, but this tool wouldn't fit or that tool ended up being broken. Even the airbags for lifting heavy objects ended up being ripped by the time they made it down through the debris. The pile was unlike anything they had ever had to work through. I couldn't help but think: *We are in the United States of America, the greatest country on Earth, and in New York City where they have the best equipment and, yet, everything is failing.* It was literally up to them to dig John and me out by hand. Tenacity is too small of a word to describe those guys. Even the request for more water became an issue because much of it was already drank by the time it arrived. People may judge this and think, "What the hell?" But the heat on the pile was getting to everyone. The soles of their boots were literally melting on their feet. It was intense, yet no one left.

"Scott, listen man, just cut my leg off; you know, just cut it off," I said. Once again, I was staring at the hole above and knew that I could get out and they could get to John sooner. "Just cut the damn thing off!"

"We're working on getting you out. Relax."

"Can't you hurry up? You got to get my partner out."

This whole time John is still silent, and my concern is growing. Paddy, Chuck, and Scott never stopped. It had been about two hours of painstakingly chipping, coughing, sweating, and contorting, putting their bodies through the mill. They were a lot closer, but there was still a lot of work to do.

"How's it going? John asked from the darkness.

The guys stopped cold and looked around. "Who's that?"

"That's my partner," I responded. "That's my partner, Sgt. McLoughlin."

They had no clue that anyone else was there, or alive. When I spoke of my partner, they assumed I was talking about Dominick, and they were trying to be respectful in answering because they knew Dominick was dead and I was in bad shape. At some point, Paddy had even covered Dom with a jacket because they knew it would be awhile before they could bring him home, too.

"How ya doin, Sarge?" Scott asked.

"I'm buried deep; I'm past Will. I'm crushed in the fetal position. I'm hurting really bad. How long before you can get to me?" John responded in a nonchalant manner.

"Is this John McLoughlin?"

John replied, "Yeah, who's this?"

"It's Scott Strauss."

"Hey, Scott, how are you doing?"

In a confused, humorous tone, Scott answered, "How am I doing? How are you doing? Listen, John, we're still working on Will. Once we get him out we're coming for you. Hang in there!"

Scott and Paddy knew John because they had done some cross-training with him at the World Trade Center. John taught repelling to NYPD in case they needed to repel the elevator shafts. "Hey, we trained with you before," Scott called out.

"Is that ol' Irish Eyes?" Paddy asked. Paddy is as Irish as the day is long. He was born on St. Patrick's Day and is a bagpiper in the NYPD Emerald Society Pipe Band.

"Yeah," John responded.

"Hey, we're coming for you. As soon as we get Will out, we're coming for you. Hang in there, Sarge!" Scott kept encouraging.

"Okay. Alright. Keep at it," John said calmly.

I was relieved again by the connection and feeling of brotherhood. Every thread of connection gave me a little peace and energy to keep going. I knew they wouldn't leave without us. This reassurance was further affirmed with chatter from above. The guys working on me were being told they need to wrap it up and get out because there was an encroaching fire on top of the pile. The sound of the fire and the efforts to fight it became louder.

"You guys gotta get out of there!" someone kept yelling down the hole.

"You're not leaving us, are you?" Will asked Scott.

"No, we're not leaving you, Will. We're with you. We'll get you out."

Scott later shared, "I didn't want to go in that hole, but I had to. I wanted to leave when they told me to leave, but I couldn't. And I got to tell you, I don't think it had anything to do with any macho bullshit. I think it was a matter of self-preservation. I don't think I could have lived with myself and gone home to hug my kids to leave these two guys to die without giving them a fighting chance. So, I think it was just a matter of me being selfish and trying to say, 'Holy shit, how do I go home and hug my kids' and say 'Hey, it sucks to be him?' I don't think I could live with myself after that. And we stayed. And in numbers there's strength."

Again, there was yelling from above, "We're ordering you to come out!"

"Go fuck yourselves! We're staying!" Paddy and Chuck yelled back.

In spite of the back and forth, everyone was still working at getting us out. The guys up above were doing all they could do. They were dragging hoses across sharp, jagged metal. Every hose they dragged up got cut on something, diverting the much-needed water pressure before reaching the end of the hose. They were even throwing fire extinguishers at the fire.

Sometimes John went quiet, and it made me nervous. He had kept me alive, and I needed to make sure he stayed alive, too. Anytime one of us called out to him and he did not respond, my anxiety peaked.

"I'm still here, Will. I'm still here." John said when he regained consciousness.

"Scott, man, just cut my leg off. I can live without a leg," I said again.

Scott firmly responded, "No, I'm going to get you out of here in one piece."

Enough debris had finally been cleared around that they were able to cut the straps from my Air-Pak. Scott began yanking on the straps, pulling the tank from beneath me.

"I'm sorry, Will. I'm sorry." Scott kept apologizing for the pain he was causing while pulling on the tank. He couldn't help it. He was lying on his side with his hands above his head in extremely tight surroundings, trying to pull a tank from underneath me and the concrete slab that was wedging us together. I'm not sure how he managed it, but thankfully he did. Removing that Air-Pak gave us an additional 8 to 10 inches of space between my chest and the slab. Paddy passed Scott some extenders, which are about 6-foot webbed straps with hooks on the ends that they use when climbing bridges, and he put them around my chest and arms. He began pulling, but his awkward position gave him little leverage. Nevertheless, he was pulling enough to create intense pain in my left leg.

"Aaaahhhh! My leg! My leg is stuck!" I screamed.

"Okay, Will, hold on and let me see what's going on."

"Cut my leg off! Get to the Sarge! He's going to die if you don't get to him." I pleaded.

"Will, I'm not cutting your leg off. I don't have anything to cut your leg off with anyway."

From above we hear Karnes call down, "Here, use this," as he lowered a Ka-Bar knife down through the hole to Scott.

"Use this? Are you out of your fucking mind? You expect me to saw it like a steak?" Scott fired back.

"Yeah, yeah, cut my leg off. Cut my leg off." I continued to push.

"Will, I'm not cutting your leg off. We'll get you out of here. We'll get to the Sergeant. Let me see what's holding it, what's pinning it down."

We all had the best intentions, but Scott was catching it from all sides, as well as dealing with his own concerns. However, he held it all together and managed the situation like a pro. He began to crawl into the space between me and the slab, trying to get to my left leg.

"Will, I can't get any clearance around your leg where it's pinned. I need an air chisel," Scott informed me. He then yelled his request to the guys above.

"How about an air bag?" they yelled down.

There's no room. I need an air chisel."

"How about a battery-operated Hurst tool (like the Jaws of Life)?" they offered.

"Well, if you think it's going to fit down here, I'll try it."

I could tell it was heavy, and Scott began pushing it over me, in a space no bigger than the space underneath a normal-sized chair.

"Will, I'm sorry. I got to get this all the way over the other side of you," Scott apologetically stated.

"Don't worry about me. Get to the Sergeant."

He started shoving the tool across my chest, and it hurt but it was necessary. There was just no room to move or to be careful. Although Scott would apologize for hurting me, he was also a fellow cop, which meant he was also giving me shit.

"Wow, I have to get the guy that eats good," Scott said, giving me a hard time.

"What can I say, my wife's a good cook. She's Italian."

Trashing each other and using gallows humor is a cultural form of communication with first responders, and it was a welcome interchange between two guys—not rescuer and victim but two brothers. Being human with one another was as much a part of the rescue as the rescue itself. Scott crawled in perpendicular on top of me, with his head, chest, and arms across my stomach. After positioning the tool in the spot he thought might work, he crawled out and yelled to the guys.

"Will, I gotta move this concrete," Scott said. "Hey, I need everyone to be quiet. Everybody, shut the fuck up! I'm going to work the tool. Chuck, Paddy, you guys need to go."

"I'm staying," Paddy said.

"Me, too," added Chuck.

Scott argued with them, "I got no idea what this is going to do. This could bring the whole thing down on top of us, and there is no use of three of us getting killed along with these guys."

"We're not leaving."

"Hey, do you mind? Get me outta here. Talk later," I said, like the smart ass that I am.

The guys never let it be known that they didn't believe they were going to make it out of the hole even as they first entered, but they entered anyway. Scott later shared that he had internally expressed his love and pre-emptively apologized to his family for dying that night as he removed his gun belt and gear to make room to fit into the entrance of the hole. Let me say it again, these men believed they were going to die, and they came in after us anyway. I felt the patriotic fire within me, witnessing the dedication these guys had. I thought, "These fucking terrorists didn't realize that this is the passion we have as Americans, not only for fellow Americans but for all human beings and for good."

Scott crawled back on top of me and said, "Will, listen, I'm sorry. I have no idea what's going to happen here. If this concrete slab breaks and everything comes down on top of us, there's 100 guys up there that know where we are, and they'll start digging for us right away."

"Just get it done and get to the Sergeant," I said.

"All right, Will, here we go."

The sound of the tool gave hope, but I didn't feel anything shifting. Scott crawled back out, which is not a good sign, and said, "Crap! It's not working."

Chuck said, "Let me try. Let me see what's going on." Chuck started gathering chunks of concrete to create cribbing to wedge the jaws against. "Try that," he said.

Scott crawled back in and positioned the tool to try again.

"Ready, Will?"

"Yeah, yeah. I'm ready." The pile had never really stopped shifting since the collapse, and there was no way to shore anything up. However, we were about to add to the instability without knowing what would happen. The sound of the machine working and things creaking reminded me of some of the noises I heard when all of this was coming down. The slab began shifting, and I could feel the wall lifting. A piece of the wall cracked and fell away from my leg. Scott immediately grabbed the straps and tried to pull again. Once again, the pain in my foot was intense and something was still holding me. They thought they just didn't have enough strength to free me individually, so Chuck squeezed into the spot, chest to chest with Scott, and they began pulling together. With greater pull came greater pain. Something was still pinning me. Chuck backed out and Scott crawled across me again with a little flashlight. Other than the battery-operated Jaws of Life, that little flashlight was the only tool they had. Everything else had been done by hand.

The farther Scott wedged himself in this space to get a better look, the more pain it caused. He finally got a view of the rebar wrapped around my boot between my ankle and the ball of my foot. He kept yanking on my foot and pants, but nothing seemed to work.

"This piece of rebar is pinning his foot down. I can't get his foot out," Scott said to the guys.

I don't know where it came from, obviously it was in the rubble, but Paddy found this perfectly sized, perfectly bent piece of rebar, and he said, "Here, try this to move it."

Scott put it in position and began to lift it up, but it was not enough. He tried again with two hands, but he just couldn't get enough leverage with his position. He could lift it enough, but he could not grab my leg and pull fast enough without losing his leverage and trapping my leg again.

"Chuck, can you get in here at all?"

"Yeah, sure. What's going on?"

Chuck climbed in, but there was just not enough room for both of them to get in far enough for one to lift up on the rebar and the other to pull on my leg.

Scott had to get creative with the space and said, "Okay, Chuck, hold on. Give me your arm. Put your hand on this. He guided Chuck's hand onto the rebar. "You've got to push up with me when I tell you to, and with my other hand I'm going to grab Will's pants leg and try to yank his leg free."

"Okay."

It took Chuck and Scott a couple of tries, but they got it. Scott kept yanking on my leg, and I was screaming. All of a sudden my leg popped free from the rebar. They had done it. They had pulled my leg free. I could tell too because the pain was full on now. I swore my femur was broken. Well, I suppose I swore in more ways than that.

Scott yelled, "We got him! We got him out!"

I still couldn't move, but I was free. These men refused to give up on me. There are no words, only gratitude. I wish I could describe the dense, jagged, and treacherous environment they were working in that could accurately portray the hellish house of cards that these men climbed through and were now tasked with getting me out. Yes, I was free from the rebar, but they still had to pull me through the hole they had barely been able to crawl through to a path large enough to use a Stokes basket, which is a device used to immobilize and transport injured persons through narrow corridors and over rough terrain. Remember, I was the guy who ate his wife's good cooking, not to mention having significantly swelled from the compartment syndrome.

Scott and Chuck crawled out from under the slab and used extender straps around my chest to pull me toward the opening. Inch by inch they pulled me toward Paddy, where he painstakingly worked on removing debris from the exit path. Additionally, Thomas and Karnes had been continuing to dig an opening from above toward Paddy.

After the initial excitement of the progress, the clarity of voices from above returned. At one point a new voice could be heard talking to the others topside, "Hey, we're doctors. Talk to us. How's it going?" he asked.

"We had some doctors on scene, Will, in case we couldn't get you out, in case we did have to amputate," Scott matter of factly shared.

I was more than willing, but I won't lie. I am thrilled they didn't have to come down. Instead, the surgeon offered up a different prescription for care.

"I've got a cell phone up here. Would you like me to call your wife?"

"Yeah! That'd be a great idea," I yelled back before giving the number. "Her name is Allison Jimeno. My name is Will." It was the first time I had been able to get word to her since I had been at the bus terminal. I couldn't hear her, but just to know she was on the other end of that conversation felt like I was closer to going home.

"Hello, Allison?"

"Yeah. Will?" she answered.

"I'm a doctor here at the World Trade Center site. I'm with your husband, Will. He told me to say that I know you have a four-year-old daughter and are seven months pregnant, so you know it's really him," the doctor said. "Listen, we think he may have a broken leg, but he's fine. He's alive. They're taking him to the hospital, and I thought you'd like to know."

"Yes. Thank you! Can I talk to him?"

"No, you can't talk to him right now," he replied.

"Can you tell me what hospital they're taking him to?"

"Okay, hold on," he said before conferring with others. "They're taking him to Bellevue."

"Thank you!" Allison exclaimed.

It was such a relief to be able to get word to Allison that I was alive. A Stokes basket was slowly lowered through the hole, and the guys wasted no time in loading me up. They basically threw me onto the basket and pushed as the others pulled.

"Sarge, hold on! They're coming to get you!" I yelled. It was a mess, but I was going vertical. I was inching my way toward home, but not without intense pain. I was yelling and unsure of the path they were pulling me out of, but I was nearing the top. I couldn't see Dom. I couldn't see John. But I knew Scott, Chuck, and Paddy were still with us.

Scott crawled back in the hole to reassure John. "John, listen. I'm physically shot. I'm no good to you. They're bringing in a fresh team behind us. Will's out, you hang in there; we're going to get you out next.

Breaking from the debris tunnel into the open air brought confusion for me. I looked up and could see some smoke, a dark sky, fire in the distance, and there were a lot of bodies standing around me. But I couldn't see anything else. The buildings were gone. Hours earlier there had been 220 stories of concrete and glass. Now, nothing. It was surreal, like a bad dream that I couldn't wrap my head around.

"Where is everything?"

"It's all gone, kid. It's all gone," a firefighter responded.

That was the first time I cried. I hadn't cried from my injuries. I hadn't cried when I realized we had lost Antonio and Chris. I hadn't cried when I watched Dom die. I didn't cry during the 13 hours of excruciating pain between the first collapse and being pulled from the pile. However, this dark reality broke me. I could only see all those people in that mall area, and we had failed to get them out. We didn't get enough people home, and I felt we failed. Hell, our team hadn't even had the chance. The tears flowed. As I cried for those lost, I was thanking those in front of me as they passed me down the line. I reached up with my right arm and touched the arms and the patches of those I passed by. A Port Authority policeman approached the basket and rubbed spit on my name plate.

"Jimeno," I said.

Sergeant Cottrell repeated it back, but with a soft G sound (like 'gym'), "Jimeno." Calling it out over the radio, he said, "8-2 Jimeno. We got 8-2 Jimeno." (8-2 is for an officer, 8-5 is for a sergeant).

I was overwhelmed with gratitude when I saw the patches from the Port Authority, NYPD, FDNY, and NJ police and rescue departments. As I was lying back and looking up, someone with a Scott Air-Pak mask grabbed my head and looked down at me.

"Jimeno, it's me! Arnold Grant!" Arnold was a classmate of mine, and he was someone that was close to me, someone I really knew. One more heartwarming inch toward home.

"Devil Dog!" I called out, referring to a nickname Arnold had in the academy. "Is that you?"

"Yeah, it's me, Will, it's Devil Dog!"

I was still filled with such gratitude for the hundreds of brothers and sisters passing me closer to home, and to be with the people I love was such a good feeling. It was incredible!

Bang!...feeling over.

Someone had slipped and lost grip on the basket, dropping me and banging the basket against the pile.

"Aaahhh! Oh my God, please don't drop me anymore. It hurts," I said in a combination of pain and laughter. In all honesty, they could have slapped me all the way down the line, and I would have loved them for it because they were bringing me home. It was a long path getting down the line to street level, but they loaded me into the bus (police lingo for ambulance).

Officers Bruce Kent and Steve DiTomasso climbed in behind the stretcher. Someone yelled to the driver, "Take him to Bellevue."

"Can you take me to Hackensack?" I asked because it is across the river and where I grew up.

The guys in the back looked at me like I was crazy. "No, we're taking you to Bellevue." Bellevue was the best place to go in New York City, and it was the place they would take the President if he were ever in need while there. The ambulance driver was looking back kind of confused. This ambulance was from upstate New York, and they had no idea where Bellevue was.

"We're not from here. Tell us how to get there."

Steve jumped out and went up front. "You guys get in back and work on Will. I'll drive us there."

Bruce was holding my hand and started collecting my IDs, the necklace that my mom and dad gave me when I graduated the academy, and my police shield (#1117). Steve took full advantage of the empty streets and put the full-on rush to get me to the hospital. Bruce just held my hand all the way while the paramedics continued to do their job.

"You're going to be all right," Bruce reassured me.

I could feel them pulling into the ER, and I felt a little guilty for hoping they could push me a little ahead of the line, knowing the ERs were going to be at full capacity. The back doors flung open, and they pulled me from the bus. There were numerous doctors and nurses lined up and waiting in their scrubs to take care of me. I wondered how it was possible all these professionals were just standing there waiting for me.

"Where is everybody?" I asked.

"You're it right now."

I cried for the second time that night. That wasn't possible. There were so many people that I knew needed help. Where were they? The absence was all the answer I received, and all the answer I did not want to know. A different kind of pain swept through me.

Reflections

1)   What role does community play in your life, especially during/after a crisis?

2) How is this integrated service community example modeled in your life?
3) Do you need to pause, breathe, reflect, or grieve in this moment before continuing?

Chapter Seven

You're Gonna Feel This

Be patient and tough; someday this pain will be useful to you. — Ovid[1]

A group of nurses grabbed the gurney and whisked me into the Emergency Room. I was amazed at how it felt like bees swarming around, poking and prodding me. A heavyset lady looked down with a comforting smile and said, "We'll take care of you, sweetie." She embodied trust and nurturance. In this chaotic environment of bodies all around doing separate tasks, a purposeful unity silently supported my fatigued and battered body.

A young male nurse sprang up on the gurney. Straddling me and looking me directly in the eyes, he said, "You're gonna feel this."

I didn't know what he was talking about or what I was supposed to feel. I was on sensory overload with everyone working on me. After what I had just gone through, what the hell was I going to feel— "Oohhhh!" I groaned. My focus became crystal clear as the nurse inserted a catheter. If I had felt lethargic at all, that was not the case anymore. I was definitely awake. People were listening for breath sounds, bowel sounds, and poking this spot and that spot. IVs were going in, and blood was being drawn. And then, everything went black. I passed out.

A couple of senior cops stood by me out of respect for their brother, one of which was Geoff Fairbanks, a mentor of mine. Geoff had been tough on me. As a rookie, I wasn't pampered; I had to earn the respect of the senior cops. When I first showed up for duty, Geoff didn't know me or if I was worth anything, and he was the kind of cop that required officers to prove their worth through action. A friend of mine, Frank Liscio, who had worked for me, was friends with and introduced me to Officer Jimmy Cosmano. Jimmy had put in a good word with Bill Finney and Ray Bryant at the Bus Terminal. Jimmy worked at the Lincoln

---

[1] Ferris, A. (2015). *Shades of Blue: Writers on Depression, Suicide, and Feeling Blue* (1st ed.). Seal Press.

Tunnel, and he graduated with Billy and Ray. He gave them a call and told them, "Hey, look out for this kid. I know you're going to bust his chops, but he isn't afraid to work."

Bust my chops they did, especially Geoff. He was the guy at a party that made the party. He had jokes. It was clear that I was not considered a peer yet but still a rookie. Geoff called me *my burro*. He was a stickler for detail, and no task was too mundane to relax the standard. We had to use an old typewriter to complete our reports, and White Out fluid was not an acceptable to use for corrections. If I made a mistake, I would have to start the report over. Geoff would call out across the room as he walked my direction, "Hey, little burro, I see you like to work." He would sometimes rip my report out of the typewriter and say, "That's no good. Start over."

At the moment, I was nothing short of furious, but what I saw later was that even though he was making me take longer and was pissing me off, he was actually teaching me to do it right. Teaching me to not make mistakes. Teaching me to take my time and make it count. Look at the wording. Look at how I'm going to make the case stand. If I make a mistake here, there's a good possibility the bad guy, the perp, is going to walk. It is important that my reports were done right, and I ended up having a friendship with him after a few months. He treated me with respect. A couple of times, I got to work with him. He taught me a lot. He taught me the ins and outs of being a cop. Now, he was standing watch over me as I lay unconscious.

My body was so swollen from the injuries the doctors had to intervene for immediate relief and care to minimize any further damage to the muscle tissue in my legs, which had been crushed for the last 13 hours. There was only one way to do what needed to be done, and it was not a finesse kind of procedure. They took a scalpel and cut my left leg from hip to ankle. When they made the incision, my leg exploded, releasing the pressure and splattering blood across the wall behind the doctor. Geoff, who had seen his share of gore, left the room. I, on the other hand, flatlined.

On the other side of the ER doors stood a sea of blue uniforms, along with Allison; my sister, Karen; and a friend of mine, Brian Boel, who also was a Port Authority police officer. Brian's brother Chris—a Little Ferry, NJ police officer—had heard over the police radio that John and I had been found, so he had called Allison to give her the good news. Chris and Allison were childhood friends, but all three of them grew up together.

Brian had been at the bus terminal when the news of them finding us had been called out over the airways. Sergeant Beverly King, a female officer who is a great, great person, knew Brian and I were tight. She found out they were taking me to Bellevue, so she called Brian over the radio and said, "You need to go to Jersey and pick up Will's wife and bring her to Bellevue."

I would have trusted any of my fellow cops to make sure Allison made it to the hospital safely, but I'm glad that it was Brian accompanying her. After all, she was about to get blindsided with the reality of the situation. Up to this point, they were all under the impression that I was being treated for a broken leg and possibly broken pelvis. Meanwhile, behind closed doors, they worked feverishly on me to regain a heart rhythm. Apparently, it was not looking good. They were struggling to regain a heartbeat.

Bruce Kent had been in the waiting room when Allison came in. They didn't know each other, but after a short wait with no staff in sight, Allison had asked him if he could go and get an update on me. He knew it was serious, but he wasn't expecting to find the situation deteriorating so rapidly. Someone in the room gave him the down and dirty on their attempts to revive me, and he turned to go back out to advise Allison.

Beep, beep. Beep, beep, the heart monitor suddenly chirped.

Bruce heard the monitor and gladly turned around just before he reached the doors, his skin already a lighter tone than just a few minutes ago. It was pretty touch-and-go for the next few minutes. My heartbeat was erratic, and I flatlined again. Allison had asked Bruce to check on me thinking I had a broken bone or two, and Bruce was turning white as a ghost, thinking, "Oh my God, I have to go tell his wife *this*?" Nothing about this day was following anyone's expectations.

The phenomenal staff of Bellevue managed to bring me back again and stabilize the situation, and they were able to bring Allison and Karen back with me. I was unconscious and a mess, but I was alive. The next day or two would tell a lot. I was far from being out of danger. Allison, nearly seven months pregnant, and Karen stayed that night in the ER, upright in rigidly uncomfortable chairs. I was unaware, but it didn't surprise me.

Some time during the first 12 hours of arriving at the hospital I was intubated, and by the next morning I had my second surgery. Allison and Karen were brought into the recovery room with me. The lethargy and mental fogginess, along with the inability to speak, was in direct conflict with my desperate need to communicate with Allison. The use of sign language wasn't productive, so I motioned for a pen and paper.

They handed me an envelope and a pen, and I attempted to let it all spill out. I was trying to tell them who I had been with, who I had seen along the way, where I last saw certain individuals, and where we were when the Towers collapsed. What seemed like a clear expression from my end was not coherent on theirs. When in doubt and with limited ability, an I love you was still the best and easiest message I could relay. So that's what we all shared for the time being before they rolled me back to the ICU. The rest of the day I slept a lot, mainly due to the medications.

Allison left for the night, but she returned first thing in the morning on the 13th. Jimmy Cosmano had driven out to Clifton to pick her up (and did so every day until I left the hospital). The medical staff removed the tube from my throat, and I was able to talk, even if it was a bit strained. Our first conversation was about the baby. I wanted her to know that I wanted the baby to be named Olivia. The next matter of importance was to, again, share as much information as I could about the people I was with, who I had seen that day, and where I last saw them. It was important to me that I try to help find them. I was trying to explain what happened. I wanted to get it out in case something happened to me. Thankfully, there were no operations that day, and we were just able to talk and be together. I finally got to catch my breath, but that would change the following morning.

The morning of the 14th and for the next two weeks, every other day would involve surgeries to debride the wounds, removing any foreign objects or muscle tissue that had died in the previous 48 hours. There had been a lot of bruised muscle tissue, so it was important to remove only the tissue that was not recovering to ensure as much living tissue as possible remained. If any tissue regained normal color and blood flow, great. If it discolored and was dying, it was cut out.

Another joyous procedure was when they hooked the Hoover vacuum to my lungs. Okay, maybe it wasn't as big as a house vacuum, but they placed this suctioning device in my mouth and were sucking rocks and gravel from my airway. We could hear the debris rattling along the tubing like paperclips in a vacuum hose. The sound was disturbing, and it was shocking to see the amount of debris that was still being removed a few days after being rescued. One of the doctors mentioned that they had to flush my lungs because my lungs looked like I had smoked for 30 years; I hadn't smoked a day in my life.

We made it through a few more torturous days in somewhat of a routine. Don't get me wrong, the staff were some of the most professional and caring individuals you would ever want to trust your health with, but what they sometimes had to do to accomplish that was extremely painful. I was so tired, yet it was difficult to sleep at night. Thankfully, I was never alone. During the day, someone from my family was always there, sometimes at night, too. Allison would stay from morning until evening, but she still needed to take care of Bianca and herself. At night, she would return home and sleep in our bed, which was helpful for her portion of this marathon. She also knew that a Port Authority police officer was always present with me. I had 24-hour protection, and it was welcomed.

Brian was assigned the evening shift. With trouble sleeping, it was good to have a friend that would listen when needed and was also not afraid to tell me to stop whining when warranted. Brian is just an awesome guy! Brian is the younger brother of Chris, and I knew Chris first. I met Chris after the Navy when I was in a class at Bergen Community College. We were in the hallway and talking with a mutual buddy, Russ Christiana, when I said, "Oh, Russ, I might be going to upstate New York to hunt on Frankie Gravina's property.

Chris asked, "How do you know the Gravinas?"

"Well, my girlfriend's parents are good friends with them.

"Who's your girlfriend?" he questioned.

"Allison Guardiano.

"Get outta here!" He started telling me how he and Allison grew up together and were close friends. The world had just gotten a little smaller.

Brian, on the other hand, sat in front of me during the entrance exam for the Port Authority; his brother Chris sat next to him but didn't introduce me to him that day. It wasn't until after I had been notified that I was selected to go through the hiring process that Allison called Chris and found out that Brian was selected as well and had to go to the WTC for the medical exam and on-boarding paperwork.

"Will, Chris's brother is going, too. Would you like to ride with him?" she asked.

"Yeah, sure. That'd be cool. Have him meet me at your parents' house in Wood-Ridge."

The following morning, I was waiting in my Bronco II when Brian pulled up in his black Tahoe, and he had a look in his eyes like, "Who the hell is this guy?" He mistakenly thought Allison married her old boyfriend and was surprised to see a person that he didn't know.

I hopped in his truck and made the necessary introductions, and we just hit it off from there. We went through the whole process of entering and completing the Academy together, and we were both working at the Bus Terminal. We leaned on each other and shared life. Brian talked to me about his mom's cancer battle while he was restricted to the Academy, and I would just walk with him and listen. We supported each other from the beginning, and here he was, again, by my side.

The social webbing of support that became so important later had been weaved between the friendship of Allison's parents and their childhood friends, Frank and Cookie Gravina, Allison's childhood with the Boel family, in a hallway with Chris at college, and with Brian at the Police Academy. The consistency of Brian's presence at night helped anchor me amid the waves of chaos.

The day shift was another story. During the day there was an ever-changing rotation of officers that would stay. Some were classmates; some weren't. The days felt like, "Who am I getting today?" I had a couple of them ask if I would put in a word for them to be assigned permanently to this duty. Something in that just didn't sit well. Maybe it was the unknown that bothered me. There just wasn't the same level of comfort and trust during the day as there was during the night with Brian. Maybe it was because I had built a relationship of trust with him. He was known, not just familiar or simply wore the same uniform. He also didn't ask for the duty, but he accepted my request. The smallest of things mattered. The days held a lot of pain, and the nights were long. I may not have slept well at nights, but I knew what to expect: Brian, quiet, and no painful procedures. Pain and the unknown seemed to be saved for the day.

Time for another IV and wound care. My right forearm had first-degree burns from the falling fireballs. Cleaning and bandage changes were beginning to heal the red, blistered skin. It was swollen and painful, but I was also reminded of how bad it could have been. I was thankful and grabbed onto every moment of gratitude that I could, but much like pain, gratitude came and went in intensive waves.

During one of my naps, someone had taped up a poster of the 37 Port Authority officers that died in the attacks. My eyes fixated on my brothers and sister. "Where did that come from?" I asked Allison.

"They wanted to show how many police officers your department lost and who they were," she responded.

I didn't see them put it up. I didn't even ask for the number. I just saw their faces, and I cried. All I could think of at first was, "What the fuck happened that this many people that I knew, or knew of, were gone? I kept staring at it. I wanted to look at each face, each person. I saw Dom, Chris, Antonio, Stuart, and Bruce Reynolds. It was mind boggling to see their faces and know they were dead. I couldn't fully comprehend it, but I continued to look into their faces. Chief Romito—I had just gone to his son's funeral a few months before. Director Morrone—the head of our agency. Lieutenant Cirri—I knew him. Captain Mazza from the Academy. My Academy instructors—police officers James Nelson, Richard Rodriguez, James Parham and Alfonse Niedermeyer. I just couldn't believe that all these people were gone. It hurt.

Officer George Howard responded from Kennedy airport on his day off and lost his life while working to save lives outside of the WTC when the towers collapsed. I would often hear stories of cops like George and others that we lost that day. Howard's mom went on to give President Bush his police shield. President Bush said, "I will carry this."

As cops would show up to visit me, I asked if they knew any of the officers on the wall. I tried to learn as much about each officer as I could. They were fellow officers. I wanted to know who they were because their lives mattered. Why were they gone and I wasn't? I would ponder that a lot while in bed. I just couldn't understand why I was still here. It just didn't make any sense. I felt it was my obligation to know a little about each one of them.

I had a lot of time to sit and stare. I was still being carved on periodically, and I couldn't do much. I am not the kind of guy that sits still for very long, so all the immobility was wearing on me. I'm also a clean freak, and I still had debris from the buildings in my hair and in my ears. The ear specialist declined to remove it and said it was less dangerous to the ear drum to let it fall out naturally. It was so annoying! I felt grimy and disgusting.

There were so many ups and downs that when I had moments of gratitude, I would cling to that like a drowning person to a flotation device. Even though my mind kept waiting for the next shoe to fall, I actively looked for things in which to be grateful. One of those moments came when two nurses walked in and one of them asked, "Hey, Will, how would you like us to wash your hair? We can do it right where you are."

"Seriously? Can you do that? I would love it!" I responded with encouragement.

They scooted me up in the bed, where my head hung over the top of the bed, and they put a bucket behind my head. The water ran through my hair, creating a flowing, black silt. It was pungent! I mean, it was really nasty! Dust, ashes, smoke, oil, and who knows what else had been there for 10 days, and the initial rinse was already relieving. I felt like barfing from the smell and smiling from the feeling of having just won the lottery. It may seem hard to believe, but I could actually feel the loss of weight on my head.

A bedside head wash isn't as nice as standing in a shower and just letting the hot water run down my neck, but it was awesome. It's the simplest of things that matter—literally, to feel clean and, figuratively, to remove some of the hold the buildings had on me. Their kind gesture helped me to feel a little more human, a little more normal. There was a long way to go, but I was fully enjoying this moment.

Maybe it was the whole hair washing extravaganza or something, but my mother-in-law, Pat, had come in and just came over to me and stared into my face. I was finally getting a little color back. She looked me over, at all of bruises, cuts, and burns, and then said, "There's not one scratch on that pretty, little face of yours. Everything is just perfect." We all just laughed. It was a tender moment that only someone who is a mother could create.

Family and laughter gave me the buoyancy I needed to stay focused on healing. My sister would visit a lot during the day, but she had a way of knowing when I was *showing* a strong face. After all, she was my baby sister, and Karen has always been protective of me. Growing up, if I had a fist fight with someone, she would jump into the fight and try hurting the person. That's my baby sister!

One day Karen came for a visit and hadn't planned on staying, but her intuition kicked in and she offered, "If you want me to stay, I'll stay." Even though I had Brian there, I needed my sister. She would sit in those uncomfortable chairs all night long and just hold my hand. If I woke up, she was right there. It was such a soothing feeling. Of course, by morning, we were acting like siblings again. I don't remember how it came up in conversation, but she recalled that I had never broken a bone in my life. I grew up playing soccer, practicing martial arts, and I drank a lot of milk. My mom would always say, "Drink milk. It makes your bones grow strong." I did. I was in probably 8th grade and my sister was in 4th, and we were riding our bikes by our home. She tells the story that I ran into her. I remember it as her running into me. Guess what, Karen? This is my story, so let it be written; it was your fault. We hit hard enough that my sister couldn't walk back to the house, so I had to carry her before sitting her down, returning to get our bikes, and then bringing them back to where I had left her sitting. We did this until we made it home.

Our dad was home and asked, "What happened?"

"Well, we kind of ran into each other," I responded.

Dad took a look at her ankle and decided she needed to go to the hospital. It was broken.

Here we were in 2001, sitting in Bellevue, and Karen asked one of the doctors, "How many bones did Will break in the collapse?" In all the first two weeks of chaos, no one even thought to ask.

"Will didn't break any bones."

Karen's face was priceless when he answered. "Hold on a second. You mean to tell me 220 stories fell on him and his sergeant, and he came out without any broken bones?"

He assuredly answered, "That's right."

"Are you kidding me?" she exclaimed. She was mad because she still blames me for breaking her ankle. Did I say she was protective of me? I guess I should have clarified that she is protective of me as long as someone or something else is the threat, not her.

"See what you get from drinking milk? You should have drunk more milk," I said with all the smugness that brotherly love could muster. It was great! Messing with my sister just gave the feeling of home for a moment. Being flat on my back, immobile, just wore on me, so jabbing my sister and us laughing together was good medicine.

Strong bones helped me through life up to this point, and they were going to be needed again in the near future. However, this day would be more a matter of the heart. Someone brought in the morning newspaper. Across the page were pictures of the hijackers. I finally got to see the faces of the cowards that had caused all this damage and unwarranted pain. I stared in each of their eyes trying to get some view into their souls. The silent questioned lingered, "What would make you do this?"

I remember there was one with glasses, and I would just look at him. I thought, "You don't look like a bad person. What would make you do this? What about your families? Did you even think about your families, the people that love you?"

I don't know why I fixated on him, but I just kept staring at him thinking how he looked like a normal guy, a regular human being. I know that I may have had prejudicial thoughts about the other guys, their ethnicity, and history, but this guy. I just couldn't let it go. I tried to get into his mind, his soul, and tried to understand the hatred he must have had to kill so many people, so many innocent people. It just didn't seem real. I felt lost. I felt helpless. I felt hate toward them. I felt like if I could go through the picture, I would kill them all over again. Right or wrong, it's honestly how I felt. There was a lot of hate in my heart toward them, and I didn't know how to resolve it—I just didn't know how to resolve it.

"Yo, Jimeno! Bro, how ya doing?" a familiar voice asked. Bill Finney walked in, and he had on this big gold rope necklace, a hoodie, and baggy jeans. Bill wore that smile of his, and I could see he was starting to tear up. Now mind you, Bill is about 6 foot 3 inches, solid, and tough as nails. I wouldn't mess with him. This guy could handle anything. He was extremely fast and was very intimidating. He made you earn every bit of credit you received, and it didn't come easy. Rookies would sometimes be swapping their highlights from the tour, and he would walk by and bark out, "Shut the fuck up. You guys got no war stories."

Sometimes I thankfully had the opportunity to go on calls with him and learn. One day at the bus terminal, I walked past three Spanish guys. One of them asked if I spoke Spanish, which I did, so they asked me some arbitrary question. The smell of marijuana wafted across my nose. We were at the bottom of the escalators by the coffee shop, next to the side entrance alleyway.

"Hey, come here. You got marijuana on you?" I questioned.

They froze. "All right, all fucking three of you up against the wall!" I threw them against the wall and quickly called for backup, as I could see their nervousness and could tell something was about to go down. Bill came running.

"What do you have?" he asked.

"I think they've got weed on them."

"All right, you fucking guys don't move!" He looked at me in an affirming way.

After searching them we found a large amount of marijuana, and it was enough to impress him. That was important to me, not simply because he was a superior but because I had immense respect for him. Now, like Geoff in the ER, Bill was standing by my bedside.

I looked up at him and said, "Finney, man, I hope I did right. Did I do good? Do I have a war story?"

Billy grabbed my hand and said, "Bro, you've got the fucking war story of all time."

I couldn't believe that Bill Finney was saying that to me. It meant the world to me.

Bill Finney, Geoff Fairbanks, and Ray Bryant were three senior guys that always had my back. Ray was a thick-necked weightlifter who was highly educated and eloquent in his communications with the guys, which is not always the case in the police world. These guys were my squad. Finney is African American, Fairbanks is White, Bryant is African American, and I am Spanish. We were all proud of our ethnicities, and we were proud to be police officers. We were brothers of different colors, and what mattered most was the dedication we had to one another.

Toughness was abundant, but mine felt like it flew out the window when I got to the stage of healing where the medical staff started applying skin grafts to my leg. I have never felt that intensity of pain, even during the collapse and rescue. The actual grafting was done while I was unconscious, but with the dressing changes they weren't so kind as to knock me out. One of the nurses came in and said, "Listen, sweetie, we need to change these dressings. This is going to hurt, and it's going to hurt bad."

"It's okay, I've been dealing with a lot of pain," I retorted confidently.

"You can hold my hand. You can squeeze my hand. Do what you need to do," she said gently.

They pulled the top layer of gauze back to expose three strips of 1x9 gauze pads covering the donor sites. I knew they were caring for me and I knew what they were doing was necessary, but that held little comfort when they began removing the strips. I was lying in a way that I could watch what they were doing. I could see them removing the gauze. The blood-soaked material was pulling on the tender tissue below, plucking at every nerve ending it could find. It was brutal. I yelled, I cried, and I almost passed out from the pain. I tried to focus by looking at the sky through the window. I questioned when the nightmare would end. I felt so helpless to *have* to have these painful procedures because of someone else's actions.

Wound care would be the gift that kept on giving. Several rounds of dressing changes happened over the next few days, and none were any less painful. When the nurse said it was going to be painful, I should have listened. Thankfully, fresh growth started to create a natural barrier to the wound, and the pain of dressing changes began slightly easing in intensity. It had been a scary experience because there was always the possibility that the grafts wouldn't take and they would need to take more skin from other locations on my body.

A day of rest, a day of pain. A day of rest, a day of pain. At least there was starting to be a rhythm to it that I could count on. When it feels like the ground you stood on has crumbled, any form of structure is important, even painful ones. The rhythm of the chaos helped me to gain a little control in knowing what to plan for and to make sure I rested the best I could in between. Hope for normalcy was starting to glimmer.

"Code Blue! Code Blue!"

The ICU started buzzing. The gentleman next to me, who had his leg broken by falling debris from the buildings, was in distress. Apparently, he had developed a blood clot in his leg due to the injury. It had broken free and put him in cardiac arrest. Unfortunately, he died of his injuries. The staff immediately turned their focus to Sgt. McLoughlin and me. They whisked us up to put in Greenfield filters, which would catch any traveling clots. I was thankful that they checked for them, but it also seriously elevated my anxiety again. Here I am thinking, okay, I made it out from under the Towers, made it through two flatlines, made it through multiple surgeries, and now I might be taken out by a blood clot. The inability to trust peace and progress never ended. I would get a foothold, and, wham, out goes the carpet from beneath my feet. I could consciously recognize that I was still alive, still being cared for, and still getting healthier, but my body was reacting in ways that did not listen to the rational side of me.

Off to my right was the entrance to the ICU. Two officers entered and walked toward me. "Hey! Scott Strauss," the first one called out, introducing himself.

I just grabbed him and said, "Thank you so much!" I had no way of recognizing him because I never got a good look at his face while we were in the hole. All I could make out through the smoke and ash were two bald heads. Can you bend down? I just want to look at your head." We both started laughing. It was so good to see him face to face and just talk.

I kept thanking him for saving my life, but true to Scott and his heart of servitude, he kindly said, "No, it was my honor."

"How's Paddy McGee?"

"He's doing fine," he answered, and we spent some time rehashing what we had been doing since the rescue, talking about our families, and just showing our appreciation for life.

His visit was so vivid. Scott was so kind, well-spoken, and humble. I felt like I was thanking an angel. I kept thanking him, and he kept handing it back to me. "Listen, stop complimenting me. You're the one that held on. You're the one that didn't give up."

Neither of us gave up, and I am grateful for that. It was a special moment when he visited.

I'm not sure how I would have been without all the support and visits, and I'm glad that I don't have to know. Especially at first, the intensity of care kept me distracted with some sleeping in between events. As the need for hyperactive care and numerous procedures started to slow, the monotony of the day would have been absolute torture for my personality had it not been for my family, Brian, visits with Donna McLoughlin (an awesome lady), and my fellow officers. I know that these human moments of connection healed me in more ways than modern medicine could have touched. Much like the raw dermis took time to grow before my skin could heal over on the outside, all the people mentioned were starting the growth that would help me then, as well as build a foundational basis for later.

A large body popped into the room and caught my attention. It was Geoff. I noticed he had an American flag patch on his right sleeve. We weren't allowed to have patches on our right sleeve. We only had one patch at the time, and it was on our left sleeve. I said, "Oh my God, Geoff, that's so good to see," pointing toward the patch. "Are you getting into trouble?"

"Yeah, I wanted to wear the American flag. I told them to go fuck themselves. I'm wearing the American flag on here," Geoff stated proudly, walking toward me. I started to cry, and I know he wanted to cry, too, but he wouldn't. His eyes started to well up, and he grabbed my hand, reaching out and giving me a hug. "My burro. You made it, man. You made it."

It was another breath of air for my soul.

As the story goes, waves come in and waves go out. Although I am a positive guy and like to look for the good in people, sometimes people behave in ways that are hard to ignore. I'm not saying the person is no good, but without self-awareness a good person can have negative effects on those around them. Occasionally, we dealt with situations and people that were unpleasant.

My mom always taught me that life gets tough and dealing with some people can be even tougher. Nevertheless, she modeled acceptance and love. Dad may have been the structure that provided safety, but her love was the fire that kept our home warm. It never mattered how old I was, she was always available to help us through. She was still working at the time I was in the hospital, so she often would come later in the day and sit with me.

Because of the difficulty sleeping I had since being in the hospital, the doctors had been using Benadryl to help as a sleep aid. They had given it to me intravenously for weeks, and it was time to start withdrawing it from my medicinal regimen. My body reacted in a really weird way to its absence: My tongue starting to swell and I had a hard time breathing. My anxiety shot up. The nurses were trying to help me, and Brian was telling me to calm down. My breathing felt restricted, which made my anxiety shoot higher. The higher my anxiety escalated, the more difficulty I had breathing. I tried self-talk and kept trying to get my breath under control, but I was just having a hard time. My mother, Emma, came to my side and began rubbing my forehead. She had a way of doing it that just immediately relaxed my breathing and calmed my body.

"There's nothing like a mother," one of the nurses said, smiling as she watched. The love in my mother's touch had such immense power to help in that moment. I realized how my mother had been able to take me from this pit of fear back to the feeling I had as a child, where I knew I was safe because my mom made it so. I also realized how I was feeling a longing to connect to something that had proceeded 9/11, something that had not been touched by it.

Alberto Martinez and I had been tight in the Navy, and I really wanted to talk to my Mexican brother, who was also the best man at my wedding. Three of the interns that cared for me—Drs. Maria Raven, Julie McLaughlin, and Lee Tessler—had been so involved in my care and offered me as much of themselves as they could, but cell phones were not allowed in the ICU. Lee heard me talking about my friend, and he somehow dug up a telephone cord that had to have been about 30 feet long, long enough to go from the nurses' station to my bed.

Lee and Allison surprised me when they walked in holding a phone and said, "Hey, we have someone on the line who wants to talk to you."

"Who?" I asked, still taking it in that they even had a phone in their hands.

"It's Albert."

"Cholo?" I said in a stunned tone. "How did you do that?"

Allison looked at me and pointed at Lee, "Lee made it happen."

Talking to Albert gave me a sense of normalcy. I was talking to a friend. I knew I should have been dead. I knew what I had gone through. But I was talking to a friend that had nothing to do with 9/11, one of my best friends in the world. Lee provided great physical care, but he gave me the real shot I had needed. The ICU staff didn't mind having to repeatedly duck under the phone line. Nobody questioned it. Nobody complained. They cared from their hearts. Their giving, and my being able to talk to Albert, was uplifting. I was going to need all the motivation I could get because they wanted to start getting me up in the very near future.

The ICU staff previously used a machine to move my leg back and forth to work my joints, muscles, and skin, and it hurt because the skin grafts were tight. Other than the machine, for the first three weeks my legs were immobile, and my left knee locked up. It was frozen. I don't know if it was because they had taken a break from the machine or what, but I knew it wasn't working. On the flip side, I was well enough to be moved to a private room. The physical therapists, Elise Carney and her assistant, started working me over pretty good with the goal of getting me up and moving. I called them the torture gremlins because they were small but gave me an ass-kicking when they came to work on me. It took another surgery and some additional therapy, but they were going to remove as many obstacles for me as possible. The wounds on my legs were healing well, and it was time.

First, they taught me to stand again. My room had a window looking out over New York City, but I had only ever been able to see the sky. However, when they helped me stand for the first time, I looked out and saw the Empire State Building.

"Oh, my god, thank you!" I said out loud. I don't know what I was thinking, but the Empire State Building now represented New York City to me as the tallest building. I ended with, "Well, that's still there," It was a very moving ten seconds for me. I stood. I saw. I was alive.

The second time the therapists pushed me a little further. They told me to stand for 20 seconds this time. Five, ten, fifteen...I passed out. I tried, but my body took a time out. My therapists never missed a beat. They simply adjusted my workouts and kept getting me up. Sometimes it was just to stand, take two steps to the wheelchair to be wheeled into the bathroom, and then reversed. Little by little, they pushed.

Next up—hallway walking. It was nice to be out of the room, but that hallway looked daunting. My steps up to this point had really been minimal, and I was looking at the length of this hall, even though their expectations were nothing of that magnitude. I was looking down toward the ICU when Sergeant Kevin Feeley came out from visiting John. Sgt. Feeley was a good cop, but he wasn't the typical tough guy cop. He was a kind man, and he watched them working with me.

"Hey, Sarge," the therapist called down to him. "Will's going to try to take his first steps."

I couldn't. I just...I think I was mentally getting in my own way and wasn't ready to try. Our eyes connected, and he gave a more stern than normal tone, "Jimeno, I'm giving you a direct order. Get the fuck up and start walking."

That was a motivator for me. Growing up with parents that taught me to respect authority, as well as having been in the Navy and with the Port Authority, when I received an order you better believe I was going to give it all I had to accommodate the demand.

I stood up. I think I took three, maybe four steps, and I was fucking exhausted. I collapsed back into the chair. It had taken all I had and felt like I had run a marathon.

"I'm trying, Sarge," I cried out. Honestly, I think I was crying because it hurt so bad, and I had given it my all. I looked at Sgt. Feeley and could see him tearing up like, oh my God, he took a couple steps. Maybe it was four steps, maybe three. But it was an accomplishment that meant a lot. He walked over and put his hand on my shoulder with a proud look on his face.

The walk wore me out, and I needed to rest. As tired as I had grown of the bed, it was a welcome site. When the pain and fatigue increased, the need for trusted comfort increased, too. My patience had grown weary with the unknowns that life was throwing my way, like the variation in day-duty officers. Grateful is too small a word for the support and care the Port Authority and my fellow officers had shown, but there were a couple that had focused a little too much on their comfort instead of the needs of the room. Allison and I had grown close to John's wife and brother, Donna and Pat, as our families were spending a lot of time together in the hospital. A couple of instances arose that didn't sit well with the variations, and our families looked out for each other in whatever way we could. A change was needed.

The change we were seeking walked in at 6:00 am. Victoria "Vickie" Lubeck, a classmate of mine from the Academy, was assigned for the day. We weren't best of friends, but she was a professional. She was caring. When she came and stayed with me, I noticed Allison getting along with her, so I asked for her to be my steady day person because I felt comfortable with her. She gave me a feeling of trust.

"Listen, would you be okay being here with me steady on days?" I asked.

She simply responded, "Whatever you need."

Vickie was a good fit with us. She was with us in the days, and Brian was with us at night. Pieces of the puzzle were fitting into place, but I still had not been able to see John other than seeing him wheeled back and forth past me.

They were ready to bring him out of the induced coma, and they said I would be able to see him the following day. John had been two rooms from me when I was in the ICU; I couldn't move, he couldn't move, and he was unconscious. It had not been a good combination for communication. However, I was excited to know I was finally going to get to talk to him. Pat McLoughlin came and got me and wheeled me over to John. Sarge was still groggy. It was very difficult for him. You could see he was out of it. However, the one thing they told me: Do not tell him that 37 cops died. They said it would be weeks before they shared that information because he was still in a fragile state of health and they didn't want the emotional stress to be addressed prematurely. He couldn't really talk at the time; he just kind of moaned. When they rolled me over and I got to be next to him, I grabbed his hand and said, "Hey, Sarge, we made it." He squeezed my hand and slowly nodded. "You know those people that did this to us? They didn't get all of us." What a moment of joy!

That was pretty much all the interaction we had because he was out of it. Over the next couple of weeks, I would go over a couple times to visit him, but it was slow going.

Everything seemed to be going slow. It had been almost five weeks since I had slept in my bed next to my wife. It had been almost five weeks since I had seen or held my little girl. I was getting irritable, and I just wanted to get the hell out of that room and out of that bed. I had several different nurses, but I remember one nurse in particular that was from the South. She made me sit up and she massaged my back, which felt really good because lying in bed had become so uncomfortable. A couple of little bedsores were starting, so they addressed them by making sure that I frequently moved my body. Although I had grown weary of lying down, I was still too weak to do much else. That limbo phase was too familiar, but I would gladly take the hospital limbo over the suspended-in-concrete-and-steel limbo any day.

Limbo didn't last too much longer. Eileen Wallin, my case manager, shared with me that we needed to start planning for discharge. I had one or two other case managers, but Eileen took over toward the end of my ICU stay. She is just a lovely person. Eileen had originally introduced herself by saying I didn't need to worry because she was going to take care of everything for me. That is exactly what she did. If there was an error in records or billing, she was on it. If any of my family had questions, she would make sure they understood what was going on administratively. When it came time to start looking for rehabilitation centers for my hospitalization aftercare, Eileen was front and center.

The only rehab center that I was familiar with was Kessler Institute for Rehabilitation. I only knew it because that's where Christopher Reeve went. I figured if they were good enough for him, I should probably go there. Eileen agreed. She said, "Listen, that's where we want to place you. However, I've got to be straightforward with you. They're very selective with who they take."

I was like, "What?"

She told me about having to submit an application, and then we would have to see if they were willing to accept me. I felt like I was going to college. I started to get nervous. I would have said I was having performance anxiety, but I couldn't really perform much in the first place. A couple of days later, Eileen came in with the news, "You're going to Kessler."

I was just so relieved—so relieved.

The past six weeks had a single constant, as far as I could tell: Each moment of peace was followed with a moment of chaos. I had hope for the day, but I expected the shoe to fall sooner or later. Literally, a couple of days before I was scheduled for discharge, the staff was unsettled by something. My ortho docs, Drs. Philip Wolinsky and Nirmal Tejwani, had seen me through this far and wanted to make sure they had covered everything. Lee came in with a Doppler machine, and he found a clot in my leg. I never really feared the clot after they had addressed the first concerns earlier in treatment, but this surprisingly rattled me.

Lee looked up from the screen and said, "You have a blood clot."

Fear ran through me. "I'm going to die?" I looked at Allison and told her, "Listen, take care of this. Take care of that." I was basically making a verbal will.

"Stop thinking that way," she said, but I couldn't stop thinking about it. I kept thinking about that poor gentleman who died from a blood clot due to a broken leg, and now I'm scheduled to leave, and they just found a blood clot. It felt like I was being handed a pardon just before the executioner released the guillotine. It wasn't rational but that didn't matter. I was terrified.

They put me on Coumadin, and Lee assured me, "Listen, you're going to make it. Look, we're going to get rid of this. It's going to start breaking up, and you've got a Greenfield filter. You're going to be fine."

I trusted Lee. He hadn't failed me yet. In fact, he went above and beyond and treated me, not just my wounds. Nevertheless, I couldn't control the worry. It was weird, but I started having other emotions coming up, too. Sometimes they made sense, sometimes they didn't. As much as I wanted to leave, I was also feeling sad about having to say goodbye to the staff that so passionately cared for me. They were kind to me and my family. I had really grown close to them, and I felt sadness in knowing I would have to say goodbye.

I started noticing things coming up on the television that would upset me. I watched the news in New Jersey, and I cried a little bit. I'm not sure if it was the emotions, something I said, or if it was protocol, but a psychiatrist came by to check on me, and he asked, "What are you feeling?"

I don't mean to be disrespectful, but he was like something out of a movie. He would just stare at me and ask, "What are you thinking?" I was thinking he was a weirdo. He had black hair, a black beard, and glasses. He just... the way he talked to me; I didn't like him. I didn't like the way he was addressing me. It was like what you would stereotypically see on a television show. Okay, so what are you thinking? Why do you think that? I remember staring at him like how the fuck do I know? You're the doctor. He would ask me questions that I didn't know how to answer. We finished with the Twilight Zone-ish interview, and he said he was going to prescribe something that would help me. He never really said what it was that he was helping me with, but what the hell.

I'm pretty good at taking orders, so I took the horse pills, as prescribed. The next day I was out of it. I think for two days I was saying stupid shit. Allison would say that I had been talking shit for years, but I'm talking specifically about the meds. I knew whatever I was saying made perfect sense, but the people around me were laughing. Allison would laugh at me. The nurse would laugh at me. Whatever I was taking put me way out there.

Brian came in that evening for his shift. The news was on, and they showed a map of New Jersey. I began crying. I started saying, "I want to go home." Brian was always my brother that would tell me straight out, no matter who I thought I was or how I was being treated by everyone. He kept it real. He looked straight at me and scoffed, "Hey, why don't you shut the fuck up? Stop fucking crying." But he did it in a way where he was busting my balls. He had always treated me like that. He would always be there to support me, but at the same time he would be the first one to say, "Hey, bro, cut the shit. Toughen up." I needed that because there were moments that I felt weak. Being on whatever drug that psychiatrist gave me was one of those times, and Brian did not fail to deliver.

After two days of being all over the board, I said, "I don't want any of that shit again, whatever he put me on." Additionally, "I don't even want to see that man. I refuse to see that man." He asked to come again, and I said, "Do not bring him in here. I don't want him in this room. I'm done talking to psychiatrists." Right then and there that put a big damper on the mental health part of it for me. That was too bad because I hadn't even realized yet how much I could have used some help at the time, but I knew I didn't want what he offered.

Allison decided it was time to take matters into her own hands and prescribe me something for my heart. It was just before I was going to be discharged, and she brought me the greatest medicine...our daughter. Bianca had two little pigtails, and she brought me a little pumpkin. She said, "Hi, Daddy!"

I started crying. It had been so long since I saw my baby girl. "You grew," I said, and I held her so tight.

"Daddy, you're squeezing me too hard," she said so sweetly, and I'm sure I was. What a great way to celebrate having made it through this part of the journey. I was being discharged from Bellevue on October 19th, 2001. I couldn't wait.

Reflections

1) What role does reciprocity play in Will's story? In your life?
2) What message does the process of physically healing tell us about healing our emotional wounds?
3) What "Empire State Building" symbolisms do you use to anchor into gratitude?
4) Do you need to pause, breathe, reflect, or grieve in this moment before continuing?

Chapter Eight

Hey, If They Can Help Superman...

Do not spoil what you have by desiring what you have not; remember that what you now have was once among the things you only hoped for. — Epicurus[1]

It was a little before Halloween, and the day had finally come. I was being transferred to Kessler Institute for Rehabilitation in West Orange, New Jersey. They loaded me up on the gurney and wheeled me outside. Outside. I hadn't been outside since they brought me to the hospital. The crisp, autumn air blew across my face, and I only had a few feet between the bay doors and the ambulance.

"Hey, can we just stop for a minute?" I asked. Apparently, they could read my body because I never explained why I wanted to stop, and they never asked. Head back and eyes closed, I just soaked it all in. It was so quiet and so simple, and it was something that I had previously taken for granted. Not this day. Not this time. This day, I felt every thermal, every directional shift of the air, and I could feel the weight I had carried being lifted by this gentle breeze.

"Okay. Thank you."

The crew carefully loaded me into the ambulance and got me situated for the ride. I couldn't really see outside the ambulance except through the back windows. As we left the hospital, it was easy to see the motorcycle units behind us, but there were just as many taking the lead. PAPD made sure I never felt alone. They continually made their presence known in assuring me I was safe.

When we came through the Holland Tunnel back into Jersey, I had a feeling that's hard to describe, but the closest thing I could relate it to was the feeling of returning home after a lengthy absence—a sort of childlike sense of knowing that safety and nurturance awaited with open arms. Kessler was in New Jersey, and New Jersey was home. Even

---

[1] Willmott, M., & Nelson, W. (2005). *Complicated Lives: The Malaise of Modernity.* Wiley.

though I would not be returning directly home with my family, Kessler offered a similar sense of safety, especially knowing that this is where Christopher Reeve was able to make progress after his horrific neck injury—Christopher Reeve, you know, Superman. Hey, if they can help Superman then I knew they surely could help me. After all, it was a nationally recognized rehabilitation center that had amazing successes.

Upon arrival, they wheeled me out to a familiar collection of blue. Fellow officers were waiting with well wishes, statements of solidarity, and a detail that would not leave me. I was taken to a private room, which I knew would be home for a while. I didn't know how long, but I knew it would be longer than I wanted. Much like the mixed emotions I felt when we were first found, anxiety creeped into my sense of comfort. What would my body be able to do? Would I be able to fully walk again? I was grateful for being there and the ability to receive that level of care, but I was also very scared. The comfort that helped carry me during those bouts of anxiety came from my steadfast cop companions, Brian and Vickie. They were my partners, whether to talk, to give me encouragement, or just to hold that space and accompany me. They worked 12-hour shifts each, 6 am to 6 pm and 6 pm to 6 am. I knew it was boring duty for them, but it gave Allison and me such comfort knowing I was covered by my brother and sister in blue. I knew if I needed something they were there for me, but my *peace* came from knowing they had me, that I was protected.

Day 1– the staff wasted no time after letting me have a night to rest and settle in. The fact that it was a weekend had no bearing on rest. Since it was the weekend, PAPD sent in replacements to assist and protect me, which provided both comfort and anxiety when facing a new change like the transition. However, it wasn't the first time I faced it, and I was still responsible for doing whatever was necessary, regardless of who was by my side.

Paul Miller, a senior cop from the bus terminal and someone I respected, was walking right beside me into the facility's gymnasium.

"Listen, we're going to get you walking," the therapist stated.

"What do you mean get me walking? I can't really walk yet," I nervously replied.

"We know. We are going to *get* you walking."

Paul, in his uniform and shoulder holster, decided to chime in with enthusiasm, "Yeah, we're going to get you walking." It was clear he was ready to assist any way he could to get me back on my feet. I took a few steps while in the hospital, but these guys weren't playing. As much as I was excited to walk again, I felt my anxiety increase with their enthusiasm. They were clear that they were there to help me walk, not to baby me. I took a couple of steps. It was painful and extremely tiring, but neither I nor the staff let that stop us from pushing me toward the goal. Again I felt the conflicting and interconnectedness of pain and relief. Grimacing, I couldn't help but think, "Wait, Will. You're on your feet. You took a couple of more steps today."

As days progressed, the team pushed me to take a few more steps, go a little further between rests. They were utilizing the persistence I showed in the rubble of going as far as I thought I could and then do a little more. Other therapists, such as my occupational therapist, Dawn Texas, taught me how to clothe myself again, take care of myself again, and even how to get in and out of a car again. Then there was Scott Zuckerman, my physical therapist. He was a *literal* pain in the ass. He worked my body, but especially my legs and hips to keep up with the growth I was showing and to assist in the healing of muscle tissue that had been so badly compressed. Dawn and Scott expected a lot and gave a lot. It wasn't just those two. There were numerous, phenomenal professionals that were passionately involved in my care, but those two just had a way.

The days were filled with physical therapy, occupational therapy, general care, and a lot of waiting. The waiting provided rest, but it also felt like more distance from home. Since I couldn't be home, my home came to me. There is no way to fully describe the consistent and loving support that my family members, from both my and Allison's family, gave each of us. It was incredible, and it was a life saver. Even though I had Brian and Vickie, there was a quiet, constant denominator in the room—my father, William. He was always there. He'd get there early in the morning and sit quietly in the corner chair. If we had something to say, we said it. If we didn't, he held silent vigil, watching over me. He was content reading the newspaper or observing the conversations of fellow officers that stopped by to visit. So many times I had felt alone, even when I was surrounded by other people, but I never felt alone when my dad was there. He sometimes gave me encouraging words, but most of the time he quietly offered his fatherly presence. All my life he worked hard and was always there for us. And, here he still was...

Having visitors helped to keep me from getting lost in my thoughts. Thinking of my team came at a cost. To see their faces again was my heart's desire, but it meant my heart broke with each remembrance of them. Sometimes I lay safely in the rehabilitation bed, but I was still in the rubble. Dom was a few feet away, and Chris and Antonio were somewhere just beyond my reach.

Ring! Ring! The phone broke the distance between reality and my mind.

"Hello."

"Is this William Jimeno?" the voice asked.

"Yeah, yeah, this is he. How can I help you?"

"Listen, I'm from such-and-such newspaper (the name really didn't matter to me), and I would love to be able to help you share your story. You're a hero, and the world would like to hear from you. Would you mind if we talked a bit so that everyone can know how you're doing?" the reporter asked, in his manipulative approach.

There was a time in my youth that I would have cherished the title of hero, but not today. Today, my heroes had been buried or returned to their departments to risk their lives for others. "Today's not a good day," I responded.

"I can call tomorrow. I can come by when it's convenient for you. Really, whatever works for you, I will be happy to accommodate."

"No thanks. I just want to focus on getting back to my family. Bye." The calls had almost become scripted.

I was asked numerous times to do interviews, to give *my* story. That just didn't sit well because I knew that my story would never have been heard had it not been for my team. My story was no more important than the others that could no longer share their stories. How do I get people to stop focusing on me? What we do is not for attention. I didn't know how to handle it any other way than to decline the interviews, but I also felt torn up that I wasn't as able to talk about the guys. Things changed when I shared this conflict with my Chief, Chief Joe Morris. He said, "Will, nobody knows who the Port Authority is or what we do. Most people see us and think NYPD. You have an opportunity here to shed some light on the department and on the men and women that wear *our* uniform."

That's when I started doing interviews with various television shows, magazines, and news outlets, including a remote interview from Kessler with Diane Sawyer. Chuck Sereika was with me for that one; it was good to see him again face to face. Each interview seemed to take the same path of focusing on me and my story. Inevitably, I tried to return the focus to the guys from my team. Rather than avoid what I didn't want to happen, I decided to focus on how I could direct it. It didn't take long for me to figure out to only agree to interviews that were live so they couldn't edit the piece to focus on me or to control the narrative. Even when they turned it back to me, I gave a little about being buried and the struggle and then turned it back to *the guys*, the true heroes: Antonio, the guy that switched spots with me to push the cart and give me a break; Chris, the guy that saved four people before running back into the building to continue his service to others; and Dominick, the guy that could have gotten out but stayed and tried to free his brothers, giving his life in the process. Being able to highlight my brothers gave me the strength to be interviewed and relive those moments. Every time I spoke about them, we were together again for a moment. Each interview felt like the emotional equivalent of physical therapy in the hospital when the staff scrubbed away the dead, burnt skin covering the tender, pink dermis below. But *this* skin was the skin of my heart. I knew there was healing with every painful scraping, but damn it hurt. Some days I didn't want to heal that much, but I owed it to my family, my team, and myself.

Interview by interview, I was able to highlight Antonio, Chris, and Dom and share their stories. I was struggling, but I was healing. Exercise by exercise, my body grew stronger. Again, I was struggling, but I was healing. However, there was a heavier focus on my physical healing, and, being the wife that she is, Allison recognized that I was depressed and decided to reach out to some of the people I admired from my everyday life: M. R. James from *Bowhunter Magazine*, the guys at Mossy Oak hunting apparel. She had heard me talking about these guys and what they have meant to the hunting industry, as well as seeing me obsessively reading *Bowhunter Magazine*, so she wrote them to let them know what they have meant to me and to share my story.

One day the phone rang, and Allison answered, "Hello?" She paused for a moment and said, "Will, it's Toxey Haas."

It took a minute to register that Toxey was calling me. Allison handed me the phone. "Hello?"

In his strong Southern accent, Toxey said, "Hey, this is Toxey Haas from Mossy Oak. How ya doin'?"

I barely got the generic "hi" out before I started crying. I mean, I literally just fell apart, and Allison had to grab the phone while I tried to calm down.

"Hold on a moment, Toxey."

"What's going on?" he asked.

"He's really emotional right now, and he's crying."

It took a couple of minutes, but I gathered myself and said, "I'm sorry."

"Hey man, what's up?"

"You know what? It means a lot that you called. You're a busy guy, and you're well known. You have your own company..."

"I'm just a redneck," he interrupted.

"No. You're not a redneck. You're a guy who's successful, and you're taking the time out to call me. You're not just a redneck. You're a fellow American taking time out of your busy day to call a total stranger, to give him some support." That really, really meant a lot. That day we started a relationship that is still going strong, and he introduced me to another great guy that has been a good friend through the years and into today, Ronnie "Cuz" Strickland.

M. R. James also reached out and said he wanted to do a story on how an immigrant came to this country, served in the military, became a cop, survived the WTC collapse, and was an avid bowhunter. I agreed. He also invited me to the Archery Trade Association (ATA) show. It was another opportunity for hope and an additional goal to look forward to that allowed me to focus on my recovery but also to see beyond the current pain.

More time was being spent out of bed than before. Each day meant more steps. Being able to take steps with a walker was humbling, yet it was so gratifying. It was a huge accomplishment! Of course, it was evident that I needed some more work on my arm strength, and the staff was more than willing to accommodate the challenge. I was on a mission because it was now November and Allison was scheduled for a C-section on my birthday, which is on the 26th.

"Hey, Will, you know the harder you work, the sooner you can get out of here and start outpatient treatment," one of the care team stated, throwing down the gauntlet before me. "You can get driven here for treatment during the day and be home at night with your family."

In my mind there was no other choice but to push. And so I did. Let me be clear: There was a team of phenomenal professionals pushing me, caring for me, and encouraging me. I had fellow cops watching my back, giving me shit, and not letting me forget that we were a team. I had my family that was steadfast in loving and supporting me through the physical and emotional pain, all trying to help me get back home to them. And, I had fellow patients, current and prior, that were examples of strength, courage, and tenacity that were my mentors and my friends. There are so many faceless people in this story who were instrumental in my recovery—faceless to the reader, but I can see every one of them. I will never forget their faces and what they gave to me.

One of those unforgettable people was Ken McGuire, an officer from East Orange who had been in a shootout in January 2001. He sustained a gunshot wound to the stomach when the bullet entered beneath his bulletproof vest, causing severe internal damage. He, like myself, had flatlined on the hospital table, but he survived and was now standing in my room. We didn't know each other, but he said he felt an obligation to come meet me and to encourage me because he knew the battle I was facing. We became friends, and he brought pizza when he visited, which was frequent. Brian was loving it, but he said, "I'm going to get fat eating all of this pizza."

We'd have some good laughs together, but Ken also shared his experiences to prepare me for what was ahead. He told me how fortunate I was and to try to do right with life. I didn't really understand what he was saying at the time.

"Will, you are going to have nightmares; you are going to have troubles," he shared. Again, I didn't fully understand what he was trying to say, perhaps because I wasn't ready to understand—yet. Later, everything really slowed down and the darkness, as I call it, came out— the PTSD. His words were illuminating at that point, and I was thankful for the seeds of encouragement he had planted during our talks.

Every Wednesday night, Kessler offered a karate group, and I met a gentleman who had both legs amputated. I honestly wouldn't have pictured that before. And there were others who were paralyzed and would never walk again, but they were still practicing karate. Awe is the closest word that could describe the inspirational feeling they gave me. I sat next to them in my wheelchair, and we practiced our martial arts movements. Brian pushed me in, and we went to break up the monotony and to feel the power of movement, in a way that was not necessarily related to pain. There was freedom in that. Brian was there every night...night after night.

I met another young man who was from Paterson, New Jersey who also had been shot. He was in a gang, and his wounds left him paralyzed. He was a quadriplegic, and all he could move was his head. He wanted to meet me, so when I finally was able to get around, I went to his room. His attitude was unforgettable and one of gratitude. He said, "I was in a gang. I was wrong for doing that, and it's taught me a lot. This is, as crazy as it seems, something that has been good for me. It made me value life."

The staff told me that he would not have a long life because of the complication with breathing that comes with being quadriplegic, but it wasn't about how long he was going to live. It was about how he spent this moment. In this moment, he inspired me. Before Kessler, he was a gang member, and I was a cop. In Kessler, we were both patients. In this room, there was a former gang member inspiring a cop. We spend too much time in this life judging one another, and it is such a waste of precious life.

The patients at Kessler, no matter what happened to them, were still living a level of conscious nightmare. Whether someone had been shot, crushed, in a car accident, or had a simple fall from the porch, we were all facing pain and limitation. One gentleman who had been paralyzed shared with me that his story was not incredible but was a stupid one. He said, "I went out to the porch to throw the garbage out. We have this wraparound porch that's maybe four feet off the ground, and I was leaning over the corner of the porch to throw the garbage bag into the trash can because I was too lazy to walk around. Somehow I slipped and fell forward off the porch and onto my chest." And he goes, "Next thing you know as I look up, I see my feet."

He had bent his back all the way over to where he was looking at his heels. He had lost the feeling and use of his legs. We talked from time to time over the next month or so, until one day I remember just looking at him like, "Oh my God, you're walking."

"The last week or so my nerves have been starting to come back."

He wasn't walking well, but there was hope. "Wow! You went through a nightmare, and you're coming out of it," I said to him.

"Yeah. They're telling me that my nerves are healing and I'm eventually going to be normal."

I remember just thinking to myself, "Wow! What a great story." And that inspired me again to keep trying to work harder for what I was doing. Inspiration is fuel. It comes and it goes. During some parts of the day, it was easier to push myself than in others because there were times that it was very depressing. Especially at night, when it was time to go to sleep, I sat there with my mind racing. There weren't any distractions to keep it all at bay—all the memories, the doubts, the fears, and the unknowns. Always at the top of my mind were my fellow officers that died and the questions about my future. Would I be able to walk again? Would I be able to run with the girls? At night, questions and doubts abounded. Come morning it was time to get back after it.

I ground it out through the sweating, the pain, the memories, and the frustrations of my limitations. I knew I was so close. I was in New Jersey for crying out loud. Step by step, struggle by struggle, and day after day I pushed until those involved in getting me on my feet came in and let me know they were giving me a pass for the weekend. They had all worked hard to get me home, even for a weekend. The idea of going home—the goal all along—was now going to be possible. Allison and I were excited at the news. And right on cue, with peace came anxiety. I don't know why I was surprised. This intertwining of peace and panic seemed to be one consistency that kept rearing its ugly head ever since

9/11. I could feel my desire to be home, but suddenly there was something holding me back. I struggled with it, and I called and told Allison I wasn't ready.

"Hey, Al, I don't know if I'm ready to go home."

"Okay, whatever you want to do. Wherever you want to go today, we'll take you. If you want to go out to a park or whatever, just be outside," she supportively replied. Through all of it she was a rock. She may not have felt that way, but for me, she was my rock. What the hell was wrong with me? How could I work so hard to get home only to avoid it when I had the chance? Whatever this was, it was pissing me off.

Allison arrived, and said, "Did you decide where you want to go, what you want to do?"

"Let's go home."

"Are you sure?" she asked.

"Yeah, I want to go home. Let's go."

After the call the day before, Allison wasn't expecting me to be coming home when she showed up at Kessler. Now she was feeling some of that peace/anxiety conflict because she had been so busy taking care of everything, and I mean everything, that she hadn't cleaned the house. She knew I was a clean freak and keeping the house in tiptop condition just didn't rank as high on the priority list with all that had been thrown in her lap over the past few months.

She was thinking (her recollection of the story), "Oh crap. He wants to go home now? There are dishes in the sink from this morning, Bianca's toys are all over the floor. I don't think I made the bed." I guess she secretly called her brother, Jerry, who lived a few doors down, and said, "Jerry, you need to go to my house. You need to clean all the dishes. You need to pick up all the toys. We're going to be there in 20 minutes. Go!" She only showed me the side of gratitude that I was coming home. She's pretty amazing!

Once I allowed the switch from anxiety to anticipation, I took it all in on the short drive home. Pulling up to the house was hard to explain. It looked normal. Everything looked like it did just before I had left for work on that morning of 9/11. Kids were playing out in the street and neighbors were outside waving as we pulled up, which was a good feeling but something didn't feel right. My mind was telling me everything was normal, but something within me was telling me it wasn't. Apparently, the surreal was the new normal.

I slowly got out of the car, and I used the walker to come around to the front. The walk from the car to the stoop was now a long walk, and it required a concerted effort to climb the four stairs that I had previously skipped down a few months ago. It was a slow go, but once I got into the house I just wanted to cry. I was home, and it felt so comforting. I had just survived a nightmare, and now I was home. That word, "home," kept reverberating through my body. Whether I was a warrior cop or a little kid, a special peace came with knowing I was *home*.

The peace soon gave way to the sadness. As I felt the love of my family and the comfort of being with them, the sadness for my friends overtook me. Antonio, Dominick, and Chris's families were not getting to experience the same thing, and this would not be the last time I felt sadness accompany my moments of appreciation.

The first night was a good night, a night of familiarity, family, and food. I settled in and tried to take it in, but also present was this persistent companion of unspeakable uneasiness that may have waned at times but never left. Nevertheless, it was better to be uneasy and in my own bed with Allison than to be in the rehab facility. I was going to make the most of it.

Saturday morning started with the usual struggle of getting up, dressed, and to the bathroom. I had one agenda for the day: to sit outside and breathe. My parents and sister, as well as Allison's parents, grandmother, and brother, were with us. I was surrounded by the people I love. Allison helped me get to the porch. It seemed like forever since I had been able to just sit and look out onto the street. I just soaked it in. The brisk air brought a special sense of clarity to the experience. The simplicity of the moment was something I had longed for, and I was appreciative. It was just the beginning of another unknowable journey, while I was still on the well-traveled road of my physical recovery. There were battles ahead that I could not anticipate.

The weekend went faster than I had hoped, but it was a welcome reprieve and re-energizing time of connection. My work at Kessler continued to be intense and lasted a couple of more weeks. Some days were better than others; the nights were the same. Nevertheless, I made it. I progressed enough to go home for good, and I did so before Allison gave birth.

The day I left Kessler—November 16th, 2001—I walked with Canadian crutches, also called Lofstrand crutches, the ones that wrap around your forearm. That was a great feeling! It was time to transition to living at home and continue my rehabilitation in an outpatient structure. I had the best of both worlds. I also began to feel the switch in the balance of physical and emotional healing.

Reflections

1) Are there people in your life that motivate you through their actions/behaviors? Do you know why?
2) What do you connect with that inspires you?
3) Are there things in your life that you clinging to that are no longer a reality, holding you back from opportunities today?
4) Do you need to pause, breathe, reflect, or grieve in this moment before continuing? What were moments of significance in this chapter?

Chapter Nine

Daddy, You Scare Me Sometimes

Honesty in love is often hard. The truth is often painful.
But the freedom it can bring is worth the trying.
— Fred Rogers[1]

It was good to be home! Although my unwanted companion, undiagnosed PTSD, remained persistently by my side, the honeymoon of returning home to family and what was similar to a pre-9/11 normalcy was welcomed, even if there was no actual returning to pre-9/11. To sit in my chair and to eat at my table, surrounded by family—ahhh…I cannot say family enough to encompass what that means to me. However, there was a loss. When transitioning back home, an in-home care nurse was needed for my daily routine, which allowed Brian and Vickie to return to their police duties at the bus terminal. They had been such cornerstones in my recovery and were like family to me; it was hard to see them go.

A nurse was provided, although it was someone with whom I had no history, and it was a shit show. It was bad. She was a nice lady, but we just didn't feel comfortable with her. Honestly, I don't know if anyone could have fit that position because it wasn't family. It had only been a week, but that was a week too long for me. What I required was a level of trust. To be fair, she never really had the chance to earn it. Allison felt uncomfortable asking her to help with anything, so she was still managing most everything herself. Regardless, I needed to feel like I had some control in my care, so I called my case manager, Eileen. She was phenomenal at her job and really went above and beyond at helping me get into Kessler, making sure my medical care was managed appropriately, and helped make a messy situation flow smoothly.

I called and said, "Eileen, I'm not comfortable with this lady, and she's really not helping me. Is there any way Vickie could come back

---

1 Rogers, F., & Junod, T. (2019). *A Beautiful Day in the Neighborhood (Movie Tie-In): Neighborly Words of Wisdom from Mister Rogers.* Penguin Books.

and stay with me during the day?"

"I think that would be a good thing, that you have someone you can trust. And, if the police force is willing to have her stay with you and Vickie agrees... let me see what I can do, Will," she responded.

It was so important to have someone I felt comfortable with tending to my medical needs, someone that Allison felt comfortable with being in the home, and someone Bianca liked. It was also important to have someone that made it a point to say, "Hey, I'm here to help my fellow officer and my classmate."

Eileen called Inspector Tim Norris, who took over the bus terminal at that time, and requested Vickie be reassigned back to working with me.

His response was simple and clear, "Whatever Will needs."

It's also important that I make this clear. These things did not happen because I was special or had power. These things happened because I was surrounded by outstanding professionals that had passion for their jobs and cared about the people they were watching over. I am forever thankful for their hearts and their generosity.

Vickie returned and was there from six in the morning to six at night, except weekends. She drove me to my outpatient therapy appointments at Kessler three times a week. She took me to interviews. She was my safety net as far as walking. If I had to leave the house, Allison knew Vickie was with me. I mean, she drove for months. I couldn't drive. She made sure that I didn't fall. I progressed from the wheelchair to the walker, to the Canadian crutches, and then to a cane before I could walk. She was always by my side. She was my safety blanket. I knew I wasn't going to fall but if by some oddity I did, Vickie was there to catch me. We all relaxed in her presence, which was especially important with Allison's due date upon us.

Allison, Bianca, and I were about to get a new addition to our family. Allison was scheduled to give birth on my birthday, November 26, 2001, and I still remember that day. Allison was admitted to Valley Hospital in Ridgewood, New Jersey, for a planned C-section. I was in a wheelchair because I couldn't stand for lengthy periods of time, but I was able to be right next to her when she gave birth to Olivia, my birthday present. I remember not looking over at the procedure; I didn't want to look over. I stayed by her head, where they had the sheet, and I remember hearing Olivia being brought into this world. There was a bit of silence until they tapped her, and she started crying. It was overwhelming. I almost missed this grand moment...almost. Trying to stay in the moment was sometimes a struggle. My mind could so easily take me into focusing on what I could have missed and where I could have been, but I was learning to refocus on what was happening and where I was right now. I *didn't* miss this. I *am* here. And, I was able to be by Allison's side for the birth of our precious daughter.

After everything we had been through, we were finally a family of four. I say *we* because I was always conscious that what happened to me happened to my family, all four of us. Whether it's the military, fire and rescue, or being a police officer, families are part of the force, too. They may not be physically present for everything a first responder experiences, but they very much are a part of our experience and suffer silent consequences (sometimes called vicarious trauma). Allison went through my struggles with me while being pregnant. And now, there we were with our Olivia. It was exceptionally special, and we were so happy. What a gift to come through—what we had and to now be holding our daughter for the first time. Life!

Allison was in a lot of pain from the procedure, but she showed her toughness again in her ability to be happy despite the pain. She took some needed time to heal in the hospital, and the doctors and nurses were awesome. Allison stayed for almost a week before being able to bring Olivia home. This home had been new to us six weeks prior to the attack, and it hadn't seemed quite the same since. But now we were bringing a new baby home, and Bianca was so happy to meet her little sister that it felt like we were getting a fresh start. It just felt right. I felt so much gratitude and thought, "Wow! Thank you, Lord! Thank you so much for giving me this opportunity."

We started a new routine, as much as could be routine with a newborn. I continued going to outpatient physical therapy, and Vickie was right by my side every step of the way. I knew how much I relied on her and how much she just fit in our home and did whatever was needed to be supportive of the whole family. However, it meant the world to me to know how much comfort she also gave Allison. Vickie and Brian seamlessly fit right into our home and our family. Brian would come over and play with Olivia, his goddaughter. Family is everything.

My parents were always there to babysit. They would rotate with Pat and Paul, each taking shifts. They would come over and just hang out, being available. My sister would come over in the evenings after work and play with Olivia and Bianca. My mom provided a constant reminder to keep my faith and to keep strong. If the grass needed cutting, my dad and my father-in-law would take care of that. If a light bulb needed to be changed, I didn't even have to ask. It was done. My father has always been the focus of strength in my family. My mom has always been the focus of kindness and faith. My sister has always defended me growing up. My father-in-law was my hunting buddy and friend, my mother-in-law was full of love and the model from which Allison's love and devotion was created, and my brother-in-law was the example of love through service.

No matter how many references to family I make, it will never be enough to express the support, the love (soft and tough), and the strength they offered through service and presence. One of those strong presences was Allison's grandmother, Julia (aka Granny). She was born in 1914, and she had lost her husband in her forties. This little, very religious woman had made her way through life without ever having owned a car. She walked everywhere, so being stagnant was going to be noticed and addressed. One night I was talking about how the wound in my leg was still not healed, and Granny immediately told me, "If you want to close up that hole in your leg go get in the bath with Epsom salt."

Man, she was a tough, old lady. She had such a positive outlook and was a kind person, but she did not settle for excuses or self-pity. She told me, "There's only so much time you can sit there and whine about stuff. You've got to get on your feet and go forward." She was old-school tough.

Don't ask me how I was so fortunate to have so many loving women in my life, but I really was and still am blessed. Not only did I have a strong and dedicated wife, but her tough and caring grandmother, her unbelievably supportive mother, my sister that was available at the first sign of need, and my mother, who was still taking care of her baby boy. Among all these women were also the three men of the family: Allison's dad and brother, and my dad. They willingly supported Allison and me and whatever the women of the family asked. They all would shop, clean, run errands; there was no need too big or small that someone in our family wouldn't handle. They stayed and kept us company when we felt lonely, anxious, or sad. They shared in our pain and our tears when things became overwhelming. Each person came with their respective skills, and together they were an unstoppable force of love, support, and motivation. It was family, and there was nothing like it!

Friday evenings everyone came over, and we played a lot of Texas Hold 'em. Mom brought empanadas and other Spanish foods. Pat and Paul sometimes brought additional games to break up the routine of card playing. Friday nights became a beacon of normalcy and were something to look forward to during the week because week by week I was getting glimpses of an increasing issue that had yet to fully surface. Per usual, I just kind of shoved it back down and focus on what I could get my hands on, what I could physically see and do.

With the functional things of life running smoothly and the continuation of physical therapy, during the next few months I was navigating getting in and out of the car better. Thankfully, my right foot still was functional and getting to the point where I could finally drive. I remember the first day I drove. It was awesome! I recall thinking, "I hope I remember how." It was such a good feeling because it didn't only represent autonomy, but it was another marker towards pre-9/11 life. Every time I did something that seemed natural to anyone else, it was confirmation that I was getting a little farther away from that dark day. It was another way to show the terrorists that they did not win. They did not kill me. They did not break me.

Every time I worked at something, I worked hard. I worked hard for my family. I worked hard for myself. I also worked hard for the guys that didn't make it because that was the least I could do to honor what they gave. However, much like the shift in balance between my physical recovery needs and emotional recovery needs when leaving Kessler and coming home, this balance was shifting even more, and I had not done such a good job at addressing it. I was physically progressing and feeling great about my accomplishments, but my anger was increasing, along with my volatility. I got very angry about little things without knowing about it. I'd get frustrated when I wanted something done in a certain way and I couldn't do it. I'm talking about things that have no real value in life, like trying to find the remote. My temper had a hair trigger, and my reactions definitely didn't fit the scenario. Vickie even tried to help me, and she told me, "You've got to calm down."

I just fired back, "What are you talking about?" I have to admit that sometimes there was vulgarity involved. It's not something I'm proud of, but it was just a peek at what was starting to surface. Another time, my brother-in-law, Jerry, and mother-in-law, Pat, came over, and I don't know what happened. It was just stupid! We had many friends randomly stopping by to drop off food for us so Allison wouldn't have to cook. That night someone dropped off a tray of Chicken Parmesan and another tray of Eggplant Parmesan. Jerry was always at our house, constantly helping (e.g., picking up Bianca from pre-school, babysitting just so Allison could take a shower, and keeping Allison company late at night once everyone else was asleep), so Allison gave him the tray of Eggplant Parmesan to take home, especially because she knew I hated eggplant. I wouldn't touch it.

"What the fuck? You're eating all the food?" I yelled. He just looked at me. He wasn't doing anything out of the ordinary or anything that would have been deemed inappropriate. In fact, he had just spent the day helping us out. I was really nasty with him. It never even registered that I was losing it over food I disliked, not to mention we had so much food being given to us that we couldn't have eaten it all.

"Will, don't be like that," Pat said. "You've got to believe in God that things are going to get better."

"God abandoned me!" I snapped back.

I'm a Catholic, and I believe in God. I know God, faith, hope, and love is what helped me through 9/11 and through that evening, but that night I was saying, "God abandoned me." That's how I felt. "Just stop fucking talking about shit. Please don't preach to me about stuff that you don't know anything about."

My tolerance for others was worn out, especially when they were trying to help with useless platitudes or empty comparisons. I told people, "Stop telling me what you think. You have no fucking clue about what I went through or what I'm going through now." My anger was no longer buried, and it had less of a healthy outlet to be channeled through as my physical recovery kept improving. It went on for probably another year. I reached the point where I was able to get around pretty well with my brace. Vickie was no longer around and had returned to working at the bus terminal. Yet, my anger and outbursts were just getting worse.

Sadly, there were times I made Allison cry for silly things. One night, I don't remember if it was the remote control setting me off again or what, but I lashed out at Allison. That's how insignificant the triggers were on the surface. They didn't even register on the rational level, but they sure registered on the emotional level, especially in the form of rage. In this particular instance, Allison had done something, and the kids were there. Olivia was just an infant, and Bianca was five years old. I was so mad. I've never raised my hand to a woman, but I was yelling at Allison and I picked up a shoe and pulled back. In that moment I realized I was getting ready to throw it at her head, and just stopped. Everything stopped, and I thought, "Will, what are you doing? This is not you." I could almost hear the internal dialogue and the confusion. This was my wife.

I threw the shoe down, turned, and left the house. I knew I needed to leave, so I got in the truck and drove up to Whittingham Wildlife Management Area, the public ground where I liked to hunt. It's about a 45-minute drive. I sat in my truck looking at the field I was supposed to hunt on 9/11. I sat there waiting for deer to come out, and a peace started to creep in. The woods became a relaxing place for me, so I sat there and thought about what had happened. Sitting alone, I said to myself, "You've got a problem, bro. You've definitely got an issue, and I don't know how to fix this. I just don't know." I knew I was angry. I knew what it was related to, but I didn't know who to talk to or what to do. I sat there until I knew I could enter the home in a better frame of mind.

After returning, I walked back in and went upstairs. Bianca was still up, so I walked in her room and asked, "Bianca, does daddy yell a lot?"

"Yeah daddy; you scare me sometimes."

It floored me! I thought, "Man, I can't do that to my kid." That's when I realized if I'm not a good husband, a good dad, a good example, then the terrorists win. I knew enough that if someone has a father who's an alcoholic they, too, might become an alcoholic. If someone has a parent that's an abuser, they might carry that on. I didn't want my kids to suffer because of my actions. There was no way I was going to let the terrorists' actions move through me and touch another generation of Americans. I would defend my daughter against anyone that tried to hurt her—even me. I was trying to deal with it more proactively, but I kept trying to do it on my own before I was ready. I couldn't deny it anymore.

I tried therapy and talked to a couple of people that were from my job. Peter Killeen was one of our Port Authority PBA therapists. I met with Peter and talked, but after a while I stopped. I just didn't want to go to the appointments. He'd ask me questions, and I didn't want to talk about it. I didn't even know how to explain it. The words just weren't there, and I'm never short on words. Nothing I said felt like it did any good, and most of the time it just felt like my anger was increasing because of my inability to express it. We worked together for a couple of months, but I felt like it wasn't helping. Sure, we'd sit there for an hour and talk about shit, but then I left and sometimes felt worse than when I went in. Peter's a great guy and he tried different ways to help me to open up, but I had to be honest with myself. I just didn't feel like going deep. I stopped trying, and it continued to get worse.

The anger surfaced, and I felt like shit. I tried to work on it, but I felt like I failed, which only increased my anger. So again my anger surfaced, and I felt like shit. The hamster wheel was exhausting, but I could not give up. My team never gave up on me. I hadn't given up on myself. My family had not given up on me. Nevertheless, the relentless anger persisted, taking the most inopportune times to express itself in damaging ways to those I loved the most.

One day we were coming from the store, turned the corner, and were heading down the street toward our home. Olivia was fidgeting in her car seat and spilled her drink after I had just told her to stop. I am not proud of this, but in an instant I turned while driving and grabbed her by her shirt as if I was going to punch her. Just as fast as I grabbed her, the realization hit me, "Will, this is a toddler, your toddler, and you are grabbing her like she is a grown man."

Allison yelled, "Will, what the fuck is wrong with you? She's just a little girl!"

I put hands on my child. I could have tried to rationalize that at least I didn't hit her, but that would have just been bullshit. I put hands on my child and no amount of rationalization would allow me to find this as acceptable. Moments like these moments of rage motivated me to seek answers, to seek help. However, they only seemed to help me initiate the work, not the follow-through.

It was time to reach out again, and it was time to get serious about facing my PTSD.

Reflections

1) Can you empathetically relate at all to Will's struggle?
2) Do you recognize moments in your life where your reaction did not fit the situation? Do you know why? What were you really feeling in the moment, beneath the expressed feeling?
3) What were moments of significance in this chapter?
4) Do you need to pause, breathe, reflect, or grieve in this moment before continuing?

Chapter Ten

Can I Come See You?

Vulnerability is not weakness; it's our greatest measure of courage. — Brené Brown[1]

In mid to late 2003, I contacted a psychologist friend of mine, Deborah "Debbie" Mandell (later, she married and became Debbie Basic), who was working at Ground Zero. She was an awesome lady. I called and said, "Can I come see you? I really need to talk to someone."

Without hesitation she agreed. Luckily, she didn't live far from me. She lived a couple towns over from Clifton, and I went over to her place to talk. I originally met Debbie in the hospital. She came in one night and introduced herself. She didn't push; she just asked how I was doing. She stopped by from time to time, but we never really got into too much because I primarily stayed focused on my physical recovery. Nevertheless, I felt comfortable with her. Comfortable with her or not, my internal resistance was waiting right around the corner.

It didn't take long before I felt like we weren't getting anywhere and that going to the sessions was just a waste of time. It was a replay of my previous involvement with other therapists. After weeks and months of talking about my feelings, the guys, and my thoughts during the day, I was in a place where I thought about ending my life. The guilt was overwhelming.

"I just wanted to go be with my friends. I should be with them. Why am I alive and not them?" I shared with her.

Debbie patiently waited and allowed me to struggle with those tough questions. Those were hard times, and feelings of suicide ebbed and flowed with countering thoughts of, "No! Are you crazy? That would have been so disrespectful." Being a gun buff, I believed that I would never turn any of my weapons on myself. My weapons were there for protection and outdoor activities. How could I ever turn one

---

[1] Brown, B. (2017). *Rising Strong: How the Ability to Reset Transforms the Way We Live, Love, Parent, and Lead* (Reprint ed.). Random House.

on myself? I think I might have been motivated more by not wanting to disrespect my guns than myself at the time. It may sound silly, but it kept me alive.

Prior to 9/11, I could never imagine that I would ever be in a place where I entertained the idea of taking my own life. I started to be aware of how often my thoughts of suicide were preceded with bouts of anger. Something triggered me, and I lost sight of all that was important, that was right in front of me. In retrospect, I questioned how it was I could lose sight of my family, which only brought on more guilt, then more anger. It was a vicious cycle. That damn hamster wheel kept showing up. Sometimes I could anchor in my family's love and my love for them, thinking about what it would put them through if I took my own life. Other times, the guilt and anger were so intense that I just wanted it to be gone, to be with my friends that died that day.

Sometimes you've just got to keep at it, keep at it, and keep at it until something clicks. Debbie had a way of creating a comfortable environment and seemed to understand not to push me too much on days I felt it was more of a chore to be there. She challenged me to find goals that I knew I wanted in life, since the one thing I worked so hard to achieve had been taken from me. It had been my dream to be a police officer, and the writing on the wall was clear that it was over. Debbie and I talked for over a year; one day she said something that resonated. She, like Peter, had said things that were meaningful at times, but this was something that grabbed me and shook me.

"Will, you're going to have to learn to live with this. We're at a point here where we can keep kicking a dead horse, or we're going to move forward and say, 'Okay, you have PTSD, you're angry. How are we going to deal with this? What are you going to do?' We talk about things. You talk about your anger, but what steps are you going to take to accept this instead of denying it. It's a part of your life, Will. How are you going to manage it?"

I don't doubt this message was part of what others had tried to get through to me, but I heard her. This cut through my resistance, and I realized I had to tackle this like I had done with my physical recovery. No matter how much physical healing I did, I would never be the same as before 9/11. I had to let go of what I had been able to do in the past to make use of what was available today. It was the only path that would help me regain the fullness of my potential. The same was true for my emotional healing. I had to engage the pain if I was going to learn how to heal and live with PTSD. I wasn't sure what this was going to look like, but I realized that reaching out was only part of the path. Taking responsibility for the actions was the other part. I had to take what she was offering, and I had to do something with it. If I wanted to live again, to have the kind of life my family deserved and be a loving dad and spouse, I couldn't do just one or the other. I needed to do both.

Over the next months, Debbie's words were taking hold: Watch for this, watch for that. She helped me to become more aware of hidden triggers and what they represented, not just what they were on the surface. I started reflecting on bouts of anger and challenging myself to work through the deeper pain that was being poked with a sharp stick. I reminded myself that to not work through it was harmful to myself, my wife, and my children. It helped me face the things I didn't want to face or feel, but it was worth it.

Debbie requested that Allison start attending some of the sessions, which she agreed to do. Debbie said it was important that she hear from my wife as well, and I painfully sat there and listened to Allison. It was hard. When Allison voiced her opinion without fear, I got mad and said, "Well, that's bullshit!"

It wasn't bullshit. It was her truth. She had her own feelings to deal with, and I had not considered them. I knew a lot of other police officers and firefighters from 9/11 who got divorced. Their wives couldn't take the anger and the depression. But here was Allison. She put up with my pain and fear, as well as her own pain and fear. She was such a pillar of strength, and I had not given her the same consideration. Besides my faith and my family, Allison was the point-person in caring for me. It was time I sucked it up and did the same for her, so I listened. I'm not saying I always did a good job. Sometimes an argument ended with me blowing up and shutting it down, which was not respectful to her. My anger overtook her anger. It wasn't fair to her. The more I listened, the more I recognized the impact this journey had on her. I knew it affected her, but I hadn't really understood it.

We continued to work with Debbie, and I was learning the importance of loved ones being able to express what they were going through so that they are not suffering in silence as collateral damage. I was also learning how to be supportive with boundaries. It helped us, as individuals and as a couple. Before therapy, I broke things, punched doors, or just destroyed things out of anger. Allison was now able to give me cues like, "Hey, you're getting mad. You're getting angry. Go for a walk." She became an extra set of eyes that helped me catch myself when I had already lost sight of where I was headed.

When I took therapy seriously, it was no joke. It wasn't about the hour I spent with Debbie, which was tough enough. It was the rest of the week that demanded personal responsibility and self-discipline. That was hard. Really hard. I was able to do it in the physical world, but the emotional and mental worlds were different. It was foreign to me, and not everything worked. I had to find what worked for me through trying things out and engaging in honest reflection, not some rationalized excuse making. What worked for me may not work for others, but actively working at it is exactly what it took.

I found doing something physical, like getting on the elliptical, hitting a punching bag, or going for a walk gave me a constructive, purposeful avenue to release that negative energy. I needed that, even if it wasn't always easy. Sometimes the situation is not conducive to just getting up and working out in some fashion, like being at a dinner or in some other public setting. However, I gained some tools, some acceptance, some tolerance, and witnessed the positive gains of the work I (we) had been doing. The more wins I had, the more motivating it was. Being in the woods was one of those things that gave me wins.

Hunting, which is more often just enjoying the serenity of the woods, was and still is a huge part of my continued healing. Most of what I needed to do, I needed to do myself. However, including Allison in therapy helped me to see beyond myself and my pain to include hers, to include that of others. My defensive, painful world was beginning to open up to see beyond the pit of myself.

Unfortunately, we lost Debbie to 9/11 cancer on December 11, 2012. She spent a lot of time at Ground Zero at night talking to first responders and trying to help. It was hard watching someone that had been so instrumental in helping me regain the living in my life actively dying from cancer, but I can fondly reflect on one specific time we were together. Debbie's cancer was growing, and she had lost her hair. She loved going to the gun range and shooting, and on one of our trips to the range we talked about something. I don't recall what we discussed, but I recall her looking at me and saying, "Don't worry about it, Will. I'm going to die anyway, and I'm okay with that. I'm just trying to live everyday till I die."

The way she said it was so genuine, so honest. In her dying she was still teaching me about living. She wasn't just talking about it; she *was* about it! She shared her pain and her life with me. There were no comparisons about loss, just shared life. Our pain is subjective and not competitive. We can learn from each other when we lay down the competitive judgment and embrace each other's humanity, each other's struggles. Her approach to therapy mirrored her approach to life. I will forever be grateful to her. Thank you, Debbie, for reminding me to grab onto life.

Reflections

1) Are there struggles in your life that you just shove aside?
2) What reasons do you tell yourself for why you don't need any help? Would you accept those reasons from a friend, or would you call them on it?
3) Is it weak to reach out, or does it just feel that way?
4) What is more important to you: your life, your relationships, or your image?
5) Do you need to pause, breathe, reflect, or grieve in this moment before continuing? What were moments of significance in this chapter?

Chapter Eleven

Hunting for My Life

A wilderness area may well have more psychological
importance than hundreds of beds in a mental hospital.
— Rod Nash[1]

Most people who know me know I am passionate about the outdoors and archery. It's ironic that the very thing that almost saved me from experiencing the collapse of the Twin Towers was the thing that helped me find my way back to living, especially considering that as a kid I had little experience with the outdoors. I played soccer and practiced karate. Other than a couple of Boy Scout camping trips, my experience with nature was limited to the suburbs. Now, I spend many of my mornings watching the sunrise from a hunting blind, glassing a field, or with my newest love, bowfishing. Most don't realize that it was Allison who introduced me to archery when we first started dating. I took her to the gun range, well, because I was a gun guy. She blew me away with a tight group at 15 yards, which was her first time firing a handgun. Of course, she was not done with impressing me. Allison followed up with a question, "Have you ever shot a bow and arrow?"

"No. We weren't the outdoors kind of family. I fell in love with guns in the military."

"We'll have to give it a try and see what you think," Allison responded.

It wasn't too long after our firing range adventure that she introduced me to her dad, Paul Guardiano, and we went to the archery range where they were shooting at 3D targets at various distances. She was a natural and had been shooting for some time. I mean, she was really good. I had always been a gun enthusiast, so when she asked if I wanted to try, I was excited. Here's this girl I'm trying to impress, so of course I took the challenge. After all, how hard could it be to pull her

---

[1] Frazier, R. (1988). Wilderness Advocacy. In *American Environmentalism: Readings in Conservation History*. McGraw-Hill, Inc.

bow back and fling an arrow. Well, it was a lot harder than I thought. I pulled as hard as I could and was barely able to get it broken (pulled back far enough where it releases some of the tension). Needless to say, my ego took a bruising, but it was totally worth it because I fell in love that day; Allison already knows I'm talking about archery.

She'll tell you I am one of those guys that goes full bore once I'm interested in something. It didn't take long before my sights turned to archery hunting. I couldn't get enough. For years I was hunting public land with my father-in-law, Paul. It was such a big deal when we booked a hunt with an outfitter in South Jersey. It was my first time traveling to hunt and use an outfitter. I was so excited that I shot a spike buck. For those that are unfamiliar, it's a young buck, but it might as well have been a Boone and Crockett (a monster-big buck). It was a thrill that fueled my love for hunting. Pre-9/11 my biggest buck was only a Jersey five-pointer. It was a nice buck, respectable, but nothing to brag about to other hunters. However, in January 2003, prior to seeing Debbie, I had taken M. R. James up on his invitation to go to the ATA show. M. R. (*Bowhunter Magazine*), Will Primos (Primos Hunting), and Toxey Haas (Mossy Oak) made it easy for me to go and enjoy, and going to that show opened doors to me in the hunting world, as well as toward my recovery, in ways that I could have never imagined possible.

I met all these guys in the hunting industry that I was watching on TV, and one of them was Jimmy Primos. Jimmy is a Vietnam vet (Marine), and I remember how instantly comfortable I felt with him. We started talking, and, of course, I'm like, "Wow! You are Jimmy Primos. It's so cool to meet you."

He just kind of grinned and was too humble to respond to my admiration. Instead, he simply asked, "How are you doing, Will?"

"I'm doing all right. I've got a limp now, but most people wouldn't even notice my brace when I have jeans on."

He pulled me aside and asked, "How are you doing up here?" as he pointed at his head. "How's it up there?"

"Man, I guess okay. I'm not sure to be honest with you."

That question really rocked my world because he was the first person beyond medical professionals to ask about my mental state. Even they had not asked in the way Jimmy just did. None of my fellow officers, not my wife, and none of my family really asked me about how I was doing mentally. Maybe they didn't know to ask, or maybe I just wore a good mask. Maybe both. They might have tried to ask, but Jimmy was the first one that really leaned right into it and wasn't afraid of the answer he might hear.

"I've seen combat. You're going to experience things that are bad. You need to get that straight," Jimmy said. He took the time to share some of his experiences and the struggles that might come my way. He spoke with such authenticity that I just listened and appreciated that he was willing to enter the darkness with me. He knew what it was like coming back from tough situations that were beyond what most will experience. Because Jimmy was willing to ask and to share, the message I received was, "You're not alone."

I'm not alone, and if you are reading this today, you are not alone either. It may feel that way, but I am reaching out to you to say, "You are not alone." I know it feels that way, especially when you are surrounded by people that cannot understand. It's a bittersweet reality when those around you cannot understand due to not having experienced something like it. On one hand it is a blessing, and on the other it is lonely. Thankfully, my family hadn't been through anything that tragic, which is a gift. But it really was lonely at times. So, when Jimmy shared his story with me and we talked about it, it helped me focus and see that this was not just going to go away. It was going to take work. I still wasn't sure exactly what that meant, but I at least knew it meant I had to grab onto life and couldn't just wait for things to get better. I had to pursue those aspects of what I said was important to me. Hunting and nature were two of them.

M. R., the Primos cousins, and Toxey were coming alongside of me and investing in my life, and whether they knew it or not, also in my recovery.

"It's time to get you out hunting," M. R. stated. "Would you let me take you?"

"Wow! Really?" I was kind of stunned. While I was trying to form the words for an emphatic yes, Paul came to mind and all he had done in teaching me about archery. "Would you mind if I brought my father-in-law?"

"Of course he can come. Hunting is meant to be shared."

It took some time getting everything set up and the people in place, but M. R. said he knew a guy by the name of Jess Moats that he had hunted with in the past, and he could arrange a hunt that would also accommodate my limited physical condition. Jess had a long-time friend that owned a ranch in Colorado, who was also ex-Special Forces, named Billy Dowen.

"They have some big deer out there, Will. You're going to love it!" M. R. said, making me chomp at the bit. Getting to hunt deer of this caliber was a dream. I didn't know Jess or Billy, but the two of them made a natural deer blind out of large square alfalfa bales. I was driven close to the blind to minimize difficulty in traversing the land, as I still had some instability in my walking. They were both good-hearted country boys that loved to hunt, swap stories, joke, and enjoy life; they started giving me shit right away. Needless to say, we jelled instantly. They allowed me the space to share my story and what I was going through. Paul, Jess, Billy, and I were all veterans. We all loved America. And, we all loved archery.

It was a great trip. I ended up taking a huge Colorado buck. I didn't even have words for what I was feeling. It was beyond what I thought I would ever get to hunt, and I got to do it with Paul and Jess in the blind. We had to wait until the next morning before we could recover the deer, so Billy and M. R. were able to be with us, too. It was a great moment; it was a great hunt. I felt so alive! It was like that first drink of water during the rescue.

That Colorado deer hangs in the center of my game room, which is one of the biggest bucks I've ever harvested and one that holds so many memories. The memories and the feelings are not even about the size of the deer; it's really about the friendships—friendships that I still have today. M. R. wrote another article, *Tamarack Buck*, [2] commemorating the hunt and allowing me to dedicate it to my team.

The hunting industry has been great to me, and I try to be a good ambassador in return. As a Colombian American, I want to share this gift with my culture, with my country, and with anyone that is seeking a greater connection to the outdoors. Nature has taught me so much, and it is my outlet. It's the place where I can go to find peace. The feeling I get from watching a sunrise or sunset is one that reminds me I am alive, that I am blessed; it gives me a feeling of gratitude that I have the opportunity to live another day and experience the things I love. Dom would be fishing right now with his kids. Antonio and Chris would be playing with their kids and bragging about them to anyone who was near. They don't get to do the things they love and be with the people they love anymore. Sunrises and sunsets bring the warmth of gratitude and the reality of the precious fragility of life.

Some have questioned me about how hunting fits into this appreciation and gratitude when it involves death. Hunting is not about the killing. Yes, it does sometimes involve that piece, but it is a source of food for my family. However, most of the time I sit in the blind and

[2] James, M.R. (2004). The Tamarack Buck. *Bowhunter Magazine, Whitetail Special,* 100–102.

just watch the woods come alive on a new day and the wildlife going about their business. It's just something beautiful that I get to experience. I just want to bottle it all up and absorb the beauty, but nature is meant to be experienced anew. It is a reminder of living each day and not clinging to the past or fearing the future, which is why nature has been one of the greatest tools for my approach at facing PTSD. It's not only a hobby but something that feels productive and healthy, which is so much better than sitting on the couch in the darkness, crying and perseverating on the past. Looking into the past had only brought further misery and, at points in my recovery, made me contemplate suicide as an escape from the pain. I didn't choose the pain of 9/11, but I sure chose how I addressed it. To choose death would mean I also lost everything that I loved and dishonored the chance that so many people gave me, with some giving their lives to give me that chance. When the darkness came, A-Rod, Chris, and Dom pushed me to do what they couldn't: live. Some days have been better than others, but with persistence, not perfection, I have had many better days in the long run.

I have been fortunate and unfortunate. Unfortunately, I had to retire in August 2004, leaving my dream job. I had to find a new dream. Luckily for me, that dream was created with my wife by making sure that I was there for all my girls' events. I am active with my kids. Nature allowed me to focus on something greater than myself, and my family gave me purpose to care for someone other than myself. I was able to go to nearly every event my daughters were involved in. Softball, cheerleading, and volleyball, I was there. I didn't miss it. There's no amount of money that could replace that time. I even saw them both shoot bows; Olivia now turkey hunts and bowfishes with me. It's been a blessing to be able to have that time as a dad and share those experiences. Hunting helped me focus on the day. The more I focused on what I could affect each day, the more happiness I was feeling and the better I could purposefully engage my PTSD.

Reflections

1) What do you find therapeutic in everyday life?
2) What can you do for five minutes that helps you feel more grounded?
3) Do you ever focus on your breathing? On a scale of 1–10, rate your current level of discomfort (e.g., anxiety, sadness, pain). Take four breaths in and out at a count of four seconds each

direction. On the last breath's exhale, breathe out for a count of six before returning to normal breathing. Rate your current level of distress again and notice the difference. This is not meant to fix anything, but it is meant to give you a calmer mind to refocus on what is in front of you right now.

4) Do you need to pause, breathe, reflect, or grieve in this moment before continuing? What were moments of significance in this chapter?

Chapter Twelve

Is It Gone?

*The more I focused on what I could affect each day, the
more happiness I was feeling and the better I could
purposefully engage my PTSD. —William Jimeno*

I say *purposefully engage my* PTSD because it is present, and it is mine.
It is something I still live with. It's not pleasant and rears its ugly head
from time to time, but it looks nothing like it had many years ago. It's
something that, at times, I'm not proud of; most of the time I am proud
because I worked to be at a point in my life where I can talk to people
who are having issues and offer them a little glimmer of hope. It feels
good to have made something from it. The idea that using my pain to
potentially help someone have one or two or three more days, or a
month, or a year, fuels me as well. Helping them have extra time to
hopefully choose to hang on and grab their life back is also part of my
healing.

When I say recover, I don't think anyone recovers from it, but we
recover enough where we could say, "I decide." It's not deciding if PTSD
affects us, but it's deciding what we will do with it when it shows up.
I've learned to live with it. I've made peace with the fact that *the day I
get over it, it's the day they bury me.* That's been *my* truth so far. I've had
enormous support, but I still had to find my own way. No matter how
many people were around me, none of them could take the journey for
me. I am grateful for the love and support I have received through the
years, and it is our hope that this book will help whoever hears its
message to reorient toward living their idea of a meaningful life.

My dad always told me, "Whatever you do, be happy at what you do
and be the best. If you're going to be a garbage man and you're proud of
doing that, just be the best at it, whatever it is. Don't do something that
you're unhappy with." After 9/11, I cannot say I followed my dad's
advice when I applied it to life. It was something I had to learn again.

One of the first things I had to do was to become more aware of my
temper and catch myself when I was getting angry over silly things. I

wasn't very good at it to begin with, and it was more a matter of seeing I had already crossed over into an unhealthy rage (e.g., not finding the remote, becoming mad about giving away the eggplant parm, Olivia spilling her drink in the car). I didn't like it, but that's just where I was. The reality was that when I was in that state, I was no good to anyone. Space was needed to help me calm down to where I could think more clearly again. Sometimes I would go for a walk, use the elliptical, shoot my bow, or take a drive. Driving is a tricky one because sometimes anger just gets transferred into road rage, so it's important to recognize if the drive is helpful or just making other unsuspecting, innocent people carry our struggles through an aggressive interaction. If ever in doubt, ask a trusted person for their opinion.

Awareness came in many forms for me. My anger seemed to come from either pain (physical and emotional), feelings of helplessness, or fear of the unknown. I had to learn the difference in how each affected me. Gaining this education did not happen overnight. Sometimes the shock factor of the speed of my rage taught me. Sometimes the space I took would assist in calming me down enough to breathe, analyze, and learn from what transpired. Breathing. Breathing is something that is easily overlooked but is so important when emotions are high. Hell, it's important when emotions are low, too. When I gave myself the opportunity to take in some fresh air, I could feel the intensity of my reactions begin to lower. The ability to check myself increased. I asked myself, *What are you really getting angry about? What about the situation would justify this strong of a response?* Sometimes it made sense; other times, not so much. The not-so-much moments usually ended in a similar manner, "Wow, I'm getting angry over that. I understand why, but it's not worth it." Those were the times I wished I could have caught it in the moment, but my anger would sometimes just flip on. My emotional dimmer switch was nowhere to be found when it came to anger, but I started learning. I didn't like how I was learning, but it was important that I kept at it...keep at it.

I started realizing that I could slowly begin to foresee how situations would trigger me, and I was getting better at feeling it and addressing it. Sometimes addressing it meant coping in a healthier way and working through it. Other times, it meant blowing it and seeing where I went off track. It took years of screwing it up, but I knew I had to keep at it. Day by day I made progress. I learned as I went. I want everybody to understand that there is no single path for healing; everybody's different. What works for me might not work for you. The outdoors is my medicine. Tennis might work for someone else. Maybe poetry. It takes effort and trying to find what feels right inside you. Again, it's a road of recovery that's long and one that is unique to each individual. Hopefully, you will take lessons from other people and learn and apply it for your life. You have to find the things that work for you because your life is an unwritten book that you're writing as you go. It's your story. There are things in life that will be a part of your book that you did not choose. However, the majority of it is up to you to write and create. In doing so, instead of avoiding the pain, fight for the life you envision to create that happiness.

Part of my happiness was getting back to my pre-9/11 morals. Bias and prejudice are difficult topics to discuss, and unfortunately we have decreased our ability in our society to have honest discussions about our own struggles in these areas. I couldn't afford to be silent if I wanted to live what I believe. One of the codes my parents instilled in me was to see the human. See the human first while including race, ethnicity, gender, class, or whatever uniqueness that was part of their lives— appreciate the commonalities and the differences. See the human. After the attacks, I had lost some of that. I'm not proud of that fact, but it's honest, and I had to be honest with myself before I could do anything about it.

Looking back on the day that I saw the photos of the terrorists in the newspaper and the fixated confusion that I experienced with the terrorist that wore glasses blurred the lines for me. It would have been so easy to just see the faces and lump them together as pieces of shit and condemn their ethnicity for what they had done. However, his normality separated him just enough to create a question. Somewhere in there I was still asking what kind of hate this normal-looking guy with glasses must have felt to do such a heinous act. I was still looking for the human. The shadow of seeing how such a normal-looking person could commit such atrocities was that I unconsciously singled out his most obvious, distinguishing feature to judge potential threats, which was his ethnicity. It wasn't intentional, but I was about to become aware of this hidden change. I struggled with the hate for the terrorists. In my mind, I did not have hate toward people of Arabic ethnicity. When in the Navy, I faced the stereotypes of being American in foreign countries and the beliefs that we are all alike. We have some knuckleheads, but we are generally good people. And that is what I knew to be true about Arabs as well.

The thing with PTSD is that it changed me. I had lifelong beliefs that I lived by, but sometimes my body reacted in opposition to what I knew to be true. I knew there were Arabs that rejoiced when the towers fell, but I also knew there were a lot that thought, "What the fuck did these people just do?" I knew and lived by my parents' teachings of having love for humanity, but I also held hate now. So much was taken from me physically and emotionally—from my department, from our country, and from the global community of immigrants that worked and lived in NYC. The pain offered an easy path to hate. I struggled with that. Hate gave me a place to hold my pain.

Living in Clifton, New Jersey, we had a large population of Arab-Americans, and they were a trigger for me at times. Sometimes I would have to remind myself to not hate. Again, I am not proud of this, but I need to be honest about the reality of the internal conflict. It would just come up, and it would have been so easy to let it just be present. It was the struggle of who I had been and wanted to be versus who I was in the moment. Make no mistake, if a terrorist had just killed people and was in front of me, I would have no issue with taking them out. Put them on their knees, and I will look them right in the eyes and put one in their foreheads. I wouldn't even think twice about it. That's how strongly I feel about what terrorists deserve. At the same time, I'm a compassionate person who understands the foolishness of hating an entire ethnicity based on the acts of a small faction. However, I struggled to navigate the conflict within.

It had been a couple of years, and I was driving to pick up Bianca from 2nd grade. It was around 2:30 in the afternoon, and the school was just down and around the corner from the house. The day was uneventful, and I was in no hurry. Life was good. Turning left into the school parking lot, I started into the entrance of the lot when an Arab woman dressed in her traditional wear was pushing a baby stroller toward the crossing. Since I had already started the turn before she reached the entrance, I had the right of way. We made eye contact, and she communicated with her eyes and her actions that she was going to pause and wait for me to go through, but none of this rational thought seemed to matter. For an instantaneous moment, my thoughts were, "Fuck you, lady! I'm going to cut you off!" No more than the thoughts presented themselves did my internal reaction of, "What the hell are you doing, Will?" come to mind. That rage was so fast, but thankfully my core belief was also quick to react. I knew that is not who I am, so I stopped and waved her through. She thanked me, we both waved, and she walked past. I'm glad she was unaware of the conflict within me because she did nothing wrong. I could see that truth from the beginning, but my body was reacting to her ethnicity. For that split second, nothing rational mattered. I thought, "Fuck you and your fucking terrorists." From the outside it looked like two people, two parents, from the same community having a friendly interaction of cordiality. That's how I wanted to act because this lady had nothing to do with my pain. My pain was my responsibility. I know, for me, the momentary satisfaction of acting like an ass to her would have had exponentially greater feelings of guilt the moment after poor behavior.

The real message here is that the struggle is real, and it is not a rational struggle. With PTSD, you change; your body changes, and you sometimes react with limited ability to think. It takes purposeful work to rewire yourself, fair or unfair. Through encounters like the one with this mother in the parking lot, I have been able to see beyond my pain. I haven't forgotten my pain or gotten rid of it, but I was learning to see beyond it. There have been times where I was with a group of people, and they would be talking about the terrorists and generalized them to anyone of Arab ethnicity, saying, "Fuck them!" I had to be able to speak up and remind them that way of thinking is what drove the terrorists to attack us. The terrorists were also thinking, "Fuck them (us)!" It only fuels the divide. If they had any conscience, if they weren't brainwashed by hate, in my opinion, they wouldn't have done it.

I think about that one, especially today when I'm presented with a situation of prejudice. I go back to that moment in saying, remember who you are. Remember who your parents raised. And I thank my parents for instilling that belief because it's easy to go to the dark side. Doing what's right can be tough. Taking the defensive path feels easy, but it has big consequences. Being purposeful is hard, but it pays dividends to one's life. One of the things that was big for me—bigger than I knew initially—was to apologize for my behaviors. I've had to do it many times, especially to Allison and our girls. I would tell Bianca and Olivia, "Look, I'm sorry that I acted like that. I was wrong." Early on, I didn't want to apologize. I had the attitude that I'm fucking mad and that's it. I think I felt like I had been handed a raw deal and it was unfair. I felt like I deserved to be mad without fully recognizing the collateral damage at the time. It was after I saw the pain that I was inflicting that I began to take ownership for my behaviors.

There was power in apologizing. Dealing with PTSD was the reason for my behaviors, but it was not an excuse. Despite not always having the ability to control my emotions, I still owned it as my process. At first, I beat myself up for it, but later I learned to use it to motivate the change I wanted instead of punishing myself. I always felt bad but stopped marinating in my guilt. I decided to use the anger in a way that I fought for my life and not against PTSD. If I fought for my life, the fight against

PTSD was a natural byproduct. Apologizing was one of those ways. I was communicating to my family that I was fighting to regain my life and to be the husband and father I wanted to be for them. Each time I faced up to a mistake, it felt like I was taking ownership of my life away from PTSD and removing the shame of my behaviors, which were a consequence of the trauma. If anyone deserved apologies, it was Allison. She took the brunt of my ugliness, and she continued to love me through it. I could not accept her devoted love without doing all I could to regain my life. Not giving up as I lay under the rubble of the Towers or in recovery was a way that I could show love to myself, to Allison, and to our girls. The terrorists caused damage, but I wouldn't settle for leaving it that way. The way I reacted sometimes caused damage, but I wouldn't settle for leaving it that way either. Sometimes those around you do not understand. My kids were young, and they didn't understand. I had to explain it to them. I had to teach them. I had to treat them with respect because I wanted them to grow up understanding, so that if, God forbid, something happened to them they could say, "My dad made it through that. I can make it through this."

Whatever *this* is for anyone, we want to encourage you that you can make it through. Whatever your World Trade Center is—a crash, a rape, war, overwhelming bills, health issues, loss—whatever it is, you can make it through. It might be messy, but keep clawing, keep fighting for your life. Be careful with being distracted by things outside of your power (e.g., others' successes, judgment from others, things outside of your control), and refocus on what you can affect today. When it comes to trauma, there is nothing fair about it. I wanted to be a cop my whole life and finally achieved it, only for it to be taken away nine months later. There was nothing fair about it, and it took me a few years to learn to accept it. Life doesn't pick and choose; life sometimes just throws things in your way. Life is a struggle. Choose where you put your energy. Physically, I was pretty dialed in at focusing my energy on healing. Emotionally, that was a different beast. Early on, I fought myself more than I leaned into it, but with each step I gained momentum and saw the meaning behind working through the pain—working *through* the pain, not trying to go around it. So what is fair? Fair is making your own choices and putting in your own effort for your own life despite the unfairness that gets thrown into the mix. Fair is giving yourself another opportunity to move forward with your life. That's what I had to do in 2004.

After surviving the collapse and two years of rehabilitation, I had made progress and was leaning into my PTSD. Allison and I decided we were going to move toward West New Jersey in Morris County. We were looking for a house with a good school district, and we ended up finding a beautiful piece of property in Chester with a nice house and friendly neighbors. It was a happy time for us. We were able to focus on making some changes that were good for the family and to focus on forward-looking goals. However, it was also during this time that I had to put in my retirement papers with the Port Authority. That was tough. Because of my injuries, the doctors informed me that I would not be going back to work as a police officer. This new chapter in our life was, again, met with happiness and sadness. We had only been in our first home in Clifton six weeks before the attacks, and now we were moving to our second home (June 2004) at the same time as I was being medically retired (August 2004). The first thing I grabbed onto was the opportunity to spend a lot of time with my girls. In some ways, it also distracted me from fully feeling the loss of being a cop.

November changed my ability to avoid feeling the loss. Even though I officially retired in August, the Port Authority held a Last Roll Call ceremony for me in November. It was a nice ceremony; they had news cameras and there were a lot of police officers that came to show their respect. However, it was hard to leave. I knew my career was over, but this really put the nail in the coffin, and I felt the physical and emotional distance on the hour-long drive back to Chester. My dream of being a cop was left at the Bus Terminal on August 14th, 2004.

When we suffer loss, we are forced to adapt and create a new way of being. Losing Antonio, Dom, and Chris left a gaping hole in my chest, and I had to learn how to live with their absence, to live with their sacrifices. Losing all those innocent people at the WTC created a moral injury[1] within me, and I had to learn how to live in a way that honored their loss of life. When I lost some of my mobility, I learned how to live with limitation and adapt. In 2004, I was losing what I had been called to be, a cop, and I had to reinvent myself. Despite all of this loss, I was the lucky one. I had to figure it out. My priority was to be a good dad and a good husband. Additionally, I started speaking more, formally and informally. Something inside me started changing. There was a healing effect, kind of like when I would learn about the other Port Authority

---

[1] In traumatic or unusually stressful circumstances, people may perpetrate, fail to prevent, or witness events that contradict deeply held moral beliefs and expectations. See Litz, B. T., Stein, N., Delaney, E., Lebowitz, L., Nash, W. P., Silva, C., & Maguen, S. (2009). Moral injury and moral repair in war veterans: A preliminary model and intervention strategy. *Clinical Psychology Review, 29*(8), 695–706. http://doi.org/10.1016/j.cpr.2009.07.003

officers on the poster and engage in conversation about their lives and their families. It resonated.

Even though it felt right to share the stories of 9/11 and of the guys, before every speaking engagement I would tell Allison about how much I didn't want to do it, how much I didn't want to rehash everything all over again. I would go anyway, and once I got started, I would get caught up in the energy of talking about serving with the best and feeling like I could bring them into the room with me to share with the audience. The story of my survival was less about Will and more about their bravery and the human aspect. Had I not pushed through the discomfort, I could have never felt the peace of reaching out to others through story, through connection.

Initially, I received feedback through kind words about the talk. Later, months and even years down the line, people started sharing with me how the message affected them and helped them to change their lives. That gave me great satisfaction. It felt like I was still wearing the uniform. Now I'm able to get up in front of a group of people, whether it be a small group of children or a large group at a military installation, and be able to touch lives.

On 9/11, I thought we were going to get everybody out to safety. We weren't able to save anyone. I learned to focus on the value of the effort rather than the outcome. The best I could do was offer what I had. The rest was out of my hands. I took this same lesson with me when I spoke. I'm clear when I share the message of faith, hope, and love that I will offer what helped me, but that it is up to those that hear the message to make use of what is helpful to them. Sometimes we work hard toward our dreams and living a good life, and sometimes our dreams and way of life gets taken from us. Over the years, I've noticed that when certain people's dreams are torn from them, it's as if their life stopped. I could have easily gone into a darker abyss, but I chose to focus on the light through the darkness. I chose to try to create a life that offered happiness as a byproduct, despite the struggle it took. My struggle at this point was to work through the pain and fear of telling the story again to see the opportunity to serve, which was the heart of my calling. Had I not been willing to feel the pain again and again, I would have never been able to redefine a calling that I thought was lost. Yes, I wanted to be a cop, but the heart of it was serving others and serving this country.

At first, I didn't speak that often and never did it as work. The requests started growing through word of mouth. Since 2004, I've had the pleasure of speaking to a lot of people in different groups from grammar schools, high schools, NFL teams, universities, military, police, fire, church groups, substance abuse rehabilitation centers, and philanthropy groups. I've been blessed in the sense that every time I speak, even though I initially feel internal resistance, the aftereffect is something that really motivates me.

I've learned a lot from the many interactions. I see the people out there struggling with some terrible things, and I see how they approach their fight courageously, despite feeling emotionally exhausted or in chronic pain. As we connect in our struggle, we help one another and even beyond. Think about the guys I met at Kessler. They shared with me, and I now share their stories with you.

Being able to speak to the Port Authority Police graduating classes was something that has meant a lot to me. I was able to still be part of the police department, and they asked me to come back once I started speaking. It stopped for a couple of years, so I spoke with other law enforcement agencies. I returned to speaking at the Port Authority in 2010. That still made me feel that the law enforcement community valued what I went through and what I learned; they wanted me to share my message with their officers.

First responders are the ones that help, so when we are struggling we often don't reach out. Call it ego, fear, or whatever you want; I did the same thing. I reached out, but I never really invested myself until I started working with Debbie. I'm thankful that I didn't wait too long, to the point of irreparable damage to myself or my family. I thought about escaping the pain. I even came close.

It was a beautiful day, we were in our new home, and on the surface we couldn't ask for a better life. There was nothing external that could be identified as distressful, especially distressful enough to contemplate taking my own life. However, I've shared that this beast would just pick at me, come out of the blue, and sucker punch me with the pain and guilt of 9/11. This was one of those days. Allison and I had an argument, and she was pushing back. I can't even remember what the argument was over, but I remember it getting heated and she appropriately wasn't taking whatever I was dishing out. Let me be very clear here; she did nothing wrong and was being my partner in conflict. I preface that because my reaction was my own.

In the heat of the moment, I felt overwhelmed with anger, like a bomb had just gone off—the bomb being me. Often after an explosion, I would experience the resulting, implosive anger reaction where self-loathing, guilt, and overwhelming sadness were all turned inward. I walked up the stairs and went straight for my bedroom closet to the gun safe. I retrieved my weapon and just held it. The gun was never pointed toward me, but I just stared at it. The pain, the anger, the sadness...it was just too much. I think about how easy it would have been to cross over and impulsively pull that trigger, but thankfully I had a great respect for my weapon. My weapon was for security, for the protection of others, for relaxation at the shooting range, and for hunting. It has never represented impulsivity, unnecessary harm to myself or others, or an escape. Judge it for what you will, but it began to help me connect back to my rational self and to the pieces of life that matter. Even though I was angry with Allison, I started to see the pain that I would cause her. In the depths of emotion the only thing I could see was the desire to escape.

What damage I would have caused to myself and to my family and friends! I understand what it feels like to only see the lies we tell ourselves in those moments: They would be better off without me, I'm a burden, there's no way out. I know what that feels like, but I also know just how untrue of a message those emotions whisper in our ears. Had I pulled the trigger, I would have never had the chance to change it. I thought about how hard I fought to live. Why would I give up now? Why would I run into burning buildings to try to help complete strangers, only to turn around and tear the hearts out of the people I love most? It shook me back to reality. I still hurt and was still sad, but I could, once again, see more than the emotional pain that had consumed me in that moment.

I shared what I had just done with Allison, and it frightened her. For the next few weeks, I could see a heightened sense of vigilance with me and that hurt. To know my actions were hurting her was hard to cope with. I had to rededicate myself to choosing how to use this pain. Do I use it to further judge myself as a burden, or do I use it to honor my wife's dedication to me and to honor my own life. I am alive. Live it. Living it meant rededicating my focus many times over.

That's why I teamed up with Michael for this book. We both have a passion to serve and both of us know the pain of loss. It's because of wonderful people in our lives that we are here with hearts to serve. It's because of those same people that we were helped along in times of pain and despair. We offer the same in this message. It is courage that says, "I need some help." I fought the same resistance to fully engage in seeking help, and it cost me and my family some undue pain. Others lost their lives because of the same resistance. I know what it means to be a cop and the stresses that go with it. First responders face things daily that others have the luxury of not seeing, not experiencing. And we gladly take that responsibility. However, we cannot serve as effectively if we do not care for ourselves—or if we're dead. When you have those feelings, learn to control them and keep pushing yourself to say that there's no shame in feeling like this. But find a way out. Find a way to anchor back to the meaningful things in life.

I think being able to speak to fellow first responders is one of my favorite things to do because we share a language and experiences. I've said, "Listen, you can work a lot of overtime and be away from your family, but the time you're away from your family, you're never going to get back. You're going to have regrets if you're missing birthdays and graduations. You never get that time back. I realized how important that is to me as a father and how important it is to my children. Some of the officers have come up to me and said, "That's a great point. I know my spouse has been telling me that for years, but I didn't listen." It's not just about what you give them. It's about being there. If you ignore what we go through, you run the risk of not being there—whether it's because of an increase in alcohol consumption, anger outbursts, physical violence, affairs, or suicide. The job is dangerous enough, but we know who the bad guy is and we have back up. What do you do when the bad guy is invisible, and you think you cannot call anyone? I'm telling you, reach out. When I was turned off by the psychiatrist at Bellevue, I stopped really trying. I reached out to Peter, but I didn't put in my full effort. It wasn't until I had seen the writing on the wall and could no longer deny it that I reached out to Debbie. Even then it was a struggle to continue. I didn't want to feel that pain and vulnerability because it felt like I was being weak. It was just the opposite. I realized that it took courage to walk into those dark places, just like an alleyway, a fire, or battle. And it was going to cost me if I didn't do it.

I wanted to give myself a chance in dealing with PTSD, but I didn't want to speak to anybody. When I first started, I thought it was a lot of bullshit. However, I gave myself a chance. Not one, but several chances and in different forms. You might have to go through five, six, or even seven people until you find that right connection, and that right connection might not be a doctor. It could be someone that just listens to you, someone you're comfortable with. We're so programmed to do what we are *supposed* to do. We come out of high school, and we're told we're supposed to go to college. You've got to do this. You've got to do that. If you have a mental issue, you have to go to a psychologist or a psychiatrist. There are all different avenues, and you need to explore more to find what works for you. Talk to a psychiatrist, talk to a psychologist. Talk to several and, hopefully, you find one that works well with you. If you don't, keep trying to find people, whether it be a priest, your parents, or a good friend. You'll be surprised sometimes who you're going to be able to talk to and feel like you're getting somewhere. No matter what your World Trade Center is, trauma is trauma and your pain is yours. You don't have to be a first responder, and trauma is not competitive. Regardless of your situation, regardless of the details, if life is feeling too much, please reach out. And keep reaching out until you find a path that works for you.

I'm no doctor. I just understand that sometimes people find their way in different manners, and getting help is more important than what kind of help. Just make sure it's healthy. Finding the right fit is so important, as well as being honest with yourself. At the time, I would use the defensive posture, telling myself that it's all just bullshit instead of owning that I was afraid and hurting. It's okay to be afraid and hurting; it just doesn't feel good. However, don't give up on yourself. Keep seeking that connection. If something doesn't work, give yourself a chance to find another avenue. The very thing we fear, vulnerability, is also the path to regaining our lives. The ability to be available opens us up to unsuspected opportunities. Therein lies the conflict.

One of the biggest burdens I carried was survivor's guilt. It took probably ten years before I began to allow myself to let go of that guilt. Again, this is not a rational issue either. I knew I didn't do anything wrong by living, but I had such immense guilt over not being able to get people out of the building. I had guilt over Antonio switching places with me. I had guilt over Dom dying while trying to free me. I knew that I had nothing to do with the death of my partners; they were my brothers, doing their job and exemplifying the definition of courage and humanity. It could have easily been me, but it wasn't. Why? Why are they dead and not me? That was an enormous weight I carried. It was almost like I was disrespecting them if I went on with my life and was happy.

Once again, change came through connection. Antonio Rodrigues's wife was a major catalyst for my ability to lay down the guilt. She told me she wanted me to be happy, which meant a lot. She was such a great example. She had lost the love of her life and made it a point to live and make a good life for their kids. I thought if she can do that, I should be able to do that. Her example and words of kindness offered me permission to see living life differently. I needed to do it for myself, my family, and for the guys. I realized that I was not honoring them with my misery and decided that my way of honoring those that I have loved and lost is by remembering them every day and living my life in a meaningful way. I'm not perfect. I don't think anybody's perfect. There are days that I fail in certain aspects, but the thing is, I get to wake up the next day, take a deep breath, and try again.

Another person of light that had a positive impact on me was Rosalie Downey. Rosalie was the wife of FDNY Deputy Chief of Special Operations, Ray M. Downey. He led the effort in the search and rescue of the Oklahoma City bombing and died on 9/11 serving NYC. I met Rosalie during an Easter Seals event full of families of those lost on 9/11. She came up to me, and I gave her my condolences. We talked about those we lost and my struggle with understanding why I was spared. She said, "Don't feel guilty. My husband would have said it was just his time." She asked about Olivia because her birth had made the news. Rosalie said, "I love that name, Olivia. Did you ever think about the name?"

"Well, my wife picked it out, and I wanted her to be happy. It's a beautiful name," I responded.

She said, "Will, listen to the beginning of the name. It says, 'Oh, live.'" She looked up at me and said, "Just remember...live." It really took me aback that this woman said that to me. After losing her husband, she told me to, "Live. Live life because my husband would want that for everyone who survived."

I've been able to forgive myself for feeling the way I did and realizing I didn't do anything wrong. What I did do was fight hard to get home to my family. I fought hard for my sergeant. I fought hard for my country. But most of all, I fought hard for myself. I think it's important to understand that moving forward encompasses so many things: hard work, faith, hope, and love. If it needs to be and you feel that way, you need to forgive yourself. I think forgiveness is one of the most important things that we can do as human beings in this world. I've been able to forgive people who have crossed me, and I realized that not forgiving has much more of an internal cost than the temporary warmth it gives you by holding bitterness against them. There's a sense of exhaling toxic smoke when you forgive yourself or forgive others.

It was around 2010 when I finally decided to stop feeling guilty, that it was all right to let go of the past with one hand and fully grab onto life today. That really helped me because I could freely be around families of other Port Authority police officers who lost their lives and look at them and think, "You know what? I didn't do anything wrong that day. I'm here for whatever reason, a reason that is beyond my understanding." If I'm lucky enough to see God one day, he'll be the One that tells me why I was allowed to live. I hope that I can look Him in the eye and say, "I hope I did good with that second lease on life."

That's important because every time that one of us goes through traumas, you do get a second lease on life. And it's a new life; it's a new beginning. We didn't ask for the trauma, but here it is. I didn't ask for the buildings to fall on me, but there I was. I think it's important that you give yourself the opportunity, a chance to make good on the second lease. It doesn't have to be a near-death experience, but something can happen in your life that's so tremendous that it changes and alters the course of your life. It could be that you are struggling with having experienced combat, drug abuse, sexual abuse, child abuse, or any tragic event. Regardless of whether you had choice in the situation, or even if it was self-imposed, start again. Do not let it define you. Today is a new opportunity, and you owe it to yourself. You're worth it!

Sometimes people say they have lost hope, but I would ask them to dig deeper, like when I used handcuffs on a wall of concrete. One could look at it and see the absurdity of the situation, but I dug with everything I had. I've had moments of suicidal ideation, but I dug with everything I had. I didn't always understand, but I dug.

There's that saying that tells us to rise above the clouds. You'll see the sun, and that's a fact. Sometimes we feel like we've lost the ability to see anything other than clouds. What if it's you and me that represent our own clouds? What if hope comes from looking beyond ourselves? A major part of what kept me fighting was my family, John, and my faith. I knew I needed to do it for myself, but when I had lost sight of myself because of my pain and exhaustion, I looked to my family and my faith as motivation. They are both a part of and beyond me.

The victory for all of us is happiness. It's not about trophies and not about money. It's not about fame. It's about living a life that offers us happiness. A happy spirit is contagious, and that's immense. But, if you are currently in a dark place, fight hard because you owe it to yourself. I hate to see anybody sell themselves short by not giving themselves the opportunity to find some measure of happiness and surrendering to the darkness.

When I say it has been a long road, I am not saying I have reached some destination. There have been many instances that challenged me to make a choice, for that moment, for that day. I give dates for reference but intertwined within these dates are movements forward and moments of feeling in reverse, ebbs and flows of grief, and trying to continue healing. Not that long ago, I was in the pharmacy picking up a prescription. My bill was a minimal fraction of the actual cost, and I said, "Thank God I have good insurance."

"Yeah, that is good," the pharmacist responded. "What plan are you on," she asked, which was a seemingly benign question.

"Oh, I worked for the Port Authority."

"Are you Will Jimeno, the Port Authority police officer?" she questioned curiously.

"Yes, ma'am."

"Well, my kids heard you speak, and my daughter came home and said such nice things. I lost a loved one on the 104th floor," she shared.

She was just making conversation and sharing her connection, just like I do when I am speaking about the guys, but it still just hit me in the chest. Even though I've come to accept many things about 9/11, the pain is still there. It mattered. It still matters. The difference is not that the pain is gone but that I have learned how to hold it and how to put it in its designated place in my heart, which is not the same as shoving it down or denying it. When I walked away from the pharmacist, I literally had to tell myself, "All right. Just go and continue to have a good day. You're okay." I have to remind myself because there's a side of me that feels bad. I wanted to apologize to the lady and say, "I'm so sorry we didn't get there." However, I've learned that I did what I could, so instead, I said, "Oh, I'm so sorry they didn't make it." She responded with very kind words, and it was good.

It took years to allow myself to feel sad without it having to envelop me. I can now let it come, speak to me, and then guide it past as I refocus on what is meaningful to me. Just like I had to give myself permission to allow happiness in my life, you deserve it, too, no matter what you've been through, even if your pain is self-induced. If there is something you need to reconcile that is in your power, by all means do it; but if your ability to set it right has passed, then use whatever pain you are going through to motivate you to create something from the ashes instead of anchoring you to misery.

I thought about a mantra every time that I needed to address my PTSD: "I'm here. I need to make my wife happy. I need to make my kids happy. I have that opportunity that my friends don't have." At both of my daughters' confirmations and their birthday parties, not a single one of those events went by without me thinking of my teammates' children. I take a moment every time to speak to my friends who didn't make it: "Hey guys, I know you're not here. I hope you know that I'm doing what I would want you to be doing if it had been you guys that made it, enjoying your families."

I didn't see any other therapist after seeing Debbie, but I also put in the work with her, and I've had to continue using what I learned every day after. Thankfully, I have a wife who is my best friend and is willing to fight *with* me. Allison has been my biggest support and listens when I need to speak. She also gives me good feedback, even though there are times I don't like it. I know she didn't like it when I was acting like an ass either, so she deserves my respect. God knows she has earned it many times over.

I do have a yearly follow-up with Kessler, but only for the physical part. Funny thing is, even today I do not have doctors ask me about my mental state. Right or wrong, good or bad, I believe it's my responsibility to seek any assistance that I need for my health and the relationships that are dear to my heart. Reinventing myself, taking care of myself, and looking for opportunities to grow is a daily process. Each passing year has brought different challenges and different rewards. I am grateful that I have been able to have additional years. I have been allowed the gift of being with my wife and watching my girls grow into young women.

In 2015, Bianca began college at Auburn University. That gave me a lot to do. Being retired and not working, I needed to keep myself motivated. I always had the outdoors and hunting, but watching our girls grow up was just an absolute gift. In fact, it was a gift that gave many opportunities. Allison and I were able to meet so many great people in Auburn, Alabama. That gave me more opportunity to connect with others and be a part of a greater community.

My passion has always been serving others, but since my ability to do it in the form of policing was taken away, I found new ways to honor who I am and what I believe my calling is. I love being able to meet people and connect, but I understand that there are so many people hurting out there that I will never be able to meet face to face. For those of you reading this today, I want you to know that from my heart I say, *you are important; you matter.* On 9/11, I saw people jumping out of the buildings, and all I could think about was a rock being thrown into a pond and the ripple of pain that would be felt with each of their deaths. Someone's mother, brother, sister, father, or friend died that day. People don't realize how many people's lives they touch every single day. You touch so many people's lives every day even though you might not think it.

I don't know what impact I will make in this life, but because of 9/11 I learned the importance of trying my best, despite my fears, in spite of my pain, to be as present as I can in the lives of others. This is especially true for my family. I enjoy my time with the ladies of my life. They each have different interests and desires. There are 365 days in a year. If I live till 90, that would be awesome. If I do the multiplication, 90 times 365 equals 32,850 days of life offered. Even with 32,000 days and change, that's not a lot of time. The problem is that we either take it for granted or see it as a burden. I'm not trying to pedal some false sense of euphoria, but I have been in the darkness and see just how easy it is to miss out on what I love most. Some days are bliss; some days I fall down. The key is to keep picking yourself up no matter how many days you fall down in a row. Better yet, don't be afraid to include those that care for you. I would not be here today if I had not allowed others to be there for me. The darkness in your life is a situation, not who you are. Don't label yourself because of your darkness. Use it. Even darkness is valuable, if you use it. If you marinate in it, it's a cesspool. But if you use it, it can give you some useful information. Embrace the bad to find the good. In the beginning, I didn't want to embrace the bad; I just wanted it to avoid it. But it doesn't go away by itself. In fact, the more you try to get away from it, the more it imprisons you.

Running from something can be situationally appropriate, but it cannot be a way of life. It will pin you in the corner. We have to face life like we face our jobs as first responders, stare it down, and make good choices. As we face our fears, we become more confident and more experienced; it's no different facing PTSD. As you pick up steam, you get stronger, you start feeling differently and begin building your life back instead of neglecting necessities in trade for trying to *feel* better. We need to be fair to ourselves to make sure we put ourselves in good positions.

Where am I at today? I thank God for where my family and I are today. It is not pain free, and there are still physical limitations and painful, emotional periods, but I am alive and have had the blessings of seeing my children grow. I have been able to be present for loved ones passing and to honor their time on this earth. Pain and happiness are not competitive. We must learn to hold both, to find the value in both. I have the same stressors that others have with everyday life, with the added exception of having lived through 9/11 and having to battle my way back. Every September 11th we get a lot of attention, but Allison and I do not look forward to the anniversaries. However, I cannot separate the discomfort of that anniversary from the gratitude of having lived through it and being able to see Bianca begin her life after graduating from Auburn in 2019, or seeing Olivia begin her education at Auburn in August 2020.

PTSD is still present in my life. It's rare to have a hard day, but even then I am happy in spite of it. I am not grateful for what the terrorists did or the buildings collapsing on me that day. However, I am proud of what I have made from it. I am proud of the people that were with me that day, the people that helped John and me from our concrete tomb, the people that helped me heal physically, the people that helped me begin to heal emotionally, the neighbors and friends that quietly supported my family and me, and my family for giving me unwavering love. I know that not everyone going through their personal trauma has the support that I have had. I wish they did. Our writing this book is our calling out to you to say, "You are not alone." It may not be the same as a family surrounding you, but we want you to know that we genuinely care for you and want to reach out to you in support, in faith, in hope, and in love.

I graduated at the Marriott World Trade Center on January 19, 2001. The Towers collapsed the morning of September 11, 2001. It's now the summer of 2021, and there is not a day that goes by without me saying something to Allison about 9/11. It lives with me every day. They attacked humanity. Those towers were falling not only on Americans, but on people from around the world. Luckily, I still have my left leg. I still face emotional pain, but I now put all of that energy into positive things in life. I want to tell the children of my team that their dads were superheroes. No comic book superhero even comes close. One thing I want 9/11 to remind us of is how we, as a nation, are united. I think we sometimes lose sight of that. Three weeks after the attacks the doctors told me, "Will, did you know we haven't had a single stabbing or shooting victim come in for three weeks?" It is possible, and we should not wait for tragedy to see each other's humanity. We are all different; we are all the same. Honor both.

I've heard hundreds of stories from 9/11 about how someone is alive because they would normally have been in the Towers but instead were stuck in traffic, their normal meeting was changed, or they happened to call in sick that day. I could have been in the woods hunting and without hearing about what happened until God knows when. But I didn't; I was there. With all that I have seen, with all that I have felt, would I do it again? Yes, I would do it again. I would do it over again because I love my country. I love my fellow Americans. I love to serve.

It's been a long road back, but I'm able to get up every morning and smile. Appreciation has been my prayer: in the wintertime I take the garbage cans out at night, and I take a deep breath of cold air, and it fills my lungs; some days, I roll my window down on my truck and stick my hand out just to feel the wind hit my hand. All those moments I try to absorb, but as much as I try I can't keep them. It's okay to feel sad, but make sure that you take the moment, every single day.

I am grateful for Allison's support, her kindness, and her love. She has put up with a lot. It's important to note that just because she put up with a lot, it was never an excuse for me to allow that. It was all the more reason for me to be motivated to reach out and get the help I needed to be the man, the spouse, and the father I needed to be for my family. She deserved the same dedication that she showed me. If I was so geared to serving, shouldn't serving my family be my priority?

Allison was so instrumental in my healing, and she did it all so quietly and without recognition. I know there are many other spouses and family members out there now doing the same thing for their loved ones, which is why we wanted the next chapter to offer a perspective from a spouse's point of view. Allison was uncomfortable stepping into the light, but she did it anyway because of her heart to serve. There are things that I didn't even know until now, so I hope that the person struggling with PTSD, the spouse/partner of that person, their family, and their friends all take what they can to help themselves and others.

Reflections

1) What surprised you in this chapter? Do you know why?
2) Is anyone coming to mind, including yourself?
3) Do you judge anyone in this section for their behaviors? Do you give yourself the same compassion or the same harshness of judgment?
4) What do you take away from this chapter? How will you use this insight?
5) Do you need to pause, breathe, reflect, or grieve in this moment before continuing? What were moments of significance in this chapter?

Chapter Thirteen

A Spouse's Point of View

To have someone understand your mind is a different kind of intimacy altogether. — Faraaz Kazi[1]

One of the components of this book that Will and I agreed on was to give a voice to a population that is often overlooked when speaking about PTSD and the struggles that coincide. We are talking about a secondary set of invisible wounds: those of spouses, family, and friends. One voice will never contain all experiences or potential experiences, but it is our goal that hearing the first-hand reflections from a spouse will offer greater understanding and empathy for those that support people dealing with PTSD.

Will's wife, Allison, graciously offered to share *some* of her experiences. Rightfully so, she also declined to answer some of the questions because it was more than she wanted to share publicly. I (Michael) have great respect for boundaries within vulnerability, and it is one of the cornerstones of how I practice when working with clients. No one has earned the right to her story. Nevertheless, she still shared in an effort to reach out to those reading this book. Some of the information will sound familiar to that written earlier. However, it will be from Allison's perspective and experience. Take time to notice the similarity to struggles that Will spoke about, even though Allison's physical experience was much different from Will's. Notice the tension between hope and anxiety, fear and confidence, gratitude and frustration. Trauma and vicarious trauma have a way of throwing people into defensive thinking and reactions. The fight to choose, when the situation creates a feeling of no choice, is experienced by both the traumatized person and by those who support them.

In Allison's own words, she recognized that sometimes the only help she could offer was to listen and not judge—listen with an open ear and an open heart. The same opportunity is offered to the reader in this

---

[1] Kazi, F. (2019). *Meant to be Together*. Macmillan Publishers.

chapter. Listen with an open ear and an open heart to Allison's experience, her struggles, her hope, and her love for her family. Take from it what you will. Allow her sharing to be hope in your life if you are struggling.

We know Will's experience of September 11th. Will you share how you experienced 9/11, Allison?

September 11th was like any other morning. Will woke up really early, as usual, got ready, gave me a kiss, and told me to have a nice day. That was our morning ritual. Sometimes he made a second round, which was appreciated but also taking up time from the final thirty minutes I had to sleep before getting up for work. Sometimes I let him know it was time to go because he had already said goodbye twice. Let's be honest, this is marriage.

I had a 15-minute commute from our home to our daughter's daycare, and I left around 8:20am. The news of the first plane hitting the WTC came on the radio on the drive to the office. The entire office was gathered around watching the news unfold. Shortly before 9:00 am, before the second plane hit, Will called me, and it was the shortest conversation I've ever had with him in my life. He had no answers to any of my questions and hung up without saying, "I love you." He never did that. I didn't realize he was heading down to the WTC, so I thought he was still in Midtown Manhattan, which ended up giving me more of the day to enjoy the denial of the danger he was in. After watching Tower 2 collapse, I left work and picked up Bianca at daycare and went home. My brother, Jerry, was there already waiting for me, and my sister-in-law, Karen, arrived shortly after. As the day continued and I had not heard from Will again, my worry started to increase exponentially. Around 3:30 I tried reaching him on his cell phone to no avail—it went straight to his voicemail. I knew at this point I needed to call Will's police department to see if they had any information they could give me, but I was scared to make this call. Until now, I convinced myself that he was just busy with all the craziness and chaos going on, but internally I knew better. It took me quite some time to get the nerve to call the PAPD. It was around 5:00 pm when I first called, and all I was told was that he did go down to help with the rescue, but they didn't have a location on him. I was too afraid to ask any more questions at this time, and they told me to keep calling back every 30 minutes or so for updates. So that's what I did.

Thank God for the support of our families. They quickly rallied around me. Our families filled the house. My parents and grandmother (Granny) were now there as well as Will's parents. Granny was such a pillar in my life. She was an example of strength, perseverance, and faith. I needed all the strength I could get, and they held me up that night. They didn't let me fall, each and every one of them.

By the time evening came and I still had not heard from Will, I was probably at my worst. I began losing hope and thinking Will may not be coming home. The information I was getting from Will's police department kept getting worse every time we called. I needed to know if he went into the buildings before they collapsed, but I had to get enough courage to ask that question. They told me yes, he did, and that he was now on the missing/unaccounted for list. As if that's not bad enough, the next time I called (around 7:00 pm), I was told that 10 police officers that went to the WTC with Will were just getting back to the police desk now. This information was given to me to show me that there was still hope that Will could be with the next group of guys that return, but in my head all I heard was that 10 police officers returned and Will is *not* one of them! I lost it at this point, dropped the phone, and ran into the bathroom and started crying uncontrollably, to the point of hyperventilating. I remember my dad coming in to console me and help me slow down my breathing. He was worried that I was going to go into premature labor. He had my mom call my OB/GYN right away to inform them what was happening and to see if they would prescribe something *just in case* we received some bad news.

Around 8:30, a close friend I had grown up with, Chris Boel, who was a police officer in Little Ferry, New Jersey, called me. I hadn't spoken to Chris in a while, but he called and said, "Over the police scanner I heard that William Jimeno and his Sergeant, John McLoughlin, were found at the WTC and are trapped but alive."

I had no idea how Will became trapped or even what that entailed, and I obviously wanted more information. But to hear he was alive gave me a shot of hope that was so desperately needed. I hoped that the Port Authority would be able to confirm this information, but they did not. I don't know why they couldn't confirm this; it was obviously true. I didn't know how I could possibly have gotten wind of it and they hadn't. Maybe they knew what bad shape Will was in and weren't sure if he would make it out alive. I have no idea. All I know is that communication was so bad that day and everyone was trying their best. But the phone lines were overloaded, a lot of calls were not getting through, and there was so much information over the police radios that it was so easy to give and receive the wrong message. Even though this information that

Chris shared with me wasn't confirmed, it still gave me the hope I needed.

I felt I couldn't get a hold on anything, so I focused on what I could take care of: Bianca. My brother lived a few houses down. His wife was watching Bianca and their kids to keep them protected from the situation and let them be kids. They were as happy as could be, watching a movie and dancing the night away.

Somewhere around 10:00 or 10:30, I began thinking that if I ended up getting some really bad news, I needed to make sure she was already asleep, so I headed down the block to my brother's house. Needless to say, the kids were having so much fun together that sleeping was not a realistic goal. I decided to bring Bianca upstairs to bed and lay down with her in my brother's room to be somewhere with the lights and TV off; the noise in my head needed a time-out. Suddenly, my brother and father burst through the front door and came running up the stairs, yelling at the top of their lungs, "He's alive! He's alive!"

That's all I heard. I hadn't even been able to get out of the bed before the bedroom door flung open and they came rushing in, "He's alive!"

They weren't even making any sense. That's how hysterical they were sounding. Someone had called my house from the Port Authority saying that Will was alive. We all ran back to my house, and I was trying to figure out, "Who'd you talk to? What was their name? Did they leave a number? Can I call them back? What do you mean he's alive?"

They had nothing. Nothing. They were so excited they didn't even ask. No name. No phone number. Nothing. They were just so excited to have the Port Authority confirm that Will was alive. I guess everything else just seemed inconsequential. I started looking through the caller ID to find the last number that called and called that number back. I began rapid-fire questioning, "What do you mean he's alive? Where is he? Can I see him? Can I talk to him?" But once again none of my questions were answered. All we knew for sure is that it was confirmed that he was alive. It was now almost 11:00 pm, and the phone rang again.

I answered the phone, and the voice on the other end said, "Allison?" For a split second I thought it was Will. My desire for it to be him was so immense, but it was actually a doctor from Pennsylvania who was at ground zero (there were doctors there in case Will's legs needed to be amputated onsite in order to get him out). He gave me information so I would know that he was really there with Will. He shared that he thought Will broke his leg. We started celebrating! I know that sounds strange but only moments ago we had all thought that Will hadn't made it. Now, mind you, I had no idea that he had both towers collapse on top of him. No idea. What we did know was that they were going to be taking him to Bellevue hospital.

Shortly after this news, Brian came and picked me and Karen up at my house and brought us to the hospital. Even though we were excited, the drive there was very eerie. New York is known for its hustle and bustle, but there was nobody on the road and there was the smell of that burning ash, which was like nothing I had ever smelled before. I can't even describe it. It was just putrid.

When we came into the emergency room's waiting area, the police officers and firefighters that were waiting there were covered in this ash that just stunk. Being seven months pregnant didn't help either. I have to say again just how eerie everything looked, how everything felt, and that god-awful smell. Brian started talking to another Port Authority Police Officer, Bruce Kent, and he introduced me as Will's wife. The officer shared they thought Will had a broken leg and possibly his pelvis, too. I remember thinking that sounds really painful. A broken leg is bad enough, but if his pelvis is broken, too, this is not going to be as easy as I thought. Little did I know the difficulty that was beyond those doors.

"Okay, well, can we go in and see him?" I asked. There were no doctors, no nurses. There was nobody but cops and firemen. We couldn't even see a hospital employee of any kind. It was really weird. I asked Bruce, "Can you go in and find out if we can see him?"

"Will do," he responded, and he walked away.

I watched and waited for him to pop back in with some news or with the approval for us to go in, but he didn't come back. It felt like an eternity. I thought, "What the heck is going on?" I'm looking at Brian and said, "You've got to go find out what's happening." I don't know why I didn't go and try to find out for myself, I think I was too afraid of what I might be told. Finally, after about 20–30 minutes, Bruce came back, and he looked like a ghost, like something terrible just happened to him.

Despite what he had seen, he gave the professional answer, "It's going to be a little longer. Somebody's going to come out and get you in a bit." It was weeks later that I found out that Bruce looked the way he did because Will had flatlined twice while he was back there, and he still had to come back out and face me. I'm not sure how much longer it was before they brought Karen and me back to see him, but I was not prepared for what I saw. I had no idea they already cut him open in the ER. I had no idea that he flatlined twice and had to be resuscitated. I had been picturing him in a chair or bed with someone casting his leg. Not a single broken bone. Instead, I walked into Will's curtained area of the

ER and faced the reality of the situation.

Due to the severity of his injuries and physical state, as well as their intentions of taking him into surgery at 7:00 am the following morning, they kept him sedated for the night. He looked bad, really bad. He was so pale and sickly looking. He looked dead actually. He was covered in ash and soot and there was blood everywhere—on the walls, on the floor, everywhere. Will was intubated at the time. He looked terrible, especially considering that I was expecting my jovial husband to only have a broken leg. I felt overwhelmed and detached. The doctors were talking to me as I stared at Will, but they might as well have been talking a foreign language because I wasn't comprehending a single word, or remembering anything they said. Not one single word.

There was a wall of policemen literally surrounding Will who hadn't left his side. Once the doctors finished explaining things to me and informing us that they were going to take him into surgery to operate on his leg in the morning, they told us we were welcome to stay there by Will's side. Only then did the group of police standing vigil exit to give us privacy while standing guard on the other side of the curtain. Karen and I sat in chairs next to Will all night. It wasn't comfortable and I had to get up to walk off the pregnancy stiffness, but it was nothing compared to what Will was going through. Thank God for Karen! She gave me the extra strength I needed to make it through the night. There was no way to imagine what the day would hold when Will kissed me goodbye that morning. I guess there never is.

So, you had your world rocked, had sat up all night in uncomfortable chairs while being seven months pregnant, and it had become clear that this was going to be a much longer healing process than a broken leg. What were the next few days like for you?

In the morning (9/12) they came to take Will up for another surgery on his leg, and I needed to handle the paperwork. As I walked with Will out of the emergency room and to the elevator that took him to the operating room, I had stopped to talk with some police officers that rotated in throughout the night, and they told me that John was on his way. Just then some paramedics came around the corner. John McLoughlin was being wheeled in and was awake. Apparently, they were about to cut his wedding ring off his finger, and John kept telling them not to and to try Vaseline instead. He was quite adamant about them not cutting it off. I'm not sure why that memory sticks out, but it was the first time I saw John, and it just stuck with me how important this was to him. The look on his face spoke in a way that words could not describe.

It wasn't until about 2:00 pm that we finally saw Will in the recovery room. He was still sedated and groggy, as well as being intubated, so there was no talking. After a couple of hours, he began waking up a bit and tried to do sign language. He asked for a pen and paper, and someone gave us an envelope and a pen. He desperately tried to write stuff down, but none of it was making sense; it was still a cherished moment because, sense or nonsense, it was my first interaction with him after almost losing him. He managed some I love you signs and started trying to give information on people that he was with and where they were before the collapse.

The medical staff kept making sure he wasn't feeling any pain, which allowed him to sleep, including most of that afternoon. The plans were to keep him heavily medicated through the night with no further procedures planned. They indicated that communication was highly unlikely that evening because he needed rest, and that we should probably go home and get some rest, too. It had been a long couple of days, and we were exhausted. So at 6:00 pm, that's what Karen and I did.

The next morning (9/13) came quick. After a shower and breakfast, we headed back to the hospital. They removed Will's intubation tube, and he could talk a little. One of our first conversation was about the baby. He wanted to let me know to name the baby Olivia. He also tried to explain a little of what happened, telling us again about who he was with, who he saw, and where he last saw them. It was important for him to share the stories and hopefully help them be found. We also were able to spend some time together with no surgeries.

Every morning I went to the hospital and then came home at night. Karen often accompanied me, and Will's dad became a fixture. The next two weeks were a roller coaster, with Will having to go back for procedures to debride his wounds. They started cleaning his lungs as well. I don't know how to describe it other than saying that they were vacuuming rocks out of his lungs. It was kind of disturbing to hear and see. One of the doctors asked if he was a smoker because his lungs looked like he had smoked for 30 years. It was a back and forth between feeling grateful to know Will was alive and the difficulty of seeing him in pain, knowing he was going to be operated on again, and learning he had irreparable damage to his body. I felt so helpless at times. Despite it all, the gratitude definitely won out.

Having our families around was priceless. Will's parents and my parents visited and made sure that Bianca was taken care of while I spent time with Will. If I didn't have them, I don't know how I would have been able to do it. They picked up the pieces wherever the pieces were falling. It was hard because I had Bianca, who was four, and I was trying to do right by her. She wasn't really understanding why dad wasn't home. She would ask, "Why is daddy not here? Why can't I go see him? What is a hospital?"

I'd never brought her to a hospital. I'm sure we told her that a hospital is a place you go when you're sick, but trying to explain why we couldn't take her there just was too big. Obviously, we didn't want her to see Will looking the way he was looking, but how do you explain that to a four-year-old who just wants her daddy? It was the everyday questioning, "So why can't I see him? Why can't I talk to him? Why can't I talk to him on the phone?"

It was hard. It was painful. It didn't matter if I wanted to deal with this or not; I had to do it for her, for Olivia, for Will, for myself. Karen and Jerry did anything needed. I was never alone. If I needed somebody or something, someone was always there, always available. I never felt alone. Even my cousins and my aunt and uncle were there for me. When I came home late from the hospital, I often found my house fully stocked with paper products. My aunt would go to Costco and buy toilet paper, paper towels, and paper plates. She did all the food shopping. There was always somebody doing something for me. I just cannot say enough or express my gratitude enough for the love and support that I had—that I have.

The first two-and-a-half weeks were probably the toughest. With every surgery, we never knew what to expect, so it was unsettling. I remember one time Will was in the recovery room following another surgery, and my dad and I were talking to Dr. Phil Wolinsky. We were trying to get an idea of how close to 100% he was ever going to get. Once we realized that his police career was going to be over, I instantly thought to myself, "Will he be able to hunt again?" I asked his surgeon, "Will he be able to climb a tree?"

He looked at me like I was nuts. This surgeon is from Manhattan, and he's wondering why I'm asking about climbing a tree. He had no clue I was talking about hunting. Context would have been helpful. I wish I could describe the expression on his face. He literally was dumbfounded. Anyway, he started explaining the situation. My dad comforted me and said, "Allison, don't worry about this. We're going to get him out there again in the woods."[2]

The doctor continued explaining that he would have a leg brace and the limitations that would be part of his life. There were some unknowns, but there were also some known limitations. Nevertheless, my dad reassured me, "Somehow, some way, if I have to, I will pull him and get him up in a tree." Now mind you, my dad had trouble getting into a tree, but it was more like, "Allison, don't worry about it, we got him. We'll get him hunting again if it's the last thing I do. I will get him up in a tree again. We'll figure it out."

That was a moment for me because at that time I felt like I was going to have to figure it all out for the both of us. I was taking care of Bianca, pregnant, worrying about Will from a health perspective, and now worrying about what his life would look like without being a cop and possibly not being able to hunt. What will he do? My mind was going crazy at that moment. When my dad stepped in and said he'd take care of it and find a way, it was just such a release.

When we were thrown into all this trauma, the smallest of details mattered. It helped us grab onto something when everything we counted on was out of control. It seemed we had a moment of peace and a feeling of hope followed by a moment of pain, fear, or unsuspecting difficulties. It was enough to remove any feeling of stability.

I would stay at the hospital all day and leave in the evening. Will didn't have a phone, so if he needed to talk to me or relay a message to me in the evenings he would have someone do it for him. One evening I had just arrived home from the hospital and was exhausted. I had left him less than a half hour ago and received a call telling me they were immediately taking him into the operating room. Electricity shot through me, and I thought, "Oh, Jesus! I just left him." It was a complete injection of panic. He was fine. A gentleman in the ICU who had his leg broken from falling debris had a blood clot kill him, so the medical staff was concerned that Will might have clots. They immediately put in a Greenfield filter to prevent any clots from traveling through his veins.

I was in my 20s and blood clots were not something I had thought about when I was younger. I assumed we had a long life ahead of us, and we would die in our 90s. We already had the ups and downs of the repeated surgeries, but then to go from progress and saying goodnight

---

[2] We talked to Dr. Wolinsky a couple weeks ago via FaceTime. We haven't talked to him in years, and he said, "That's still the one thing that, in my career nobody's ever asked me, especially coming out of a historical event like that." He's just like, "That's what you're going to ask?"

after a good day to rushing him to the operating room for potentially death-inducing blood clots, it just felt like I could never let my guard down. I couldn't fully enjoy the progress he had made.

I was worried, but I kept focusing on having a positive attitude to help me get through. I had my moments, I had my days, but I kept trying to bring it back to the fact he was alive and improving, which was more than most were able to have following 9/11. We were waiting for him to be out of the woods. Thankfully, Will had a lot of visitors, which not only benefited him but was a blessing to all our family. A lot of times when people came to visit Will, he wasn't there. He was either in the operating room or the recovery room, so they wound up talking to us. It was a pleasant distraction. Otherwise, we sat there twiddling our thumbs and waiting. It was very comforting.

You mentioned feeling helpless, as well as gratitude. How did you face the feelings of helplessness? How did those terms fit together?

Watching Will go through everything was so hard. I didn't feel like there was anything I could do to help him with his pain or his sadness. At one point, Will had strong cravings for Hawaiian Punch. He kept asking for it; however, nobody knew where to get it. He became really grumpy about not getting any Hawaiian Punch. At the time, I had no idea where this craving came from because he did not typically drink Hawaiian Punch. Apparently, a week prior to 9/11 he had been working on an investigation regarding a missing youth and walked into a bodega (a small Spanish mom-and-pop convenience store) and saw a Hawaiian Punch. He hadn't had one in years, so he bought it and thoroughly enjoyed it. That feeling of satisfaction must have stuck with him, so one day I went on a quest to find him some. I searched every floor, every vending machine, every part of that hospital for Hawaiian Punch. I didn't give up until I found a vending machine that had it. It was like finding a needle in a haystack but felt like winning the lottery! He was so happy to have his Hawaiian Punch, and it made me feel good that I was able to do something that helped him feel better, even if the feeling was short-lived.

After finding the Hawaiian Punch that made him so happy, I made sure that after leaving the hospital that I made a special trip to the supermarket just to stock up on Hawaiian Punch. Well, wouldn't you know it, his craving had already come and gone. He was over it... I was so annoyed!

As far as how the two terms go together, I would say that ever since day one I was so grateful that he was alive, even though we spent much of our time in a hospital room. I was so grateful I was not planning a memorial service, like so many people were. On the other hand, especially in those first couple of weeks, I was scared that he wouldn't make it through one of his surgeries or would take a turn for the worse, and I had zero control in that.

What did you do to take care of yourself?

I made a point to go home every day. As much as I worried about Will, I knew I needed to take care of Bianca and our unborn child via taking care of myself. In the evenings, even though it was hard for him to sleep, I knew there wasn't anything I personally could help him with. He was never left alone, which was a huge comfort to me. He had family, friends, or a police officer—somebody was always by his side. Sleeping in my own bed was necessary to sustain the long journey ahead. I could have never done that without the help of the Port Authority Police, our families, friends, and even our neighbors.

It was funny, but my neighbors, whom I didn't know well at the time because we had only moved there six weeks prior to 9/11, even found ways to help us. One day coming home from the hospital, I saw my garbage can out on the curb. I didn't think much of it. I didn't even know when garbage day was to be honest with you. The next day I noticed that the garbage can was back on the side of the house. I wondered what happened. It was one of those things I didn't really think about because I was already overwhelmed with all that was going on, but I later found out that it was one of my neighbors who secretively supported us through this kind act.

I think being pregnant with Olivia forced me to make sure I was taking care of myself and staying focused. I've always lived life with the understanding that I either go forward, forging forward and pressing through, or I don't. If I don't go forward, I go backwards. My baby needed me. I couldn't afford to go backwards. I think it would have been easier for me to stay in that dark place that a lot of people can go into if I hadn't been pregnant. I really do. I think being pregnant with Olivia helped me.

I am grateful for all my family on mine and on Will's side. However, my mom was my anchor. She was always my first go-to person. If I had a question, if I needed help with something, if I was lacking the strength to get through the day, or if I just needed a hug that only a mother could give, she was the person I could always depend on. My mom stepped up to the plate to remind me that I needed to take care of myself. Even though I knew it, she was my accountability partner, watching to see if I had eaten, got enough rest, or was drinking enough water. After all, she was looking after her baby to ensure that I was taking care of my own baby.

What were you noticing about Will's emotional state? What were you noticing about your own emotional state?

I didn't have major concerns regarding Will's emotional state while at Bellevue, at least nothing indicating what we were in for. He was at times very emotional and sad, but not more than what I would expect from someone who went through what he did. I think that for me one of the first things was going from, 'Oh, thank God he's alive' to 'Okay, what's his recovery going to be like; that was a quick switch. I was happy he was alive, but then I started to worry about what his life was going to be like. I was concerned about him not being able to go back to work as he had done before and worried about what he would be able to do and how that would affect him. I didn't have any indication as to what we were about to face emotionally. We were so focused on his physical healing and were trying to understand what to expect.

That uncertainty prompted a lot of questions to his doctors: Would he make a full recovery? What kind of issues is he going to have in the future? That's where my mind went. I started thinking, 'Okay, what's our future like here? What are we talking?' I remember from day one the doctor explained that he would have injuries to his leg that would prevent him from making a full recovery. That part was hard. I had to get over that little bump. I had to learn to accept it. Knowing that he probably wouldn't go back to being a police officer like he had be, not be able to have fun living his dream, it started to prey on our minds, and we were going to have to figure life out.

You had a lot of uncertainty. What did you ground yourself in with all the unknowns?

Yes, a lot of uncertainty. It caused anxiety, but I was thankful that Will was alive. I knew that whatever needed to be figured out would be figured out. He was alive. We could work on the rest. And we had our family.

What was it like making the transfer to Kessler?

The first thing that comes to mind was seeing how happy Will was. He looked forward to leaving New York and heading back to Jersey. It was the next step to being a little closer to home. At this point, we were not so much concerned anymore for his survival; he had a clean bill of health. He made it through all his operations, and it didn't look like he would need any more, unless it was for cosmetic reasons. Those were all great, but at Kessler we transitioned to concentrating on how he was going to get back on his feet. He wasn't walking yet, beyond a few steps.

I felt mostly positive. He had police officers, who were great friends, with him around the clock. Getting to Kessler was easier and quicker for me even though it was about the same distance as Bellevue Hospital. I could drive myself to Kessler and come and go whenever I wanted/needed to. I was with Will every day, but I didn't stay there as long as I did while he was in Bellevue. I was able to bring Bianca more often, and it was great for them both. It was a relief knowing that Brian was with him after I left and stayed with him all night long. I tried to be as supportive whenever and wherever I could, but I also had my moments. I worried, I cried, and I kept refocusing on what needed to be done to move forward. Will had a lot of ups and downs, some good days some bad days. Some days he was frustrated with his progress; some days he was happy. He was sad at times, too. I'm pretty sure he was keeping a lot of his emotions from me because he knew that I had a lot going on, and I know he was worried and concerned about me.

In the hospital Will was pretty much at the mercy of the doctors and what they were doing to help him heal, but he felt pretty helpless overall in having any sense of control in his life. At Kessler, he had goals and was active in his physical rehab. It helped him mentally because he had some control in his life, but it also continued masking what we would eventually face. The focus was on the physical work at Kessler.

We started to see how physically difficult this was going to be for him to get back on his feet again. Learning to walk again was a long process. It was a matter of how far he wanted to go with rehab. He has always been a determined person, but he set a goal to be by my side in the hospital when I had Olivia. My due date was December 2nd, but at some point my doctor suggested that I have a C-section due to the difficulties I had with Bianca. I agreed, but I told him it had to be on November 26, Will's birthday. He now knew how long he had to get back on his feet so he could be there, which he succeeded. It was not easy.

What did you experience the day Will was discharged to go home?

Elation! He came home from Kessler the weekend before Thanksgiving, and I had Olivia the Monday after Thanksgiving. He was not walking well, but he was able to stumble from the car to the hospital to be there for the delivery. We truly had a lot to be thankful for!

Will was open about how the darkness descended after he got home and had fewer distractions. What did you notice?

It was such a blessing to have Will home. He was still going to Kessler three times a week, which helped, but other than that he had nothing to do. Nothing to distract him. I saw the sadness and some irritability in Bellevue and Kessler, but I had never witnessed the anger, the rage. Other than the few hours a week he spent going to physical rehab, he had 24/7 to think about not having a job and this horrific experience that kept circling in his brain. And he couldn't even get up to go into the kitchen to get himself a snack if he wanted one. Then throw in the chaos of an infant and a four-year-old in the mix and a wife who is recovering from surgery, as well as family members in the house trying to help. It was too much for him. We said time and time again what a blessing it was for family to be so supportive, but being in that situation, he sometimes couldn't see it as people being helpful. He saw people as being a nuisance, being intrusive. He had a different pair of glasses on. He saw the world differently. He didn't see what was actually happening. He didn't see our families taking time off from work to help him. He saw that he couldn't help himself anymore. It was rough.

I don't think about it anymore, to be honest with you, because it was a horrific time. He always seemed upbeat, and he is upbeat, but there was a darkness with him that not everyone saw that was there for so long. Now and then, he says he has these PTSD moments. I think it's normal, to be honest with you. It's more of a normal frustration with things, not so much bringing him back to that day. That was a different time.

Will shared a story about how he had not worn his vest that morning and that you would have, jokingly, killed him had you known at the time. The story may seem insignificant after the fact but tell us about it.

Oh, the vest? Oh, don't even talk to me about the vest. It's still a sore point today, and I am *not* even joking. Between him not having his cell phone on him and not wearing the expensive, ultra-lightweight vest that was a lot of money for us at the time—thankfully, I didn't find out about that until months and months later when it was okay to be mad at him again. In the beginning, I didn't care about anything other than he was okay. Months later when he was home from the hospital and doing well, he was talking to one of his friends when I realized that he had not worn his vest that morning. I literally could have hit him over the head.

Once the honeymoon was over, did you have moments of your pre-9/11 relationship?

Absolutely. We had some great moments, including the moments where we could laugh, tease, and be angry—whatever we had done before. However, we had to deal with something we weren't used to dealing with, and that was the PTSD.

What has been your experience with Will, in dealing with someone struggling with PTSD?

The easiest way to sum it up is by saying that once I saw this anger, which probably wasn't diagnosed right away as PTSD, I became aware of how quickly it's like a light switch. It's like he was fine one second, the switch gets flipped, and it's like a different person. I guess what I did for however long, even today, to be honest with you, is I've learned how to make sure the switch doesn't get flipped on. This is the best way I can explain how I have lived or changed or dealt with this. I try to prevent the switch from being flipped, which is a really difficult way to live.

It sounds an awful lot like walking on eggshells. Is that accurate?

Yes. There are times when I see he's getting annoyed, so I try to not continue the argument because I see it's going south. Even today, I try to avoid where it's going. In the beginning stages, I did everything in my power to avoid the switch being flipped, which, let me tell you, was extremely exhausting. It's silly things. It's things that any person without having lived this kind of trauma would have been able to handle.

For instance, my daughter spilled nail polish remover on a table and it made a mark. Will already had this thing for glitter. He can't stand glitter. She had a school project, and there was glitter on the table. I'm frantically keeping him out of the kitchen to clean up the glitter before he sees it. It's things like that. I mean, pre-9/11 it would just have been an annoyance. That was no longer the case.

One time he yelled at my brother. Will and Jerry had and still have a great relationship. Jerry was at the house a lot since he lived a couple of houses down. He came over almost every night for coffee. If I had to run out to the supermarket, and Will was all propped up and resting, he would just sit in the house with both my kids so I can run and take care of business. People were always bringing food over because that's what people do to help, which was always exceptionally nice and appreciated. But sometimes there was too much food. We couldn't have eaten all the food people were bringing. We always had family members over taking care of us, especially my brother, so I was constantly giving him some of the food. He was working full time, had three kids of his own, and he didn't have time to do stuff for himself because he's doing stuff for us.

Will hates eggplant. He won't eat eggplant if he's on a stranded island. He won't eat it. There's no way he's ever going to eat eggplant. Someone brought over a whole tray of eggplant parmesan, as well as a tray of chicken parmesan. My brother was over, as usual, helping. I gave him the eggplant parm. Will just flipped out. He flipped out on my brother for taking the eggplant parm. There's no rhyme or reason, at least that we could tell. Something happened. Maybe he thought there wasn't going to be any food for himself. Who knew? This is how easily his switch would flip, and it usually did not make any sense to us because it seemed like it was over things that were so insignificant or silly. For the longest time, I would do whatever I could to avoid that switch from being flipped. It was exhausting, I have to tell you; it was exhausting.

Do you realize that there is a thing called vicarious trauma?

No. I didn't know there was an actual name for it, but I could imagine there's something because it has an effect on everyone that it touches. It really does.

It does. Allison, it's been my experience that most of the time spouses and family are overlooked, or they don't seek support themselves because most of the focus is on the person with PTSD. However, there is a trauma that happens to spouses or people who are around those dealing with the primary trauma. It sounds like walking on eggshells had not been your normal approach to a healthy relationship, but that's where you ended up. Will was constantly on guard and hypervigilant toward the smallest of chaotic details, and you became hypervigilant of his mood, temper, and reactions. Does that sound familiar?

Oh, absolutely. Yes, without a doubt. I really don't like talking about myself like this because I don't want to come off as bragging or something, but I know this is important and hopefully will help someone else that is currently where I've been. I think I had the right personality to deal with a situation like this, which is not to say if you're struggling that you're weak. Not at all. I struggled immensely. When I am reflecting on that time in our lives, I am speaking about how I believe my confidence helped me despite feeling insecure at times—anxious, afraid, and all the other emotions that make us uncomfortable.

I think I'm a fairly self-confident person. I am whole. I didn't need any validation for what I was doing or going through. It was tough, but I saw it as something that just needed to be done for my husband. I am truly a happy person within myself, and I didn't need any sympathy, such as "Look what she's going through." For me, I just needed him to be better. Mind you, I also was not alone. I had tons of support.

Everybody's in a different situation, but a lot of times when I hear other women so jealous of another woman because of this, because of that, I'm always thinking, 'It just sounds like this person is unhappy with themselves and who they are, and that's why they're having difficulty with whatever it is.' Since I am truly happy with the person that I am, I'm able to do more or get through more.

What I hear is an internal framework, that your internal sense of confidence grounded you. Even though Will hurt your feelings off and on throughout this, it sounds like you did not take it personally. You didn't internalize it. Even in the walking on eggshells, it wasn't about trying to avoid getting your feelings hurt, but it was more about taking care of him. Does that resonate?

Yes. I don't think I ever took anything that he did personally. I knew it was an issue he was dealing with. I was more concerned with others and their reactions, especially those closest. I didn't want it to affect anyone else around us: my children, my brother, or anybody in our family. When they're not living with somebody and they don't see the daily issues, it's hard for someone to understand—even his own parents, his sister, or anybody who loves him to the core, when they don't see it every day. They don't understand why he behaved the way he did sometimes.

When he would have rage, they were still thinking of the old Will they knew versus where he was currently?

Yes. For instance, my brother, who loves Will and they have a great relationship, couldn't really understand the problem with the eggplant. You know what I mean? It wasn't about the eggplant, but you don't get that if you don't see it every day. It's so hard to explain to somebody because they just see it as, "What's his problem?"

One of the things Will shared that really made the difference for him, that he's had to do, was the day that he had talked to Bianca, and she said, "Daddy, you scare me sometimes." He said that just broke him. From a mom's perspective, what were you seeing, and how did you see it affect them?

I know there were times when our daughters saw Will getting mad and upset and they were confused as to what happened. From their perspective, nothing happened, so why all this? I did my best to deflect. I was big at deflecting. To be honest with you, I don't even know how much they saw of it because often it was really behind closed doors, or I was able to see it coming and either get them away or get him away and let him deal with it privately. He understood because from the moment he realized, "Oh, I'm scaring my kids," or if he became aware I was trying to get the girls away, somewhere in the back of his head something started to click and he would let it go. If he could become aware in the moments, he would go his own way. There were times that he wasn't able to stop it before the rage came. However, he always stopped before getting physical. There was some awareness he had about our physical safety that would break through and stop him. I am thankful for that because I know that's not always the case for some families.

You have shared with me that you have your own feeling of survivor's guilt, of how when you see other families whose loved ones didn't make it through, you would see them looking at you, and it felt like they were looking and wishing they could be you and Will. You had some strong feelings about that. Can you just talk a little more about that?

From the beginning, whenever Will was invited to go anywhere or be a part of anything, I would try to go as much as I could. It was hard because it was painful to be in the presence of so many widows. I could see the hurt in their eyes, how much they... I mean, there weren't many Wills. There was Will and John, and that was it. To see the look in their eyes. Once, a widow called me lucky or told me how lucky I was, or something to that effect. You could see she just wanted to swap places with me so badly, and now we're in a group. There's a group of people, not just her and me. You could feel everyone around you, everyone's emotion. What do you say? What do I say? There's not much I could say. Nothing I could say would've helped. Nothing. After that, I avoided putting myself in that position because it was just too painful. I could feel their pain. I could feel it. Through their eyes I could feel it!

I struggled with what I could offer. When they spoke to Will, it was different. Normally, when they were talking to him, either Will had some information to give to them, which they were so happy to receive, or he could share a story that he knew about someone. For him, it was meaningful and cathartic. For me, it just felt painful, and I felt helpless. I had nothing that could take their pain away. I never labeled it as survivor's guilt, but I would say that's probably what it was. It always felt like, "Why are we so lucky? Why were my prayers answered?" There were thousands of people praying that day. Whenever I have mentioned this, people say the same thing, "It just wasn't his time. It wasn't..." They give the same answer, the same spiel, but it never makes any sense. What do you mean it wasn't his time? Why is it not his time, but it was this person's time? None of it really makes any sense. I always felt it hard to accept that Will's meant to be here for some reason and someone else wasn't meant to be here. It was too difficult to take that as a reason why he's here, but the guy that was standing next to him isn't. That answer never felt right. It was hard in the beginning, I have to say. At this point it's been so long, Will's done so much good to help others, that I have found some acceptance in the reality. It has been a painful process.

It sounds like when you do feel it, it's manageable in the sense that you're able to just let it be a feeling of empathy for their loss instead of feeling guilty.

Right. I remember when we moved to Chester in 2004. In this small town that we live in there was a widow from 9/11. I didn't know her, and Will didn't either. However, John McLoughlin had been friends with her husband. She went to the same church that we did. That was hard. She was a nice person. She never made me feel awkward or anything. She was always very kind, but when I saw her at the supermarket, even though we were both there just to get groceries, I would suddenly feel horrible. I now can feel for someone's loss, instead of feeling guilty.

I felt a separation in your statements. When you talked about when the widows talked to Will versus when the widows talked to you. It sounded like you felt Will was able to give them something or in some ways was able to represent their spouse. They were able to feel closer to their spouse for a moment. However, when they talked to you, they were reminded of their loss and reminded of the separation.

Exactly. It's true. I mean, that's the impression that I always got. I would see their face light up when he would talk to them because he always had something good to say or something good to represent, but I didn't.

Well, perhaps you couldn't. It may not have mattered what you said in some ways, because indirectly you both were connected to a shared trauma, but with different outcomes. It was a reminder for both of you, and it was wrapped in immense pain. Until we work with it and learn how to live with it and with each other, we tend to just react to it.

True.

Both your daughters are now young adults. One has graduated college, and the other one is still in college. Time has gone by pretty fast, in spite of how slow some days may have passed. Just taking all of that in, what do you experience today in your life as it relates to the shadow of 9/11?

Both Will and I have reached a point in our lives where we really realize how fortunate we are—how blessed we are, and how thankful we are that I did not have to be a single mother to these two young girls. They're still young, obviously, but getting them through childhood into adulthood and knowing that we did it together, honestly, it makes waking up every day easier knowing how thankful and blessed we have been these last now 20 years.

Knowing what it could've been like had he not made it, how difficult it could have been, how hard it would have been, thinking back, we are immensely grateful for each day. Olivia would have never known her father. Bianca probably would have had little memory of her father. Just knowing that they both have had all these years of having their dad here, we have been blessed despite all we went through. Since he did retire so young, not only was he alive, but he was able to attend all their recitals and plays and all those things that sometimes dads don't get to see. I can honestly say we wake up every morning just feeling so blessed. It makes waking up easy. It really does. But, to be honest, it's scary at the same time because we also know we're at a point in our lives, we know how lucky we've been. So sometimes I wonder, when does that luck run out?

When the fear comes up, what do you do with that, Allison? How do you handle that?

That's a hard one. When I find I'm dwelling on something that I don't have the power to do anything about, I keep going forward. I find a way. Just like in the hospital, I have to remind myself of what we have instead of the what-ifs. It may be a simple idea, but it isn't easy. It takes work. Going through this COVID pandemic, we had to deal with it and find the positives. Obviously, I don't wish anything horrible like this, but it was so nice getting to spend so much time together, the four of us, before Olivia had to leave for college. Instead of everyone just running to a different room to watch TV or do something different after dinner, which sometimes can happen, we played board games. We watched a movie. We would play cards together. It's probably something we wouldn't have done if this pandemic didn't happen. We find a way to find the good. We felt so fortunate to have this time together.

I heard four different things that you do with the fear. One, you recognize it. You're aware that "I am afraid of this." Two, you accept the fact that you don't really have any control of it. If the shoe's going to fall, it's going to fall. Three, you tend to put yourself back into the day instead of the future, the what-ifs. Four, I heard gratitude is a huge anchor for you.

Absolutely. Whenever I feel overwhelmed, I can honestly say, "What am I overwhelmed about? Look at this life I've had for the last 20 years with Will by my side. If we can get through that, we can get through anything." I'm not the type of person to worry about things that I cannot prevent anyway. That's not in my nature. I do worry about a lot of things, don't get me wrong, but I don't let them bog me down if it's something that I can't do anything about.

What did you notice about yourself having gone through the struggles following 9/11?

I would say I had never realized I would be able to go through something like that and come out stronger. I had always felt I was an independent person, but I also realized how much I needed to rely on people when this happened. I had managed life pretty well up to that day, but there was no way to prepare for what came. When my family helped support me and took some of the basic demands of life from my plate, it allowed me to face the fears I was experiencing at a whole new depth. Clearly, it made me a stronger person, a more aware person. Since going through this kind of situation, I became much more aware of things, especially recognizing when things are unimportant and insignificant.

Any other changes?

Yes, absolutely. I was never the type of person to hold anything back, especially my feelings. I am one of those people where you never had to second guess what I was thinking or feeling. You know how people say things because they're trying to be nice? I am more the kind of person that if you don't ask my opinion, I'm not going to give you one. If you ask my opinion, I'm going to tell you as kindly and politely as I can, but I'm going to give you my truthful opinion. Going through what we did, the experience changed me because I had to withhold a lot of things that I normally would have spoken freely about to Will, such as things that bothered me, annoyed me, or that I had issues with.

Without a doubt, I had to bottle stuff up because I knew it was going to be a switch flipper. That was a change for me. I have to say, it's been a long road, and he is much better. I don't hold back anymore. I let him know what's bothering me. Just ask him; I'm sure he'll tell you. However, I learned a better way of going about it. There's always going to be arguments and disagreements, but I do know I have to, or I try to, take a better approach to avoid an unnecessary argument.

What made the switch for you then, Allison? What was it that helped you make the switch to say, "I'm not going to do this anymore. Enough is enough. I need to get back to who I am and who we are."

Well, quite honestly, it wasn't me. It was more Will. Once he got to a point where he was able to process and handle his own frustrations better, it made it easier for me. For him, it's always been better to talk things out. Sometimes when he gets frustrated or feels like something is going to blow, he'll go for a walk or whatever. He'll just leave. Whatever the situation is, he just leaves and lets himself cool down. And that seems to work for him.

Over the years, as he found whatever worked for him, it became easier. As it got easier for him to not blow up, and as he learned how to deal with it himself, I want to say it made it easier for me to be more me.

As he made more space, you were able to step back into it?

Absolutely. When he's good, I'm good, and vice versa. That's just how we are with each other. When the other one's not doing good for whatever reason, the other one feels it, too. Although he was the one with PTSD, I don't want to say I had it because I didn't, but I was affected by it.

Speaking from your heart, imagine speaking to another spouse that is struggling and facing this right now with their spouse who went through a major trauma and is suffering from PTSD. They reach out and say, "Help. What do I do? How do I make it? Tell me something that will help me get through this somehow."

Wow! That's a tough one. I'll tell you why it's tough because, honestly, I am not one to give advice. I guess it really depends on what the situation is, right? How bad the situation is? I know that physical violence is a real possibility, but I never had to deal with that.

Because it worked for Will, I guess I would suggest that this person with PTSD speak with someone. Is there anyone they can talk to? Does it help them when he talks about it? For Will, the more he talked about it, the more it helped him. I guess I would start off there. It is a tough position to be in because sometimes there's not much you can do. It really has to come from the person that's going through it. You do feel helpless because if the person that needs the help isn't getting the help, what is there left to do? I don't know. Does the person leave? Do they get a divorce? Do they separate? Does the spouse leave to figure it out on their own and realize that it is really that bad? I don't know. I mean, it's such a weird position to be thrown into. I guess I was lucky because Will recognized what his issue was, how he needed to get help, and what he needed to do to get the help.

Knowing what you know about yourself, I am going to ask a hypothetical question. Do you think you would still be holding things in had Will not sought help and made changes?

I think, at some point, things would have become so bad that ultimately a change would have had to be made. There are countless scenarios that could have happened, some good, some not so good. We can only imagine, at this point. However, I believe somehow we would have still arrived at the point where we are today, whether it was Will initiating the need for change or myself.

What did it mean to you as a wife for your husband to make the choice to change, to fight for change?

I feel very blessed, fortunate, grateful, and I could go on and on with many more adjectives. It truly meant the world to me that Will was able to find a way that helped him fight for change. The one thing I knew about him and where he got his motivation from was that he did not want to let his family become a victim of the tragic events of 9/11. He could not live with letting the terrorists affect another generation, his children.

Did Will talk to you about what he was going through?

Yes, but not fully. He would explain to me as much as he could, but no matter how much he would share with me I was never going to completely understand what he was going through. I can know his story but not how it made him feel. I will never be able to feel that. I'm glad, though, he was also able to talk to John. They had each other, and I thank God for that because only the two of them could fully understand what the other one was feeling and going through.

You made a clear distinction when you said, "I can know his story, but not how it made him feel."

Exactly. I can't feel what he feels. There's no way. I know his story; I repeat it verbatim, but I can't feel what he's feeling. The closest I can get is by listening. I'm a pretty good listener. I just listen because I know by him going through the motions of telling me, it's helping him somehow. I don't have to know how; I just need to listen.

Allison, your words remind me of a quote for which I have great respect. It also reminds me of how Will described Debbie and the work they did:

> The friend who can be silent with us in a moment of despair or confusion, who can stay with us in an hour of grief and bereavement, who can tolerate not knowing, not curing, not healing, and face us with the reality of our powerlessness, that is the friend who cares.[3]

If you were to create a mantra that would sum up your approach to surviving and growing through tragedy/struggle, what would it be?

This is a tough one for me because I'm still not completely sure how I was able to get through what we went through. However, there is a saying that I read that resonates with me on how I was able to get through each day: "The struggle you're in today is developing the strength you need for tomorrow."[4] I remember my mother-in-law telling me that on 9/11 she didn't just pray for Will to be alive but she prayed for God to grant her the strength that she needed for whatever the outcome might be.

It sounds like you kept your feet planted in today and what was in your power while keeping your hand touching the hope of tomorrow. I think you just expressed the concepts of faith, hope, and love in a single sentence: Faith in the value of the struggle you have today; hope in having a tomorrow; love for self/others, which gives you strength to hold on to both.

Yes, I would say that is pretty accurate. Actually, I would say you nailed it.

Reflections

1) What did you experience in hearing just Allison's voice?
2) What stood out for you in her message? Does any of this relate to your life?

---

[3] Nouwen, H. (2020, June 23). *The Friend Who Cares.* Henri Nouwen Society. https://henrinouwen.org/meditation/the-friend-who-cares/
[4] Morgan, E. M. (2016). *Change for Health, Vol. II: Making Positive Changes In Your Life and Health with Brief Inspirational Messages.* Nagrome.

3) What are three or four words that describe what you found useful in her navigation of their process as a couple dealing with PTSD?

4) Do you judge her, connect with her, or both? Do you know why? Use your why answers to reflect on your own struggle.

5) Do you need to pause, breathe, reflect, or grieve in this moment before continuing? What were moments of significance in this chapter?

Chapter Fourteen

A Psychologist's Point of View

*Sometimes you've got to cross boundaries to know where
they're at. — Jesse S. Moats*

It never fails to make me laugh inside when I see the facial expressions of a stranger at the moment they find out I (Michael) am a clinical psychologist. Two things consistently happen. More often than not, their eyes will slightly widen with a subtle backward flinching of the head, accompanied by a longer than usual pause. This is many times accompanied by the nervous joke about how they better be careful because I am probably already analyzing them. Second, I get a more welcoming tilt of the head, with a breath of relief, which is typically followed with a life history or a story about someone they know who has sought therapy. First responders typically fall into the first category. If you laughed or nodded, you know exactly what I'm talking about.

I (Michael) live in the Colorado Springs area; it is the home of 5 military installations (Peterson Air Force Base, Fort Carson, Schriever Air Force Base, the United States Air Force Academy, and the Cheyenne Mountain Air Force Station) and is the second largest city in Colorado, which means there is a heavy concentration of first responders living in the area. I feel blessed to have such a strong presence of men and women who do what they do to help protect and care for our community, our state, and our nation. However, we also are confronted with the reality of PTSD and the struggles that exist, including among the often forgotten population of spouses, children, extended family members, and other helping professionals that are dealing with vicarious trauma, sometimes called secondary PTSD. Although there is a difference between the two, they are often interchanged when speaking about anyone other than the primary person.

Not everyone will experience PTSD or vicarious trauma, and for those that do, not everyone will experience it in the same way. However, it can be useful to better understand potential symptoms, how others experience them, and how others deal with them. We will use examples from Will's and Allison's stories, as well as unidentified examples from the therapy room. My hope is to offer an introductory understanding of PTSD, a bridging between Will's message of faith, hope, and love and psychological concepts, as well as remove some of the stigma about therapy for those that avoid seeking assistance.

First and foremost, for those who are dealing with effects of trauma exposure, you are not weak and there is nothing *wrong* with you. Something has changed, but I want to remove the judgmental label from what you are struggling with so we can refocus on working toward where you want to be. Instead, it's important to realize and hang onto the fact that what you are experiencing is a natural response to an unnatural situation. It can make a person feel crazy, but that is not the case. It is our body's way of trying to deal with the painful circumstance that we have experienced, as well as trying to figure out how to live with the changes that have been created within us. *Feelings* of weakness are natural and are indicative of the courage it has taken to stand in the face of fear without answers and continue working through the struggle. I know this flies in the face of what most of us were taught growing up, but I assure you that the feelings of weakness do not directly equate to weakness of character. The symptoms are a direct reflection of the pain and struggle that you or your loved one is going through, especially when trying to regain a sense of normalcy in life. To engage one's symptoms produces distress and often invokes feelings of fear. If it was easy, courage would be unnecessary. You have already lived through the worst of your experience. Now let's work at living with it—and beyond it.

First things first, this chapter is meant to be informative and, hopefully, helpful. It is not meant to be an exhaustive text about trauma. Although I will be sharing information, theory, and stories, my goal is to make it as digestible as a good piece of cake that goes down smoothly, leaving a desire for more. My therapeutic approach, whether formal sessions or just being in a healthy relationship, is to be as real, honest, and as encouraging as I can be. Sometimes that means challenging, too.

Much of my approach to life and to therapy was formed by being brought up in a culture that believed if you couldn't sit down over a cup of coffee and go face to face *with* someone, credentials meant nothing. And some of my best teachers in the field of psychology never finished high school. They were dirt-poor elders of mine that knew about living and surviving life: the pain, work, joy, struggle, community, love, hope, support, grief, and faith. They didn't speak the actual word *trauma*, but the meaning of it was integrated within the teachings of their stories. It took grad school to offer the formalized concepts and operational definitions. I'll do my best to offer a mix of theory and research, but in a less formal and sometimes story-telling manner. Eat the meat and spit the bones.

The ability to have a common language to understand such complex concepts like PTSD is invaluable to medical and mental health clinicians, much like first responders have their own language. However, in the medicalized approach there has also been a shadowed stigma that has been present in the dialogue of symptoms and treatments.[1] The person is labeled with a *pathology* instead of a human struggle. PTSD is called a *disorder*, rather than a *reorder*.[2] Our brains are unbelievably adaptive, and we are sometimes able to process and encode trauma—singular or plural—in a way that has minimal impact on our daily functioning, not to be confused with suppressing and denying, which will be covered later. However, sometimes the situations we have faced are just too big and powerful, and we get stuck in a mental loop of attempts to remedy the situation, leaving our psychological well-being in a heightened state of distress. This may be a result of a single instance (i.e., acute), being exposed to multiple traumatic events (i.e., complex), or a combination where a single instance busts the dam that has been holding back the accumulation of trauma. Until we can find a way to resolve our trauma, we are geared for defense, which can present as visual and mental reminders of the event (e.g., intrusive thoughts, images, sensations), aggression toward self or others, isolation, avoidance of situations and reminders of the event(s), poor sleep and concentration, lack of interest in activities, reckless behavior, and being startled easily.[3] With aggression, there may be nothing immediately present to defend against, at least externally. The battle is primarily within, and the most innocent of instances can trigger an outburst, whether the trigger is internal or external. Additionally, it can appear as a slow, consistent hollowing of one's soul or character. When attempts to reconcile these symptoms

[1] Elkins, D. (2016). *The Human Elements of Psychotherapy: A Nonmedical Model of Emotional Healing.* American Psychological Association.
[2] TEDx Talks. (2016, March 14). Understanding PTSD's Effects on Brain, Body, and Emotions / Janet Seahorn / TEDxCSU [Video]. YouTube. https://www.youtube.com/watch?v=BEHDQeIRTgs
[3] American Psychiatric Association. (2013). *Diagnostic and Statistical Manual of Mental Disorders* (5th ed.). Author.

are not successful, many individuals will self-medicate with alcohol or drugs, increase thrill-seeking behaviors in spite of safety risks, detach from friends and family, or self-harm.

Part of the difficulty that PTSD can offer is a self-generating feeling of guilt and shame. Conceptually, there are different forms of guilt, including what we call healthy guilt, which falls more in line with remorse. However, for this discussion I use the term guilt to mean a destructive, internalizing responsibility and blame for something that one wanted to do but couldn't (i.e., get everyone out of the Twin Towers) or for surviving when others did not. Not only does the individual feel guilt resulting from the trauma, but they often begin compiling guilt for feeling bad and behaving in a manner that was not typical for them. It's easy to judge and say just go get help, but the added component of shame is a toxic protector of the emotional wounds, which causes many to try to push it down and hide it. I liken shame to mold; the more you keep in the dark, the bigger it grows and the more damage it does. The catch is that it's an upside-down, emotional attempt to prevent anyone from seeing or touching this deep, hidden wound. The short answer that I give clients comes in the form of a question, "Do you want to do what is needed, or what feels better?" Although I usually get "neither" for the initial answer; most people, especially first responders, inherently know that what is needed is the right path toward safety, even if it initially brings greater discomfort. This is a very small, but very significant, step.

Many come into my office able to recite a litany of traumas, in order, front to back and back to front, by grouping, or however it is requested. This give the impression that the person resolved these injuries and is no longer affected by them. This is not likely. It is more likely that they have disconnected in a way to *manage* their histories in a cognitively defended manner. It's as if to say, "If I can recite them, they don't bother me anymore." In an effort to control their pain, the person has used powerful survival skills of compartmentalizing and denial. Reciting gives the illusion of acceptance and serves as a defense against prying any deeper into their wounds in an attempt to convince themselves and others that the wounds have healed. What does "healed" even mean? That's it? It's over? No! A minor bruise may disappear with no observable discoloration remaining, like an offhanded argument with a friend, but a trauma that causes a puncture, slicing, tearing, or mutilation is going to leave a scar. The wounds may heal, but there will be a scar that expresses a past injury. Sometimes there are new limitations to what one was once able to do, even one's way of life.

However, none of this defines your life. It can have serious affects, but it is up to you to determine how you ultimately define your life, despite the circumstances. Emotional wounds are similar.

I generally believe that no one gets out of this life without scars. This is not to minimize the impact of life's pain, but more of an acceptance of the reality of suffering that life provides. Victor Frankl, who spent a total of three years in four different concentration camps, spoke about the meaning of suffering. He also spoke of the courage to suffer, which does not mean needlessly. However, he also reminds us that we still have choices available to us, even when surrounded with limitations.

> There are always choices to make. Every day, every hour, offered the opportunity to make a decision, a decision that determines whether you will or will not submit to those powers that threatened to rob you of your very self, your inner freedom; which determine whether or not you would become the plaything of circumstance, renouncing freedom and dignity to become molded into the form of the typical inmate.[4]

Frankl's thinking is a paradigm shift within a traumatic situation. His ability to find meaning was not in the absence of misery (e.g., imprisonment, torture, starvation, death). The concentration camp honed Frankl's ideas about finding meaning in life despite difficult and painful circumstances. It was not in reference to his prior freedom (e.g., who he used to be, what he used to have), but it was connected to his current reality, which included suffering. It included context because being in the concentration camp was not spoken of with fondness, yet Frankl sought out ways, through choices, to find personal meaning and existential freedom.

First responders are portrayed as those who throw caution to the wind in a valiant effort to save everyone at all costs, but this is not true. They are highly trained professionals that want to return to their families at the end of the day, the shift, or their tour. Yes, they run into places where others are running out, but they are not doing so haphazardly. They are taking risks that others would not, but they are also making calculated decisions and using their training to make educated risks in volatile situations. Their focus is on how to save as many as possible while also returning home, which still puts them in an emotional conflict. Although they can logically understand that not all

---

[4] Frankl, V. (2006). *Man's search for meaning.* Boston: Beacon Press.

can be saved, the inability to save or to witness the pain of others is a cut every time emotionally. They are taught to first assess and then utilize critical thinking to minimize emotionally reactive decisions that could put themselves or others at greater risk. Sometimes no amount of decision making can prevent bad things from happening, and for some, they may have to do things or take risks they would rather not. Sometimes things work out, and sometimes they don't. Sometimes, first responders make mistakes. It's all so very easy to judge from a rational, safe seat after the fact, but it can be hell in the split-second moment with conflicting needs for career, for family, and for self.

Training doesn't necessarily assist with what they will emotionally experience in a situation, a day, a tour, or a culminating career. To do their jobs, they have to somewhat disconnect from the risks (e.g., denial or acceptance), what they may have to do (i.e., war), or what they may not be able to do (i.e., could not save a victim or a partner). Unfortunately, disconnecting doesn't effectively work with processing or healing trauma. It's important to understand how a person views the trauma they have experienced, the actions they have taken or didn't take, survivor's guilt, or the injustice of it all. They definitely have to use a Zhi Mian[5] approach, or *to face directly*, entering their darkness with eyes wide open and taking protective gear while doing it, just like the functional part of the job. Sometimes it feels as though their gear has been scattered about, hidden within the darkness, leaving them vulnerable and resistant.

This is where Will's message of faith, hope, and love comes into play. Allow me to play devil's advocate for a moment. If Will came into my office and recited faith, hope, and love were all you needed to treat trauma, like he read it off someone's Facebook meme, I would tell him he's full of shit and it's time to get real. However, listen closely to what is deeper within the message. His message of faith, hope, and love offers both nouns and verbs in each word. Using them as nouns, they are like lighthouses that offer markers of guidance and safety. Having been adrift and pummeled by the tumultuous waves of your storm, you seek a harbor, a place of respite, safety, and nourishment. You may have an idea of where that might be, but without the proper instrumentation or light, you are left feeling adrift in the darkness. Passively waiting for a

---

[5] Wang, X. (2011). Zhi Mian and Existential Therapy. *The Humanistic Psychologist*. 39, 240–246; Dueck, A., & Wei, G. Q. (2019). The Indigenous Psychology of Lu Xun and Xuefu Wang. In L. Hoffman, M. Yang, M. Mansilla, J. Dias, M. Moats, & T. Claypool (Eds.), *Existential Psychology East-West* (Vol. 2; pp. 17–46). University Professors Press.

Sunrise Through the Darkness

sunrise has proven to be ineffective, especially when our situation is dire, so what are we left to do?

Too abstract? Okay, let's make it more relatable. We've all been in situations where removing one of our senses, like when the lights unexpectedly go out as we're walking through a room, causing a mild feeling of anxiety and resulting in us fumbling around slowly, unsure of the movements we had just been making with complete confidence prior to the darkness. The loss throws us into a situation that causes less trust in our movements and anxiety about feeling that blinding pain catching the corner of the coffee table in our shin. Now let's talk about something real, like trauma. Some describe it as a dimmer switch turned down, others like complete darkness, and some as the feeling of a slow slide into an abyss. None of these can be argued against, but they *are* survivable, even if they do not *feel* like it.

Faith, hope, and love demand that you take action. Much like priorities or values, when put into place they begin to make decisions for you, especially in times of doubt. They don't lay out the whole picture before you, but they begin helping you make one choice at a time, creating a path that will likely be difficult but rewarding. The old adage in physically working out—no pain, no gain—comes to mind. When we feel weak, working out is not pleasurable. But if we keep at it and use awareness and good sense with the pain, we find our healthy struggle begins to show results, which in turn begins to motivate us a little more. It still hurts, but we now can see a little further beyond the pain. Will's message is all about action. It's all about struggling, but doing so purposefully. The phrase I share in therapy that speaks to this is, "If you're already feeling miserable, you might as well make it useful."

Will speaks from the heart and in a manner that is relatable. The concepts sound simple on the surface but have a depth and richness within the story. Let's go through some of Will's story to give context to how faith, hope, and love were lighthouses in his darkness. If you cannot currently find your own, use his until you can get closer to finding your own.

Trying to escape our reality (e.g., what is, where we are currently), we often pour over the past (e.g., what was, what we have lost and now long to regain) and think of things that could have been different (e.g., leaving the vest and phone behind, Dom staying, Antonio switching spots, compounding regrets due to behaviors from PTSD). But it doesn't help; it just keeps us trapped in the darkness. In life, we all have myths,[6]

---

[6] May, R. (1991). *The Cry for Myth*. London: W. W. Norton & Company.

beliefs that provide structure and a sense of trust that guide us in our daily living. We could also use Will's concept of *faith* to describe myths. Faith is not just a spiritual concept, but a belief in anything that we can anchor to and value. At one time, people freely and without fear walked in and out of the Twin Towers, knowing they were safe. In fact, people from around the world would purposefully visit them to take in their majestic view of the city. Will also had this myth, this faith, that the buildings would never come down, even after seeing the damage from the planes. When the buildings fell, so crumbled his myth, which was symbolic of the shattering that happened within his life. He believed, in spite of fear, that he and his partners were going to get everyone out, which was what helped him enter the buildings, even though he was already surrounded with such devastation (e.g., knowing people had already died from the attack, having watched many jump to their deaths). His belief—despite the damage to the buildings, the painful presence of death, and the unknowns that awaited—gave him motivation to enter the belly of the Twin Towers.

September 11th shattered his once-established structure for living: his calling to be a police officer, his physical abilities, his joy for life, and believing he and Allison would grow old together. In the rubble and the years after the rescue, he had to learn how to recreate these into new forms. In my practice, I face a large amount of trauma and grief. Analogies often provide tangibility to the concepts that we discuss, and one of them that I use is a vase. Imagine that you cherish this vase and it is invaluable to you. Somehow, whether because of you or someone else, it gets knocked over and shatters. It doesn't just break into pieces, it shatters. You know what I'm talking about, where the little shards seem to explode in all directions and end up in places that you didn't know were possible? Yeah, like that. Once we are over the initial stunned feeling, the feelings of loss pour in, but we no longer have a vase to contain them, no structure to help us know how to hold it. So, we begin to sweep up the debris and collect it in a pile. Painstakingly, we try to put it all back together, every piece, every sliver. However, no matter how intently we focus, no matter how hard we work, we can never regain the polished and unblemished vase that once stood proudly on display. There are cracks and missing pieces. When we try to recreate what was, we are left in despair. Instead, I offer two choices for recreating one's structure for living.

The first option is to use the pieces that we have and make something that resembles what was. Instead of trying to create an exact replica, we allow for the change that has occurred. An ancient Japanese art, Kintsugi (金継ぎ), involves using gold to put the broken pieces back together, highlighting the scars rather than trying to make them vanish. Our pain is part of our story, and there is no need for shame, including self-imposed pain. The depths of tragedy only stand to highlight the summiting changes that we make in our lives. Every great novel is based on tragedy. *Les Miserables* is a story of redemption that is overwhelmingly full of pain and despair. In fact, it sometimes feels like it's hard to catch your breath before the next wave is presented. However, it was the choices within the pain and struggle that eventually offered the light of redemption, which made it even more beautiful, in a way that could not have been imagined while in the darkness. I am not suggesting to just start breaking things to see what happens, but I am suggesting allowing your scars to become badges of honor that encompass your pain rather than feeling ashamed by them. Your pain is because of loss, and no amount of shame will ever repair that. For Will, this book is one of the gold highlights of his life. He no longer hides the ugliness of his struggle but offers it up for viewing, no longer allowing shame to cover him and prevent him from fully living.

The second option is to take the pieces and begin going through them. Decide which pieces to keep and which pieces we can no longer hold onto. As painful as it is, we must let go of those pieces. When we are speaking of people that have died, we are not talking about forgetting them; we are talking about letting go of their physical presence in our lives. The other pieces (e.g., who we are because of them, memories, our children, the impact they have made in others' lives) are the parts that we retain. As we sift through the pieces, the edges will be sharp. We will get cut, and we will bleed. It is painful. If we tend to our wounds as we go, we eventually have the foundation of what we are about to create. Instead of trying to recreate the vase as it was, make a new work of art, perhaps a mosaic. Use the pieces to create something that fits your life, encompassing its limitations and changes. For Will, his life's passion to be a police officer was cut short. He had to create a new work of art from the pieces of his heart for serving. In doing so, he learned to share his story with others in an effort to protect them from self-harm and to serve their humanity through connection.

When trauma creates a shattering in our lives, we are left feeling adrift. We try to get the scattered pieces reorganized, labeled, and put back together. It is not an easy process, and it is not fast. In this process, we find that some myths are no longer sustainable and some are still standing. Filtering through these is a remodeling or recreating process, referring to the vase analogy. For Will, the buildings were gone and they could not save everyone. Those myths were important for a time but are no longer sustainable. Trusting in the expertise of his sergeant was not about a guarantee but was a belief that if anyone could help them be successful, it would be John. That one stood the test of time, and it is still one that Will believes in and holds close. Antonio, Chris, and Dominick died that day, and they believed John was the best leader to follow for their survival. Their death does not make their belief invalid. Sometimes situations are just that big and out of our control.

Our attempts to reclaim our lives are not held in what was. It is in what we create, each day offering another chance to shape it a little more. It's not a place in which you arrive; rather, it's a journey of sorts through the unknown of what will be. Norbert Wiener stated, "Every creative act must pass through a moment when it is neither seed nor flower...through the nothingness that is the hidden source springs of everything."[7] Some things look familiar, but some are out of place or are missing. Picasso remarked, "Every act of creation is first of all an act of destruction,"[8] which means stop fighting what has happened and cannot be taken back and focus on what your unwritten chapters might say.

It's your story. Get off chapter five. Quit rereading the same pages over and over and expecting your story to change. Start writing on the pages that are still blank and waiting for your pen to move across them with fluidity, anger, confusion, and happiness. Let others read it, literally or figuratively. If not, why are you reading this? Your story is just as valid. Your pain is just as real. Your life is worth living and worth sharing! Write not because you know the ending, but because it is an adventure yet to be discovered. You may be in the valley now but keep walking. You may have to go uphill, but the view will open up the higher you climb. As first responders, you would have climbed that mountain, that ladder, or those stairs for someone in need. Treat yourself with the same respect and compassion that you offer others on a daily basis.

For some, the words I am speaking will not carry the same weight as that of a brother or sister of the same uniform. Let me offer the following from a fellow sister in the fire services:

Flame Eternal[9]

---

[7] Medina, M. (2008). Everyday courage: Living courageously without being a hero. Existential Analysis: *Journal of the Society for Existential Analysis, 19*(2), 280–298.
[8] May, R. (1975). *The courage to create.* New York: W. W. Norton & Company.
[9] Rosemond, K. (2015). Eternal flame. In L. Hoffman, & M. Moats (Eds.), *Capturing Shadows: Poetic Encounters Along the Path of Grief and Loss.* Colorado Springs, CO:

Kat V. Rosemond

For brother and sister 9/11 firefighters and EMTs

We are never too old and it is never too late to truly live...
Not while our eyes are open and we still draw breath.
Hope is a flame eternal
Faith is the sturdy stone pathway
Love is the greatest power in all the universe
Not even death can break or overcome it

Brothers and sisters of the firecross, lifestar, and shield
Keepers of the terrible little known tragic life-truths
Though the deepest dark surround us
Though death should snap with sharp cold jaws
Nothing can break our bonds
We are never alone

Take up the flame eternal
Keep your feet on the path of sure stone
Keep open the doors of your heart to the greatest power
Beat the dark walls that would hold and snuff you
Until they break utterly
And you are free and alive once more

Without knowing the circumstances surrounding the respective pain of each reader, I still say this: Shouldn't trauma hurt? I won't say to what degree, but let's generalize for a moment that when we speak of trauma we are speaking of personal, significant pain. Whether we are talking about being injured, being a victim of crime, witnessing the death or pain of another, having to appropriately perform an act of violence in the line of duty that still hurts one's soul, being helpless in an attack on oneself or others, or the accumulation of any of these, isn't it appropriate to allow ourselves the reality that these experiences are painful? It seems exceptionally human to feel sad or maybe even horrified about any of them. However, here is the catch: It's what you do with the pain that matters. Trauma involves loss (e.g., death, physical abilities, sense of confidence, moral injury). Loss involves grief. Grief hurts; stop trying to escape it. Instead, we have to actively and purposefully work through it. If you don't know how, beyond trying to cover it up or ignore it, then it's time to reach out. Step into your darkness, but don't do it alone. This book, for example, is based on connection (e.g., Will and the Port Authority, Will and his team, humanity). It was made possible through connection (e.g., Will and Michael, Michael and the publisher), and even the title was inspired by connection to another man's story of traumatic loss, Jerry Sittser, who wrote, "In choosing to face the night, I took my first steps toward the sunrise."[10]

Chasing the sun only leaves exhaustion and feelings of failure or despair. The outcome remains consistently waning. However, turning into the darkness may initially invoke additional feelings of fear and uncertainty, but it also offers hope for a sunrise, for something different. If you are deep enough in your own darkness, it's pretty clear that there is no sun on the path you are walking. Turn around. You now, at least, have one marker that gives you valuable information: Death, this way; opportunity, any other direction.

I am reminded of a client that I worked with that actively thought about suicide multiple times a day. I wrote of our interactions in a chapter called, *A Walk in the Dark: Accompanying Clients as They Investigate Their Relationship with Suicide.*[11] A part of that story follows; it has been included to demonstrate what therapy might look like and how open it can be.

***

I asked, "Sarah, I know you think about suicide. Would you tell me how often these thoughts are present?"

Stammering with hesitation, she shared that she thought about it multiple times a day and had for years. She described an embedded coping style that primarily relied upon the option of suicide. Sarah admitted, "In some ways it's the only thing that has kept me alive, knowing that I *could* always kill myself."

"It sounds like you have found a dark cave that makes you feel safe. I think we need to explore the cave together. After all, there is a lot to be said about having company when we explore, don't you agree?"

"Yeah, but what do you mean about exploring the cave?"

Sittser, J. (2004). *A Graced Disguised: How the Soul Grows through Loss.* Zondervan.
Moats, M. (2019). A walk in the dark: Working with suicidal clients. In L. Hoffman, & M. Yang (Eds.), *Existential Psychology East-West* (2nd ed.). University Professors Press.

"Well, this cave, this darkness, has provided you with a sense of safety, but my concern is that it offers no nourishment, no connection. I think we need to see what else it can provide. Likewise, I think we need to find an outlet for emotional nourishment and connection. Does that make sense?" I inquired.

"Yeah, kind of."

I shared, "As we go along, we are going to try to learn about your pain and why death, the cave, seems less frightening than life, the light. Maybe in doing so we can shine a little light within the cave, so that it becomes more supportive to you and your needs while providing you freedom to come and go from the outside into the darkness and from the darkness into the outdoors."

"But I don't want to get rid of the cave."

Reassuring her, I said, "Oh, I'm not talking about getting rid of it. I am talking about feeling more comfortable with moving in and out as you see fit. I don't believe the cave is all bad, but I do believe it is limiting you as you are using it currently."

What I was asking Sarah to do, in challenging her perceived sense of safety, was going to take courage, and courage requires risk. Philosopher Paul Tillich believed that the "courage to create implies the courage to replace the old by the new—the new for which there are no norms and criteria, the new which is a risk and which, measured by the old, is incalculable."[12]

This interaction with Sarah is no different than I would have with anyone that has contemplated suicide. Because I believe that a healthy relationship requires honesty and transparency, I also am very clear with my boundaries around mandatory reporting. We have the same laws about self-harm, but it has been my experience that the manner in which it is practiced varies greatly. I realize I am taking a risk of scaring people away from utilizing therapy by talking about mandatory reporting, but if I am going to ask you to take a risk then I must also model that willingness to face my own fears. In my practice, I deal frequently with suicidal ideation. What I have found is that the more I try to control a situation or practice out of fear of losing my license, the less available I am to my clients. I have boundaries, and I am very clear with them up front. My goal is to provide a clear line so that the clients are empowered to make their own informed decisions within therapy. It is true that some therapists will call 911 when a client states they have been considering suicide. My boundary is wider than that. The

---

[12] Tillich, P. (2000). *The Courage To Be* (2nd ed.). Yale University Press.

point I am making is not about saying I am better or that another clinician is wrong, it is to inform you to ask questions and assess the situation to see if the relationship is capable of holding the space you need to process. Don't assume it's okay. Don't assume it won't be. Seek it out and be active in your own rescue.

Sarah and I had covered these boundaries, and she tested them from time to time to see if they still held true. It was quite the journey. Continuing with the story:

We had traveled through some very unstable ground while in the darkness and made it to a more solid and brighter piece of ground on which we could catch our breath before moving forward in a continued *obstinate attempt of two people to recover the wholeness of being human through the relationship between them.*[13]

With an encouraging voice, I verbally nudged Sarah, "I think it's time we go for a walk and explore, kind of like how I shared with you what I do when I go for a hike. What d'ya say?"

"Explore what?"

"Let's explore your darkness. Let's explore this relationship you have with suicide," I said.

"O...kay?"

"You've already shared what your goals and desires for life are. You love your fiancé and want to grow a life with her. You want to go back to school and become a cardiologist. You want to travel and see the world. Tell me about why it would be good to die. Give me three good reasons to kill yourself," I said matter of factly.

She stared at me with a stunned look and gave a mixed exhale and nervous laugh. It was visually clear that she was rattled by the openness and in-your-face reality of the question, and it became verbally clear by her following statement:

"Ah, man! That's messed up!" she blurted out.

"Messed up? What's messed up, Sarah?"

"That question. It's, uh, it's really tough."

"It is, Sarah, as it should be. We are not talking about a decision of what kind of bread to buy or if you want to take a nap or not. We are talking about life and death. Do you really want to make a decision of this magnitude without having really thought about the choices?" I honestly asked.

"Yeah, but...that's messed up," she reasserted.

We continued the dance, in which she tried to hold out, and I had to

---

[13] Laing, R. (1967). *The Politics of Experience.* Pantheon Books.

remain calm and steady until she was able to give some reasons she thought were worthy of death, which primarily were to escape emotional pain. It was only when we could establish this honest dialogue that alternatives became available. I continued with the following comment:

"The reality is that you have held tightly to the belief that if life felt too hard you could ultimately take your own life and escape the pain, yes?" I said, asking for confirmation.

"Yeah."

"Well, much like hiking through the mountains, in life we have high points, valleys, cliffs, sun, darkness, dangers, beauties, caves, and different paths we can take. I see that you have a very worn path between the dark cave and the cliff's edge, with minimal travel in other directions. How about we continue exploring together? Let's learn to map the cave and let's see what else is around here, beyond the cave."

"Okay," Sarah agreed.

***

The story of Sarah and me is one that I carry with me because she gave to me as much as I helped her explore her pain and darkness, her cave. We did so through connection in the rawest sense. To sit in that space of painful intimacy requires an unknowing process of trust in ourselves and each other. As her therapy was ending, I used poetry to reflect, process, and contain our therapeutic experiences. In our last session, I read the poem I had written to her, and we used it to process together, as well as grieve the relationship that was ending. Learning to grieve is part of what I do with all clients upon termination. The poem, *Adrift*,[14] utilized being alone in the middle of the ocean and drowning, until learning how to relax and float with the waves from a sun-bleached board passing by. The final stanza read:

A current of determination creates peaceful freedom. "I don't know where I am going, but I know the sun rises in the East. If I die it will not be because of my decision. It will be because it was inevitable." And so, she swims.

---

[14] Moats, M. (2017). Steadiness in the Midst of Chaos. In M. Yang (Ed.), *Existential Psychology and the Way of the Tao: Meditations on the Writings of Zhuangzi*. Routledge.

In that stanza, it was *hope* that Sarah's *actions* would take her to land. Hope is the meaning you have currently, and it is not passive. Sometimes it's for the day because it's all that can be held, and sometimes it's sustained over a longer span of life. Sarah's was to swim toward life, but yours may be more of a life calling, like being a police officer. Or it may be as basic as getting out of bed today and trying to be present for a moment of potential motivation. Notice, I said basic, not easy. It's all valuable, especially depending on where you are in your life.

The unique nature of being a first responder is that this chosen career field is often tied to one's identity—not what one does but who one is—which is a large, structural framework for a life narrative. There are exceptions, but the sample I interact with identifies with the career choice as more than a career. Within this framework often comes multiple traumas, some obvious and some that are dismissed in a manner of coping. Other times there may be a singular event that gets tied to one's framework of identity. The complexity of these two situations with first responders is that it isn't only tied to experiences; it's also tied to their identity, which can begin to erode the foundational belief and fortitude for going into situations that others flee. Sometimes it's experienced as a blown tire; other times it may feel like the dimmer switch to the light is slowly being turned down. Without healthy intervention, reactive course correction can cause the blown tire situation to become a roll-over, and the dim lighting can cause one's motivation for life to slow. So, what's a person to do?

For some first responders, mentioning their struggle is met with regurgitated cliches and defensive happiness. Others find themselves fielding a barrage of misguided advice or declarations of magic fixes, such as "just change your attitude." And yet others find the threat of losing a career that they love and that gives them the only meaning that is keeping them clinging to life. Sadly, some face all three.

In my office, I have heard depths of despair and hopelessness that took the air from my chest. However, I also have met some of the most courageous people to cross my path. These courageous, hurting souls are still fighting, still seeking, and still reaching out from their darkness, mustering the strength to hang onto the fragments of hope that somehow remain.

It is in these moments that weakness and courage get confusing. The confusion comes in defining weakness from a physical state or a feeling that drives a belief about oneself. The other is recognizing courage as an action rather than a feeling. I have spoken to many Special

Forces (SF) soldiers and stated, "Courage doesn't show up until you're afraid." Without hesitation, they agree, although usually through a head nod or an affirmation of few words that is very convincing. These are people that fly, repel, fall, walk, and run into some extremely dangerous situations, not in the absence of fear but despite it. However, you do not have to be in SF or be a first responder to experience this feeling of having to choose a course of action while facing intense fear, especially when dealing with trauma. Sometimes the best course of action is to turn and avoid it in order to catch one's breath (e.g., going into the woods to watch deer while deescalating, going for a walk). However, too much of this course can further ingrain the reaction of avoidance or flight. Many times, we use aggression to clear space in an attempt to remove the threat or feeling of helplessness, which is still avoidance (e.g., the eggplant parmesan story, the remote control story), but it is through fight instead of flight. Keep in mind, some of these instances are not being actively chosen by the person.

The reactions within PTSD can seem confusing to the observer, as well as the person dealing with them. It's not what others are literally seeing as the details or the problem, it's what the details represent symbolically. This symbolism taps into deep pain, fear, the trauma, and the details happen to touch this root, or nerve, firing off the brain's defensive system. Even though Will dislikes eggplant parmesan, he exploded. The feeling of something being taken away from him (e.g., control, food as a first tier on Maslow's Hierarchy of Needs,[15] feelings of powerlessness) taps into this other trauma root/nerve and causes a reaction that makes no sense on the surface.

The brain registers a threat and does not differentiate that it's only a misplaced remote control or an overabundance of food that a person doesn't even like. It's what it represents, and regardless of whether it can be understood rationally or not, it activates the fight or flight response. We don't always have a choice of our reactions in the moment, but we do have a choice to address it once we are aware.

Sometimes leaning into the fear and marching forward in the direction of the subjective goal for life and healing is the choice that takes the most work but also offers the most reward (e.g., investing oneself in therapy, using pain to make something meaningful). And sometimes when running away is not warranted and walking forward feels beyond one's capabilities in the moment, the courage to stand firm

[15] See Hoffman, L., Lopez, A., & Moats, M. (2013). Humanistic psychology and self-acceptance. In M. Bernard (Ed.), *The strength of self-acceptance* (pp. 3-17). Springer.

on trembling legs is still a valiant action and investment in one's own pursuit of regaining the joy in living. This is the courage I often see in my clients. They sometimes *feel* too weak to continue, so they stand, and they take steps—like coming into the office knowing they are going to be challenged—to lean into what they have been avoiding. This is no small feat!

The willingness to fight for one's life and to reclaim the desire to live and thrive is meaningful. *Meaning* drives us through the pain, through the suffering, through the unknowns in a desperate attempt to see our potential realized. Sometimes life runs us over and causes us to be disoriented and amnestic. Most of us call first responders when that happens. Who do they (you) call? There is pressure in the assumption that they are supposed to have it all together, to be the rescuer, to be the badasses that don't let anything get to them. Well, let me tell you something I have learned: the biggest badasses I have ever met know that having it all together is recognizing that sometimes they don't have it all together, or can't; that we all need help at times; and that not letting things get to them is really a very fragile veil masking their fear and a pathway into danger.

First responders must honestly evaluate situations and make tough decisions, including those that cause trauma in themselves by having to do something (e.g., shoot someone, tell someone their child is dead) or not being able to do something (e.g., not rushing into a fire, not being able to save someone, especially children). They are still tasked with making choices that are geared toward coming home safely to their families, albeit in the context of their dangerous jobs. Use these same skills that are used on the job to come back home emotionally to your families. We cannot be the same people that we were before doing these jobs, but we can come home with a great depth and capacity to integrate our pain with our joy instead of straddling the fence. In the country, we would say, "If you straddle that barbed wire fence and try to walk, it's just going to be painful and you won't go anywhere." It's time to do something different. Toss a leg and start walking to the life you want to see.

Trauma often brings a feeling of detachment to those people, things, and activities that we enjoyed and loved, which brings us to the final domain of *love*. Love is about compassion and connection to something or someone greater than oneself (e.g., service to others, family, team, spirituality), which is also tied to meaning. Additionally, it is love for self because without love for self, we cannot fully connect with others. Desmond Tutu believed, "we are made for fellowship because only in a vulnerable set of relationships are we able to recognize that our humanity is bound up in the humanity of others."[16] It is painful when we are experiencing this severing of connection within ourselves and with others. We are grieving people who are standing around us, as well as grieving the person we were.

It's hard to appreciate much when you are in pain (e.g., family, friends, career, prior passions, or hobbies). If you don't believe me, take your shoe off and kick the corner of a piece of furniture or the wall, and now turn around and try to smile and notice the beauty of the day. Let me save you the trouble and some pain; it's not going to work out for you. Sometimes PTSD is felt in intense, jolting pain (e.g., panic, flashbacks, nightmares, rage) and sometimes it's more of a persistent, internal gnawing of your heart and will (e.g., feeling of emptiness, no joy, lack of any form of passion or interest, meaninglessness). It's hard to appreciate life and what life offers when in pain. It's hard to feel the love that you know is there but is seemingly just out of reach. Keep fighting. You need them, and they need you—whoever them/they are. Notice what you have been trying to do to address your PTSD and ask yourself if it is truly working. You may find that some things are and some aren't working, or you may find that none of it feels productive. Then let's try something different. Try reaching out. Just like being part of a team, we are stronger together than individually. Seeking help may feel foreign and unsettling, which is a hard thing to reach out for when life already feels unstable. Again I say, "If you already feel miserable, you might as well make it productive."

Is there anything greater than love and connection? The older I get, the more I am impressed with less. As the shininess of things fade, the depth and value of relationship continues to hold its luster. It's part of why I am a psychologist, and, I am guessing, why some of you chose to be first responders: You value others. However, everything has a shadow. It costs to care, especially in times of tragedy, and first responders have a front row seat and daily dose of tragedy. For those who aren't first responders, let me reassert that I am not saying their trauma is greater. Again, it is not competitive, but it has been my experience that first responders are less aware of the daily doses because it is a chosen career field and they often dismiss the impact of what they experience as a choice they made, which they have to suck up and be tough enough to handle. But handling it frequently means

---

16 Battle, M. (1997). *Reconciliation: The Ubuntu Theology of Desmond Tutu*. The Pilgrim Press.

dismissing their humanness and the toll tragedy takes on the heart and mind, which is ineffective. If you want to give to others, you must feed yourself first. Self-care is not selfish, and you will sacrifice yourself and your relationships if you do not take this challenge to heart. You are worth it. Your relationships are worth it.

It was the love for his family and his sergeant that helped Will survive his 13 hours buried in the rubble. It was his relationship within his faith that gave him rejuvenation in his fight for life. It was the love for his family, himself, and for the sacrifices of his team that gave him strength to fight in his recovery. And it was his love for humanity that gives Will the strength to continue sharing his story with others today. We are not as alone as we feel.

If you feel you are alone and feeling hopeless, that there's no one who understands, please hang onto this, and then reach out for help:

Today,

I'm Still Here
I Still Remember
I Still Share
I Still Love
I Still Cry
I Still Dream
I Still Struggle
I'm Still Here.
If You're Reading This,
You're Still Here.
There Is Hope...
If you don't have it,
I Will Hold It For You,
Until You Find Your Own.

There is entirely too much information to cover to comprehensively discuss the many facets of trauma in this chapter. However, I want to just touch on some domains that I speak of when providing therapy. Adding to one's coping strategies is one of the first things I try to implement (e.g., de-escalation, distress tolerance, increasing one's support network, sleep hygiene). It's important to find a therapist that is comfortable with the tough discussions of suicide and trauma because you need to be allowed to safely tie off to them while you swim through the waves of your trauma and grief. Although my bias and practice is from an existential framework, others practice from other orientations. Some practices are presented as gold standards, which is a farce, but they all hold value. It's important for client and therapist alike to be open and flexible to the path(s) that are travelled.

Two words that I spend many sessions on are *acceptance* and *forgiveness*. How a person defines those words allows them to be words of freedom and growth or resistance and rage. These two words, in my experience, are often misinterpreted, causing greater frustration and the possibility of creating a barrier between client and therapist. Many of my clients have told me that they disliked the word acceptance because it meant that it was okay or that they had to be okay with the trauma. This is not the case. In short, acceptance is no longer holding onto any other version of a story than what is presented today. It is not about approval. It simply means that we see the situation for exactly what it is and that we are at a place where we take it in and make decisions on how we integrate it as part of story, rather than feeling divided by it. It's when we begin to really move forward with our lives instead of feeling like one foot is stuck.

Additionally, clients have shared that forgiveness has meant a similar feeling of saying it's okay that someone got away with such atrocities. That is also not the case. However, one prison that I have found that holds people back in their processing of trauma is the need for justice. It is completely warranted but sometimes impossible to achieve. The result is that the only person who is held for punishment is the person who was hurt by the trauma because they are held captive by the need for justice. This is one of the places that I found forgiveness to be useful. Forgiveness in this context is about letting go of an uncollectible debt that is owed. It's freeing you to pursue more valuable endeavors of life that offer reward, instead of costing you more of your life by holding onto something that you may never be able to receive. It's a valid feeling to want justice. However, the idea of grieving the need for justice (i.e., through forgiveness) may just be the key that lets you out of your own prison.

These are topics that would benefit greatly from speaking with someone and being able to expand the discussion beyond overviews. Although I naturally have a bias toward mental health clinicians, I also know the value of a good friend, clergy, and family. I also know the value of therapeutic interventions that are not formal therapy, such as an organization called Huts for Vets (https://hutsforvets.org), in which we take veterans into nature. We walk through the wilderness, read philosophy, feel the physical challenge of hiking at altitude, read poetry, and engage nature in an experiential manner rather than just observational. There are many modalities for working with PTSD. If one doesn't fit, don't give up on yourself; find the one that does. You are worth it!

Will thankfully had a great support system. Even though they were there, he often felt lonely. He was not alone, but the disconnect within and with others created loneliness. Will credits much of his recovery to Allison, which is a motivating factor in making sure that she had a voice in this book. As a psychologist, I work with a lot of spouses that feel guilty for their own struggles because they believe they don't have a right to struggle since they did not go through the trauma first-hand. Are you hearing the theme that trauma offers: guilt, shame, dismissiveness of self, pain, struggle, confusion, fatigue, and sometimes depression. Allison also shared her immense appreciation for the support of her family, who gave her strength to continue her fight for herself and her children. She had the fortitude to be patient while Will struggled, as well as standing firm when he crossed a boundary. He, in turn, chose to respond, not react. It took many steps, but with each one he gained resilience, strength, direction, and healing. Like grief, it is not over; it is a process. To have lived through the trauma and to dismiss the lessons that helped him create something beautiful would mean the trauma simply remained a tragedy. However, to highlight the cracks with gold or to create a new work of art from the shattered pieces is a triumph.

It was faith in Will's spirituality and in himself that allowed him to believe he could do better. It was hope to see his children grow, to grow old with Allison, and to serve his community and nation that prompted change. It was love that gave him the permission to live when his friends did not, to share his story with others, and to seek help when he saw his pain and the pain he was causing. It wasn't his fault and it wasn't fair that he had PTSD, but it wasn't his family's either, so Will did what he had to do. It was faith, hope, and love that guided Will to the life he loves today. It is faith, hope, and love that can guide you to your sunrise.

Reflections

1) Are you surviving, or are you living?
2) Is it possible that there are alternatives beyond your current understanding (i.e., your horizon)?
3) What does acceptance mean to you?
4) What does forgiveness mean to you?

5) Do you allow yourself to believe that you have no choice or can't do something?

6) How are you hypocritical in the care you give yourself compared to the care you give to others?

7) If you were to think of one thing you would like to see different in your life, what would it be?

8) If what you have used to make change in your life has not yet worked, is there a reason you don't try a different approach, even therapy or a different therapist?

9) What would be important to you in connecting to a therapist (e.g., personality, background, practice orientation, gender, age)? Do you know why?

10) Were there other insights that you had that I did not mention? Connections to your own life?

11) What else would you like to learn about trauma or treatment? There is so much more available, so please do investigate.

12) Do you need to pause, breathe, reflect, or grieve in this moment before continuing? What were moments of significance in this chapter?

Chapter Fifteen

A Final Word from Will

As we come to the last chapter in this book, I want everyone to know that this is not my last chapter or yours. As long as we are alive, no matter how bad things get in life, we have the opportunity to write a new chapter every single day. We all have an unknown amount of chapters left to write in our lives, so I hope that you take away some lessons from this book that will help you when, unfortunately, the chapter you are currently writing is difficult, or you're dealing with a long series of struggles.

This book is a project that I have been trying to put together for years. The thousands of people that I have had the pleasure of meeting along the way was the motivation to put myself out there and let people see the ugly side of what I had to deal with as a survivor, as well as what my family had to deal with as survivors. With each speaking engagement, I shared my story, and those present also shared their stories with me. We kept building a community of support through the commonality of pain. They told me that my message helped them to find renewed strength at a time they were starting to let go, and they helped me never give up and provided the motivation to complete this book for others to use. I thank you for that! Because of our interactions and because of your feedback, I feel like I am wearing the uniform again. I never imagined having this feeling again all those years ago. It was beyond the limitation of my sight.

On September 11th, I thought we could save everyone—I was wrong. I couldn't imagine a scenario where we would lose almost 3,000 people that day. It was unfathomable. There were times that I could not imagine ever feeling the satisfaction of living again and allowing myself to feel the joy of waking up, being with others, or finding a new way to serve. Once again, I was wrong. What we believe can be both supportive and can imprison us. When we get locked in depression and despair, we often believe there is no way out. Instead, we have to step out into the unknown and try every day. If something is not working, try something new. We already know that some of the band-aids we use to feel better are not getting us where we want to go, and sometimes it only gets us in deeper. That's where I was.

I never set out to do speaking engagements or share my story. It came from wanting to help children live a fulfilling life without being sidelined by fear. Yet, as I continued to do speaking engagements, I kept getting more invitations and had opportunities to meet so many people who would come up after I finished speaking to share their stories. Some of the stories were heartbreaking, and I started realizing that we all have scars, and we think we are alone. You are not alone. The more I share and listen, the more surrounded and supported I feel. Our stories are unique, yet shared. So many of us have scars from the darkness in our lives. Allow me to share a few from courageous individuals that have walked into their own darkness to find their sunrises.

One day, I spoke to an American military group of about 1,200 people. Afterward, I stood outside with a piece of World Trade Center steel that I bring to every speaking engagement. I share with them that I want them to feel a piece of U.S. history from September 11th. When I was in the Navy and in Hawaii, I saw the USS Arizona, and it meant a great deal to me. I now make it a point to share a piece of 9/11 World Trade Center steel that is cut out into a cross.

Following the speech, there was a long line of people, and I greeted and talked with each of them that came through. One lady gave me a big hug and told me, "I needed to hear what you said today about having faith, hope, and love, about overcoming darkness. I recently lost my job, my son tried to commit suicide within the last month, and my daughter is addicted to drugs. I feel like my world is coming down on me. I feel like I have a World Trade Center coming down on me!"

I gave her a hug and told her that it's not going to be easy, but you'll find a way to overcome. You will find a way to help your daughter cope with the drug abuse, and you will find a way to help your son realize that his life is precious because he means a lot to so many people. You will find a new job! We cried together, and it meant the world to me to know that by sharing my story, I was able to help this lady in need. I know I cannot save the world, even if it's my heart's desire. However, if I can light a small fire that will grow within a person to help them overcome their darkness, my pain was worth it.

Another story I would like to share is when I was asked to speak at a youth rehabilitation center. I was informed that the students that I would be addressing were young adults struggling with alcohol and substance abuse. I arrived at the campus early to learn a bit more about who they were, what they were going through, what help they were receiving, and where they were in their treatment, as well as in their lives. The friend who invited me and the head of the program, who is a survivor of alcohol and substance abuse, shared that I would be speaking to their graduating class. They shared that many of the students had made great strides in overcoming their darkness, but some were still in a battle for their lives.

One young man was on his last strike and was known for being hard to reach. He had been in and out of rehabs for heroin use, and jail likely was next. After sharing my story, the normal line of people that want to engage formed, and we had some great interactions. As most were departing, the young man who had been identified as high risk, asked if we could go off to the side and speak privately. He began by thanking me for taking the time to speak with him. The young man shared that he really did not speak with anyone there and felt that he was a lost cause. Several attempts had been made to end his pain through suicide, but he had not been successful. It truly broke my heart to hear such a young person with so much life ahead of him feel so much despair and hopelessness. I asked him to please share his story with me so I could better understand.

He told me that he came from a wealthy family, and anything he could ever want or imagine was at his disposal. Yet, he still sought something more and found heroin. Once he started, it grabbed him and wouldn't let go. After several stays at rehabs, he lost hope in his ability to break the hold it had on him.

I asked him, "What are looking for?"

He responded, "I do not know or care. I just want the pain to go away."

"I am going to speak from my heart. The pain will never go away without fighting for it. I know it is easier said than done, but anything worth fighting for will never be easy. First, you have to find a purpose worth fighting for because you are important to this world. You have so much life ahead of you. I understand that you can have any materialistic thing since you come from a wealthy family, but that stuff is meaningless, especially if you are not alive to enjoy it and do something good with it.

"You need to fight for yourself. I believe in you despite the numerous failed attempts to kick this. We all fail, sometimes more than we care to admit, but through failure we find strength and must keep moving forward. Otherwise, there is nothing left, and you deserved better for yourself."

He listened, and then said, "You having reached a point in your life where you're happy after being in such darkness, gives me hope for finding my happiness, and I want that."

"There you go. You have found something to fight for!"

He smiled and we chatted for an additional 20 minutes about other things pertaining to his pain and addiction, but in the end, he hugged me and gave a heartfelt thank you.

Afterwards, my friend and the program director were shocked that we spoke that long and that this young man opened up more than he had ever done before. Those of us who have been fighting and continue to fight the darkness are just human beings who can relate because of that darkness and pain. Instead of avoiding it, learn to use it. I was at the right place at the right time to be available to this young man. Had I not worked with my own darkness, I could not have come alongside him and helped him to understand he was not alone and offer some guidance. Once again, I felt like a cop but, more importantly, like a person who made something from my own pain to make a positive impact on another person's life.

A final story that frequently motivates me was not included in this chapter. I purposefully left it out because I asked this person, a Marine, to write the Foreword for this book. If you have not read the Foreword, please do. His name is Mauricio Henao, and he says he is thankful that I crossed his path. I would say that it was my blessing to have crossed his.

I'm no different from them or you. I truly am not. I want you to know that if you're struggling through any type of darkness—whether it be mental health, PTSD, child abuse, drug or alcohol addiction, anxiety, depression, anger, or grief—you, too, can overcome the darkness and get to the sunrise like I did. Many times, people ask for the formula. The closest thing I have found to a formula would be to never give up on yourself! When you feel weak and surrounded by darkness, that's a tough thing to do. But you owe it to yourself. You are worth it. You are not alone.

I had so many people tell me that this book would probably not come to fruition, but I kept believing in it. Thankfully, when speaking with Michael we talked about it, and we both thought it was important because we had a shared passion for serving others. We both have felt pain and despair. We both have had wonderful people in our lives offer support and lend their strength when we felt our weakest. We worked together to reach out to you.

Don't try to go through the darkness alone. Reach out to people.

Don't allow your fear to keep you down. Sometimes it sucker punches you and will take you down—quickly. Catch your breath and get back up. Whatever you try might not always pan out the first, second, third, fourth, or even the fifth time, but keep trying because you owe it to yourself. You are a special person; you mean a lot to many people, even if you are unable to see it right now.

September 11th changed my lenses. I learned in a deep way from going to different funerals that it didn't matter if the death was from cancer, suicide, a car accident, or just old age; every single human being touches so many other lives. Never make the mistake of disregarding how much your life impacts others. That belief is just the limitation of your sight.

People have told me, "Will, I can't believe you had 220 stories fall on top of you. That's the worst thing anyone could go through."

It's dramatic, but it's not the worst. Our traumas are not competitive. My World Trade Center trauma is mine. Whatever your World Trade Center story consists of is yours. There is no need to compare; that's wasted energy. What you do with yourself once that World Trade Center comes down on you is what's important. No one gets trophies for trauma. Your reward is creating the life you want to see. In 2020 the whole world had a massive World Trade Center fall on all of us with COVID-19. Did we take an unimaginable loss? Yes, we did. I'm proud to say that many people rose up. It wasn't without struggle or conflict, but people demonstrated how resilient they are and how they were able to cope with such difficult times from losing jobs, being stuck at home feeling like prisoners, and facing the unknowns, which were plenty.

No matter your darkness, you can overcome it. Never give up on yourself and keep moving forward! Claw your way if that's all you can do. It breaks my heart to know I had friends who chose to give up on themselves. Honestly, it breaks my heart to know that anyone does. If you know someone who is going through their own form of darkness, make sure you take the time to check up on them. Be there in support by talking to them or, more importantly, by listening. Let them know that you love them. Telling people you love them and truly meaning it is so important and often underutilized. It could be a family member, a close friend, or it could be a total stranger. Letting them know that they are loved just for being a human being has such great power. The more love we share with people, in any form, also has the power to change the person offering it. A simple smile may be that gentle gesture that changes another's outlook for the day.

There was a time that I really thought about ending my life because of struggling with PTSD and survivor's guilt. I felt overwhelmed. I say *felt overwhelmed*, rather than *was overwhelmed*, because I never gave up. Somewhere beyond was what I felt was the truth—that I still had more in me. On the days when you can no longer see the truth beyond the feelings, surround yourself with people who believe in you, who will challenge you to keep fighting while also being willing to give you a hug, or simply hold space for you. We all feel stronger when someone has our back.

I always end my speeches with this quote, often attributed to Edmund Burke, "The only thing necessary for the triumph of evil is for good men to do nothing."[1] In my heart, I believe that there are good men and women who will never stand by and let evil win. When I speak of evil, I am using this term as meaning anything that holds us back from living the lives we seek, even if the darkness is self-imposed or unrealized. Evil, our darkness, comes in many forms: child abuse, sex abuse, alcohol and drug abuse, terrorism, bullying, racism, and domestic violence.

In my heart, I know that there will always be good men and women who come to aid in fighting evil, and that means you. Remember to take this day, whatever is left of it, and turn into your darkness. Stare it in the eyes and say, "It's time to take a seat. I'll take it from here." Begin again. There were so many instances of ludicrous attempts I made during my survival, when we look at it on the surface (i.e., trying to bust concrete with handcuffs), but the very act, ludicrous or not, kept me alive and still trying until they found us.

Keep fighting. Reach out. Make tough choices and start walking through your darkness to the life you want to create. Live a beautiful life; you deserve it! You may say you have no faith. Just because I spoke of my spiritual faith, I am not limiting it to that. I am speaking to the Atheist, the Buddhist, the Islamist, and to everyone, regardless of affiliation. Faith may be believing in your own ability, believing that hard work pays off, or that time, opportunity, and action will push the odds in your favor. Faith is believing in something more than you can prove at the moment. And if you don't have hope? Then borrow someone's. Let them hope for you, but keep trying. I knew my family was hoping for my return from beneath the rubble, which helped me when I would lose my hope. Okay, what about love? You are loved, even

---

[1] Burke, E. (1999). Thoughts on the Cause of the Present Discontents. In *Select Works of Edmund Burke* (Vol. 1; Liberty Fund ed.). Liberty Fund. (Originally published in 1770)

if you can't or won't allow yourself to see it. Do not believe in the lie that others would be better off without you. That is just a distortion of thought to make it easier to let go. If you can't find faith, grab onto hope. If you can't find hope, grab onto love. If you can't find love, start over and seek faith again. Do not give up!

We only have so many days on this earth, so make them worthwhile. Make them something that you can look back upon with pride. I am not proud of everything I've done in my life, but I can honestly say that when I look at it all, I am proud of my life. I am proud of what I fought through to make it to today. You can do it, too! Our time will come on its own. When it does, leave a lot of love behind. When we leave this earth, we can't take our materialistic things such as money, cars, homes, or job titles. However, we can enjoy the knowledge that we had a fruitful life of investing in others and making a positive impact on the way they lived.

I am no different from you. I'm just the guy who had a dream of becoming a police officer. I worked really, really hard to achieve that dream. After nine months, it was ripped away from me, and I needed to find a way back to living again, not just *existing*. I have been able to do that with a lot of support; some of it I avoided for a while, which only cost me and the people I love. Some of you might not have the support I have been fortunate to surround myself with but go look for it. Do not cheat yourself. Do not cheat those around you who love you. Go out there and find those individuals that are going to uplift you, support you, and love you. It doesn't have to be family. It doesn't have to be friends. It could be your priest, a counselor, an organization, or someone you haven't yet met.

I wish each and every one of you the very best. I love you! I believe in you! You mean a lot to many people, and I wish you nothing but happiness because you deserve it. Never forget to have faith, hope, and love and to continue to fight to find the sunrise through the darkness.

God bless you. God bless your families. God Bless America. And God bless all humanity. From the bottom of my heart, I wish you much peace and happiness!

Will Jimeno

Reflections

1)   What is life asking of you today?

Photograph by Olivia Jimeno

When I walked through my darkness, this is the sunrise that awaited.

Setting the Context: Before and After

After reading this book, complete the following sentences below:

On September 11, 2001,

I thought:

I felt:

I was:

It held:

- Once completed, reread what you had written before reading this book and compare it to what you have just finished.
- What do you notice?
- What changed? Do you know why?
- What stayed the same? Do you know why?
- Has your experience allowed more room for the feelings resulting from 9/11, or do they feel more restricted? Explore your answer.
- Is there anything you learned that you can use for your life today? What is it, and how will it be used?

Activities

As with any activity, we ask you to use these as prompts for exploration rather than as prescriptions. The variation of activities presented are to offer availability to experience the book in a different manner that is more engaged with the hope that the experiential knowledge may be used in your life or allow you to come alongside the life of a loved one. If doing these activities creates strong reactions, please reach out to a resource for assistance.

Experiencing This Book

Take a moment to reflect on your experience of reading this book. Did you notice physical sensations, emotional changes, or thoughts that came up for you? Did it take you back to that day or the first time you saw news footage of the attacks? Beyond sympathy, were there other feelings that were primarily felt? Did you connect in a way that offered insight into your own life? Your own struggle?

Write or draw something that represents any of the answers that you have to the questioning prompts. Do not worry about form, grammar, spelling, or any other mental limitation "should be"s. Allow yourself the freedom to write a big F-U across the page if you want. Let your heart speak first; you can always clean it up after...or not.

Physical Movement

Empathetically place yourself in a physical position that you feel represents Will beneath the rubble of the Twin Towers (only do this if physically capable and it is not harming to you). Hold it for ten seconds, if possible. Notice what you feel physically, emotionally, and in thought. Now, empathetically place yourself in a physical position that you feel represents Will today. Hold it for ten seconds, if possible. Notice what you feel physically, emotionally, and in thought. What changed? Did pain linger? Was there a release? Was there both?

Now imagine your own World Trade Center, your own struggle in life today. Place yourself in a physical position that represents you beneath the weight of your own WTC (only do this if physically capable and it is not harming to you). Hold it for ten seconds, if possible. Notice what you feel physically, emotionally, and in thought. Now, place yourself in a physical position that you feel represents you in the life you seek. Hold it for ten seconds, if possible. Notice what you feel physically, emotionally, and in thought. What changed? Did pain linger? Was there a release? Was there both? What is one thing you can do today to walk toward that life? No longer look at your struggle with disdain but as a marker on your path to where you are going.

Surveying the Scene

Take a moment to personally detach yourself from your life. Put on your first-responder goggles and observe the patterns you see in your home, in your relationships. Survey the scene. What do you see? Let's get real here. You already see the ugliest of what life has to offer when you do your job. Don't shy away now. Use the same courage to make an honest assessment. Can you see changes in your behavior? In your drinking? In the way you interact and communicate with your spouse, family, and friends. Do you see changes in your family's behaviors toward you, possibly being hesitant or avoiding? Are you doing the things you love anymore? Are you already feeling detached from the ideal of fulfillment in your life? Are you surviving the day?

Part of the training for first responders is to make an honest assessment of the scene and take action on the facts presented, even though there are also unknowns. Dire situations are tough, yet you still try. Will you apply this same approach to your life that you have for the sake of others? If you are honest with yourself, could you use some backup? Will you reach out?

Lessons Learned or Lost

What have we learned from September 11th? What have we forgotten? In tragic times, society often comes together for a time; however, in personal tragedy, we often feel fragmented within ourselves. Using what we know to be healing in society during tragedy, how can you apply that knowledge in your life today?

Mindfully Walking vs. Taking A Walk

Go for a walk around the block, at the park, or on the nearest trail. However, this time take a deep breath before you start and make a mental note that you are here now for the purpose of walking. Begin to walk at whatever pace you like. Notice how your feet connect with the ground. Feel the changes in pressure across your feet, into your calves, as well as the swinging of your arms. Are you breathing through your mouth or nose? Is the air warm or cold? Notice smells in the air. Take the time to look at the underside of a leaf or the variations of blue in the sky. Are you noticing any stiffness, any relaxation, any...whatever? Just keep noticing. If thoughts of other things interrupt you, as they most likely will, do not push them away. Rather, notice them and mentally guide them to your side, as if using a swim stroke. If they come back, notice them again, and repeat. No agenda, no pressure, no hurry. Just experience.

What did you notice physically? Is there anything there needing to be addressed? Did you have a hard time connecting physically to your body? Were there recurring thoughts that were intruding? Is there something that needs addressed? How did it feel to not just walk by a tree or bush but to experience it? What smells did you smell? What do they represent to you in your life? Did it make you aware that you have been too busy or too detached to notice? Is there something that needs addressing?

We have a way of cognitively defending against potential threats to our way of being, but they sometimes are overused in a detrimental way; this leads to an unconscious burden that drags us slowly down into anxiety and depression. Become more aware; become more powerful in your own existence. The feeling of weakness is not weak. It takes courage to address that which we shove down and avoid.

Poetic Reflection

Please read the following poem and notice what you feel as you read. Whatever the reaction, it is valid; it is yours. Take some time to write a few things down about your experience. Did you notice thoughts that surfaced, feelings, physical reactions, or did you just judge the poem?

September 11[1]
David N. Elkins

Those planes, those buildings, those fireballs,
Those people jumping, that thick dust rolling,
Those crashing towers, those people inside,
Those firefighters, those families watching in terror
  at home, knowing their husband, wife, father, mother,
  or friend was inside those buildings, on those planes.
The Pentagon, the black scar where the plane hit,
The ones inside who never had a chance.
That Pennsylvania farm. "Let's roll," he said,
  and they did – right into eternity – and into our hearts.
Images – forever cut into the soul and history of America.

And then came the politics.
Americans – and allies around the world – divided, polarized.
French fries or freedom fries, take your pick and show your
patriotism – or maybe just your ideology.
Shock and Awe – and we watch it on TV.
Popcorn, anyone?
Blood on the popcorn? Don't worry. We've hired a PR firm to
  wipe it all away.
What? No weapons of mass destruction? But I thought...
Flawed intelligence or cynical politics – our nation divided,
  still torn in two, even to this day – about that day.

Sandy was 18 and Jim was 20 – and in the National Guard.
The wedding was already planned but Jim said,
"Wait until I'm home for good. I don't want to be separated
  after we're married."
He made it through three tours of duty but in his fourth the
  wedding plans,
  along with Jim's Hummer, exploded
  and Sandy and Jim's dreams broke into pieces and
  flew 2,000 feet into the Iraqi sky.
Two weeks later, Sandy bought a one-way

---

[1] Elkins, D. (2015). September 11. In L. Hoffman, & M. Moats (Eds.), *Capturing Shadows: Poetic Encounters Along the Path of Grief and Loss* (pp. 36–39). University Professors Press.

ticket – some called it an overdose – to go see Jim.

But maybe today, maybe today, more than a decade later,
   maybe today we can remember:
How we came together.
How we spoke to neighbors.
How we filed onto sidewalks, into city streets and parks.
How we shook hands, or gave strangers – who somehow were
   not strangers – a hug.
How our souls became one giant Soul
How we were one people. How *E Pluribus Unum* jumped off
   our coins and into our hearts.
Black and White, Latino and Asian, Christian and Jew, Hindu
   and Muslim,
Straight and gay, republican and democrat.
A melting pot – a true melting pot. And we had only one name:
Americans
– Or better yet: human beings.

And remember how friends around the world – people in
   other countries – sent faxes and e-mails by the millions
   saying,
"We are so sorry. So sorry – and we are thinking of you,
   praying for you, Americans."
No longer were we "ugly Americans." The truth came out:
They were our friends – there for us when the chips were
   down.

But perhaps the thing that tore our hearts out were those
   lost people, wandering aimlessly in the aftermath, at the edge
   of the ruins, looking for any sign of their loved one.
And those notes on the fences, fluttering in the New York
   breeze, saying things like:
"Bill Johnson, if you read this, please call your family."
"Maria Gomez. If you know where she is, call me at 776-8843
   – I'm her mother."
And "Here's a picture of Daddy and me last Xmas. If you see
   him somewhere, maybe in the hospital, tell him Tammy loves
   him and really, really needs to see him."

And then those readings of the names. Hours just reading

names.
Names of husbands, wives, children, brothers, sisters, uncles,
   aunts, cousins, grandmothers,
grandfathers, friends, firefighters, policemen, flight attendants,
   pilots, passengers.
Would they ever stop reading those names?
Would the list ever end?
Would the pain spreading out like ripples on a lake to
   immediate families, extended families, close friends, other
   friends, business friends, church friends, temple friends,
   mosque friends –
Would the pain and the ripples and the names ever stop?
Would the ponds and lakes, the seas and oceans, ever be calm
   again?
Those names, Those beautiful names, Those beautiful,
   haunting names.

So here we are, more than a decade later. Remembering.
Trying to say something – anything – that might pay
   tribute, honor, to those who
Just wanted to drink their morning coffee,
Just wanted to check their overnight e-mails
Just wanted to call home to remind their husband to go to the
   cleaners,
Just wanted to say hi to their kids because they had left for
   work that morning while they were still in bed.
Yes, here we are. More than a decade later – with no words
that even come close.

When Aldous Huxley was near the end of his life, the great
   philosopher said that it was a bit embarrassing
   that he had spent his entire life working on the
   human problem and that he had nothing of substance
   to offer but this:
   "Try to be a little kinder."

Perhaps Aldous had it right.
We did it on "9-11." Perhaps we can do it again.
And maybe that would be the best memorial of all:
"Try to be a little kinder. Just – "Try to be a little kinder."

For the next week, take time to allow your thoughts and feelings to become present. At the end of the week, reread the poem and notice what you feel this time. Is there a change? Take some time to write about what is different, what is the same. If you are comfortable, ask a trusted person to read the poem, as well as your notes. Discuss them.

Resources

If you or someone you know is considering suicide, please call 911 or go to your nearest emergency room (ER). Additional resources are also provided for different purposes. It's always possible that the numbers and web addresses will be changed over time, so if the one you are trying to use is no longer valid, please do not give up. Reach out through another avenue or to another resource, a friend, the ER, or call 911. You are too important not to do so.

National Suicide Prevention Lifeline
- Call 1-800-273-TALK (8255)
- Text "help" to the Crisis Text Line at 741-741
- Call 988, starting July 16th, 2022
- Go to suicidepreventionlifeline.org for Lifeline Chat
- For TTY Users: Use your preferred relay service or dial 711 then 1-800-273-8255

Veterans Crisis Line
- Call 1-800-273-TALK (8255), Press 1
- Text support at 838-255
- Go to https://www.veteranscrisisline.net/get-help/chat for Confidential Veterans Chat

National Domestic Violence Hotline
- Call 1-800-799-SAFE (7233) or 1-800-787-3224 (TTY)
- Text START to 1-800-799-SAFE (7233)
- Go to https://www.thehotline.org for live chat

National Sexual Assault Hotline operated by RAINN (Rape, Abuse & Incest National Network)
- Call 1-800-656-HOPE (4673) to link victims to counseling and legal advice
- Go to https://hotline.rainn.org/online for live chat

National Child Abuse Hotline
- Call 1-800-4-A-CHILD (422-4453) if you suspect a child is being abused, if you fear you might hurt your child, or if you have been abused

Psychology Today
- Go to Psychologytoday.com to find a therapist in your area, which can also be filtered by reason for a visit, insurance, and zip code

In Honor Of

We wanted to honor those who died on September 11th by listing all their names. But even using triple columns, the added page count would have been 55. The names of those that died on September 11th filled 55 pages! This does not include people like Debbie or the many others that ended up giving their lives due to their tireless efforts at removing debris from Ground Zero, supporting those working on-site, or the many that were digging through the pile to bring home the lost loved ones that hadn't escaped in time. We made the final choice to not add the pages, but we still want to honor those that died and their families. To learn more about the 9/11 Memorial and see a list of the names, please visit https://www.911memorial.org.

About the Authors

William Jimeno is a retired Port Authority of New York and New Jersey Police Detective, who survived the World Trade Center attack on September 11, 2001. After being buried in the rubble for 13 hours, Will had a long recovery, in which he now uses as a redefinition of serving others in his struggle with PTSD and the importance of never giving up on yourself by anchoring into faith, hope, and love.

You can follow Will Jimeno on Instagram, or contact him for speaking engagements or book signings at the email listed below:

Instagram – @wasparcher
Email – willjimeno26@gmail.com

Dr. Moats is a clinical psychologist in Colorado Springs whose passion lies in working with clients who are learning to redefine their lives and create new meaning, especially those dealing with grief and loss in its many forms (i.e., death, divorce, job loss, recent move, natural disaster, war). Michael believes that every instance of loss is new, is not competitive, and offers a gift wrapped deeply within the pain.

You can follow Dr. Moats at the following social media links, or contact him for speaking engagements or book signings at the email listed below:

LinkedIn – Michael Moats
Facebook – @DrMichaelMoats
Twitter - @DrMichaelMoats
Instagram – @drmichaelmoats
Blog – www.drmichaelmoats.com
Email – drmichaelmoats@gmail.com

Please follow Sunrise Through the Darkness on its Facebook page: https://www.facebook.com/SunriseThroughtheDarkness

Other Publications

By Michael Moats

Capturing Shadows: Poetic Encounters Along the Path of Grief and Loss
Louis Hoffman & Michael Moats (Eds.)

Our Last Walk: Using Poetry for Grieving and Remembering Our Pets
Louis Hoffman, Michael Moats, and Tom Greening (Eds.)

A Walk with Nature: Poetic Encounters That Nourish the Soul
Michael Moats, Derrick Sebree, Jr., Gina Subia Belton, & Louis Hoffman
(Eds.)

A Walk in the Dark: Working with Suicidal Clients (Chapter 11).
In L. Hoffman, & M. Yang (Eds.), *Existential Psychology East-West* (2nd
Ed)

White Privilege: A Multifaceted Responsibility (Chapter 8).
In L. Hoffman, H. Cleare-Hoffman, N. Granger, & D. St. John (Eds.),
*Humanistic Approaches to Multiculturalism and Diversity: Perspectives
on Existence and Difference*

Steadiness in the Midst of Chaos (Chapter 3).
In M. Yang (Ed.), *Existential Psychology and the Way of the Tao:
Meditations on the Writings of Zhuangzi*

Humanistic Psychology and Self-Acceptance
Louis Hoffman, Abraham J. Lopez, & Michael Moats (Chapter 1).
In M. Bernard (Ed.), *The Strength of Self-Acceptance*

By Will

*Immigrant, American, Survivor: A Little Boy Who Grew Up to Be All
Three*
William Jimeno & Charles Ricciardi

Suggested Readings

Man's Search for Meaning
Viktor Frankl

A Grace Disguised: How the Soul Grows Through Loss
Jerry Sittser

Rediscovering Awe
Kirk Schneider

Crucial Conversations: Tools for Talking When Stakes Are High
Kerry Patterson, Joseph Grenny, et al.

The Body Keeps the Score: Brain, Mind, and Body in the Healing of Trauma
Bessel van der Kolk

A Grief Observed
C. S. Lewis and Madeleine L'Engle

Tuesdays with Morrie: An Old Man, a Young Man, and Life's Greatest Lesson
Mitch Albom

Wilderness Essays
John Muir

CPSIA information can be obtained
at www.ICGtesting.com
Printed in the USA
BVHW050447220921
617191BV00014B/1073

9 781939 686992